Fieldwork in Developing Countries

Fieldwork in Developing Countries

Edited by
Stephen Devereux and John Hoddinott

LYNNE RIENNER PUBLISHERS
Boulder, Colorado

First published in the United States of America
In 1993 by
Lynne Rienner Publishers, Inc.
1800 30th Street, Boulder, Colorado 80301

Typeset in 10/12pt Times by Keyboard Services, Luton

Printed and bound in Great Britain by
Hartnolls Limited, Bodmin

Library of Congress Cataloging-in-Publication Data

Devereux, Stephen.
Fieldwork in developing countries / edited by Stephen Devereux and John Hoddinott.
p. cm.
Includes bibliographical references and index.
ISBN 1-55587-392-8 (pb : alk. paper)
1. Social sciences—Developing countries—Statistical methods.
I. Hoddinott, John. II. Title.
MA29.D395 1992 92-16847
001.4′222—dc20 CIP

5 4 3

Contents

Notes on Contributors

Garry Christensen is a Senior Research Economist with the Food Studies Group at Queen Elizabeth House, Oxford University. His research interest is the study of household behaviour.

Lucia da Corta is a Research Associate at the Department of Economics, University of Manchester. She is currently working on a Leverhulme Trust funded project on economic mobility and crises in drought-prone villages in south India. She is concurrently working for her doctorate at St Antony's College, Oxford.

Stephen Devereux is a doctoral student in economics at Balliol College and a Research Associate with the Food Studies Group, Oxford University. His research interests are in famine and seasonality in Africa.

Elizabeth Francis is a Junior Research Fellow at St Anne's College, Oxford. She carried out fieldwork for a doctorate on the economic and social impact of labour migration in Western Kenya, 1987–9.

Barbara Harriss is a University Lecturer in Agricultural Economics and Fellow of Wolfson College, Oxford. Her research interests – agricultural commerce, gender and malnutrition – have been pursued using fieldwork since 1971.

Judith Heyer is a Fellow of Somerville College, Oxford, and a University Lecturer in Economics. She did fieldwork in rural areas of Kenya in 1961–2, and in Tamil Nadu, South India, in 1980–2. She also supervised fieldwork in Kenya for research projects she was running in 1968 and 1974, and has supervised several students doing fieldwork of their own in Africa and India during the 1980s.

John Hoddinott is a Research Officer at the Centre for the Study of African Economies and College Research Lecturer in Economics at Trinity College, Oxford. In 1988, he carried out fieldwork in western Kenya on migration, accumulation and the role of children as old-age security.

Matthew Lockwood trained as an economist, and carried out fieldwork in eastern Tanzania in 1985–6, researching into relationships between fertility and household economy. He is currently a Research Fellow at the Centre for African Studies, University of Cambridge.

Wendy Olsen, originally of Bloomington, Indiana, studied at Beloit College, Wisconsin, and Hertford College, Oxford. She did primary research in south India during 1986 and 1987. She now works in the Faculty of Economic and Social Studies, University of Manchester.

Shahrashoub Razavi is a research student at St Antony's College, Oxford. She is currently working on her D.Phil. thesis. Her research has been funded by fellowships from the British Institute of Persian Studies, the British Academy.

Davuluri Venkateshwarlu is currently working for his Ph.D. on social mobility in coastal Andhra Pradesh, in the Department of Political Science, University of Hyderabad, India.

Ken Wilson is a Research Officer with the Refugee Studies Programme at the University of Oxford. He has undertaken fieldwork in Sudan, Zambia, Malawi and, during two of the three years that he lived there, rural Zimbabwe. He has used a variety of research approaches, usually as part of teams including local people.

Acknowledgements

The genesis of this book was a workshop on locality-based fieldwork in developing countries, held at Queen Elizabeth House, University of Oxford, in April 1990. We would like to thank Queen Elizabeth House, and also Oxford University's South Asian Studies Committee, which generously funded the workshop's administrative costs. The Centre for the Study of African Economies, the Food Studies Group and Trinity College, Oxford, provided administrative support.

Six discussants at the workshop provided incisive comments on the papers, which are reflected in the revised versions of those papers, as included here. Our thanks are due to these discussants: Janine Aron, Fareda Banda, Andrea Cravinho, Georgia Kaufman, Jovito Nunes and Fiona Samuels.

Introduction
Stephen Devereux and John Hoddinott

Fieldwork is not a science. If it were, a standard manual would have been written decades ago. Many books exist that are worth consulting on research methodology, but we generally found these to be too narrowly focused once we experienced fieldwork for ourselves, in all its uniqueness and complexity.[1] And while anecdotal accounts or 'fieldwork diaries' can provide a flavour of life in a Third World village, they are often too idiosyncratic, amusing or terrifying to be of practical use.[2]

All the contributors to this book look back on their fieldwork as an exciting and memorable life event – much more than merely an intellectual exercise. But fieldwork also subjects everyone who undertakes it to varying degrees of physical and psychological stress. Nigel Barley was undoubtedly exaggerating when he commented that perhaps 1 per cent of his time in the Cameroons was spent doing research, and the rest 'on logistics, being ill, being sociable, arranging things, getting from place to place, and above all, waiting' (Barley 1983, p. 98), but these practical factors certainly are major components of any fieldwork. Indeed, the researcher's physical and social environment inevitably have an important bearing on the nature and interpretation of the data collected. Accordingly, this book differs from others in the genre by arguing that the context within which fieldwork is conducted is absolutely integral to the research process. 'Contextual' and 'methodological' considerations should be considered jointly, not as two distinct categories in which the first obstructs the pursuit of the second.

Although every fieldwork situation is unique, many features are common to all, and Part 1 offers an introduction to these, as well as examining several topics ignored by other texts. 'The context of fieldwork' discusses preparing for, experiencing and returning from fieldwork, while 'Issues in data collection' narrows the focus to specific methodological matters. For stylistic reasons we have divided Part 1 into two chapters, but we regard these as fundamentally interlinked.

Part 2 consists of eleven case studies, in which our contributors draw on their personal experiences to examine a variety of fieldwork issues. Again, these relate both to the conduct of research and to questions of lifestyle and interactions with the local community. Rarely is a single 'correct' approach advocated. Fieldwork is about weighing up the pros and cons of decisions such as how long to stay in the field, how to remunerate assistants, what kinds of data to collect, and how best to collect these data. The authors invariably present alternatives rather than prescriptions, in the hope that these contributions will stimulate critical thought on fieldwork method (broadly defined) as well as suggesting possible solutions to common problems.

The ordering of these case studies is partly 'chronological', in the sense that specific aspects of fieldwork are discussed more or less as they occur. Thus population enumeration and sampling issues are treated in the early chapters, followed later in the book by interviewing techniques. The final chapters address broader considerations such as the nature of data, fieldwork ethics and doing fieldwork more than once.

This book has been written with several types of reader in mind. The immediate and most obvious audience is the neophyte fieldworker, but this category extends to academic supervisors or employers, researchers who have previously undertaken fieldwork, and lecturers or instructors who teach courses in research methods. Although most of our contributors are economists or anthropologists, the lessons learnt apply equally to fieldworkers from related social sciences and other disciplines – agronomists, demographers, geographers, political scientists, nutritionists and epidemiologists. Finally, fieldwork is undertaken not only by doctoral students and academics (either abroad or in their home countries), but by consultants and employees working for government ministries (of agriculture, health, planning and others), research institutes, international donors and non–government organisations.

Development policy and analysis rely increasingly on primary research at the household or community level. These studies can easily be misused or misunderstood, particularly when the reader has little conception of the context in which they were undertaken. By highlighting these concerns, we hope to contribute to a more informed understanding of the strengths and pitfalls of this type of research. This book is therefore also addressed to a broader 'development' audience – academics, practitioners and the interested public – and we hope that they too find the discussions that follow helpful and stimulating.[3]

Notes

1. Among the most popular texts are: Casley and Lury (1987), mainly used by economists and strong on the empirical and theoretical aspects of sampling; Ellen (1984), used by many anthropologists. A recent addition to this genre which bridges the disciplinary divide is Gregory and Altman (1989).

2. 'Amusing' because they can provide witty (if occasionally tasteless) commentaries on cultural differences between fieldworkers and respondents, 'terrifying' because the catalogue of disasters these writers describe is enough to put anyone off doing fieldwork at all! The best-known contemporary example is probably Barley (1983). Older accounts which fieldworkers still cram into their rucksacks include those by Bowen (1964), Levi-Strauss (1973) and Rabinow (1977).
3. In fact, many topics addressed in this volume apply to community-level research anywhere, not only in developing countries – especially technical questions relating to s rvey design, ethical concerns and the subjective nature of data.

PART 1

Overview: fieldwork from start to finish

1

The context of fieldwork

Stephen Devereux and John Hoddinott

Introduction

The topics selected for discussion in this chapter reflect a range of practical and personal matters which significantly affected the contributors to this volume before, during and after their fieldwork.[1] In highlighting potential problem areas, our intention is not to be alarmist, nor to imply that all these difficulties will be faced by any one fieldworker. Rather, our ambition is simply to bring to the reader's attention various problems that might arise, and to offer suggestions for dealing with those that do. We should also emphasise that there is rarely a single perfect solution to any dilemma or difficulty encountered during fieldwork, so that what we offer are guidelines rather than golden rules.

This chapter divides into three sections: pre-fieldwork and post-fieldwork issues ('Getting there' and 'Coming home') being first and third, while life in the field is discussed under the heading 'Being there'. 'Getting there' looks mainly at logistical aspects of fieldwork preparation. 'Being there' divides into two sub-sections: 'Living in the field' (lifestyle and health) and 'Living with others' (relationships with assistants, respondents and officials). 'Coming home' briefly addresses questions of personal and academic readjustment, and post-fieldwork obligations to the research community. Issues directly concerned with the collection of data are deferred to Chapter 2.

Two arguments motivate this structure. First, many texts on fieldwork limit themselves to discussions of technical matters – how best to collect and then analyse data. While there is nothing wrong with this approach *per se*, our experience suggests that fieldwork is much more than a data-gathering exercise. Anyone who has done research outside his or her home community knows that questions relating to lifestyle and personal relationships loom as large as narrowly defined technical issues. Rather than restricting our attention to methodological concerns, therefore, we aim to describe fieldwork as a complete experience – from start to finish.

A second, related objective is to question the conventional definition of 'methodological issues' as referring only to sample selection, questionnaire design, interviewing techniques and statistical analysis. Fieldwork, especially as practised by economists, is predicated on the assumption that the researcher is collecting 'facts' and observing 'truths'. Yet, in some (or perhaps all) circumstances, this view is deeply questionable. The *context* of data collection (how the interviewer is perceived by respondents, for instance) can be as important in explaining the data as the data themselves. A case in point is Matthew Lockwood's discussion of obtaining data on respondent ages, in Chapter 11 – systematically different responses were recorded, depending on who was asked, and who was asking, the questions.

This also means that the distinction between methodological and other questions is at best blurred. The way we have separated the discussion in these two overview chapters is itself rather artificial, for this reason. Everything about life in the field influences the professional goal of collecting 'accurate' data. The most important methodological fact in a fieldwork experience may be something seemingly peripheral – that one assistant was replaced with another halfway through, say. Unless and until this contextual dimension of data collection is fully recognised – and accepted as integral to the process – fieldwork results risk being reported in a way which is misleadingly 'precise' and 'objective'.

1.1 Getting there

This section addresses matters which mostly affect those fieldworkers (often but not exclusively Westerners) who set off to do research in a foreign country. For researchers working in their own countries, questions such as applying for visas and raising money for air fares will probably not arise. For this reason, the principal audience for this section is assumed to be expatriate prospective fieldworkers, although some topics, such as choosing a research site and theoretical preparation, should be of interest to a wider audience as well.

Fieldwork begins at home, not in the research site. By the time any researcher arrives in the chosen village (or district, market or town), a number of decisions have already been made that will greatly influence the subsequent research. These common preliminary matters fall into the broad categories of financial, bureaucratic, theoretical and methodological preparation.

1.1.1 *Financing fieldwork*

Unless the research is part of a larger, institutionally funded project, the fieldworker must somehow raise enough money to finance the expedition. This can be a laborious process, and is especially difficult for first-time researchers without a proven track record to back up their applications. Two aspects of financing fieldwork are considered here – sources of funding, and budgeting.

Sources of funding

Funding sources can be divided into major institutional donors, which give big grants, but have strict application procedures (such as the Economic and Social Research Council (ESRC), the Economic and Social Committee for Overseas Research, Overseas Development Administration (ESCOR-ODA) and Wenner-Gren in the UK, and the Rockefeller and Ford Foundations in the USA); and miscellaneous donors, which offer smaller amounts, but require only brief proposals and give grants unconditionally (charities, and university research or travel grant committees). Whatever sources of funding are approached, it is vital to begin this process long before departure, ideally up to a year in advance. Many agencies have a single, annual closing date for applications, and the whole exercise is much more time-consuming than might be anticipated.

Major donors often have complex, standardised application forms, fixed research priorities and rigorous report-writing requirements. They demand detailed proposals that can take weeks to prepare. For this reason, it is advisable before preparing requests for funding to find out about the institution's theoretical interests and disciplinary bias. Some major donors are well known for being 'pro-economist' and 'anti-anthropologist', for instance. Writing the perfect research proposal for an agency which has no intention of financing it is simply a waste of time, irrespective of the quality of the application.

Lists of miscellaneous sources such as charities can be found (for the UK) in the annually updated *Grants Register* and *Directory of Grant-Making Trusts*.[2] It is slow and often tedious work going through these books, copying down the names and addresses of dozens of potential donors, and then sending out a mailshot of begging letters. But this time is almost always well spent. After all, charities exist to give away cash, so there is no harm in asking for some! A well-drafted letter which happens to reach the right organisation at the right time could reap a sizeable donation. One of the editors of this book sent requests to 105 UK charities and trusts in 1988, and received cheques of £500 each from two of them, with no strings attached.

The main disadvantage with these sources, apart from the 'pot luck' element, is that they rarely offer full financial support for a research project, but instead make useful contributions towards expenses. Five hundred pounds or dollars may seem like a lot of free money to a struggling student, but it is not enough to cover the air fare to Papua New Guinea, let alone the costs of living and working there for a year or longer. Securing a single, sizeable grant is preferable to trying to scrape together enough money from several small donors.

A final option is bank loans, but this is not recommended until all other sources have been exhausted, for two reasons: first, because the temptation is naturally to ask for as little as possible, hence to skimp on research expenses and (crucially) on funding for post-fieldwork analysis; and second, because pressure to pay back the debt may force the researcher into employment too soon after returning from the field, and to defer writing up indefinitely. One or two contributors to this volume arrived home impoverished and indebted, and spent anxious months looking for employment or further funding. But writing up fieldwork is such an intensive activity that trying to do it part-time, while holding down a full-time job as well, is virtually impossible.

Budgeting

Virtually all donors require a budget to be submitted along with any research proposal. This can be difficult to do in advance, especially for fieldworkers who have never done fieldwork before, nor visited the country concerned. For informed and up-to-date estimates of living expenses, it can be helpful to consult nationals of the country involved, while academic supervisors and other researchers can provide advice on likely research costs. Intelligent estimates are needed, not just for the total sum required but broken down by category. Some donors are inflexible about moving funds between categories of expenditure – so that overspending on one item cannot be offset by underspending on others.

Unless the total requested needs to be kept beneath a particular ceiling, it is advisable to allow for unforeseen contingencies, particularly in those categories which are most difficult to cost. Also, as suggested above, doctoral students and freelance researchers should strive to secure financial support for data coding and analysis, and for writing reports, papers or theses after returning from the field. A useful rule of thumb is that it takes approximately twice as long to analyse and write up the data as it takes to do fieldwork itself. A popular strategy for fieldworkers whose funding does not stretch this far is to take on short-term consultancies or part-time teaching contracts until writing up is completed. This keeps them alive but is less disruptive than full-time employment.

On a positive note, it is much cheaper living in most African, Asian or Latin American communities (particularly in rural villages) than in Europe or North America, the more so the better integrated the researcher is with the local lifestyle. Living expenses can be minimised by buying food in village markets rather than imported tins in city stores, travelling around by public transport rather than hired Landrover, and living with a local family rather than among rent-paying expatriates. Moreover, currency devaluations can provide windfall gains to Western researchers. The biggest single expense most expatriate fieldworkers face is simply the air fare there and back.

Finally, it is worth noting that institutional donors often demand receipts against claims made. Accordingly, it is vital to collect these while in the field, and to keep accurate records of expenditures, no matter how small. A few donors also state that any equipment purchased with their funds remains in their possession after the project is completed. Though this is not always enforced, it is a good idea to check before giving away bicycles and pocket calculators purchased with grant money as farewell gifts to assistants and respondents!

1.1.2 *Research clearance and visas*

Expatriate fieldworkers need to obtain permission to enter the country in which they hope to work (visas), as well as permission to carry out the research itself (research clearance). Even resident nationals often require official permission to do fieldwork in their own countries. Before applying for visas and/or research clearance – indeed, before selecting a research site – it is useful to investigate the nature of the bureaucratic process. Some governments discriminate against researchers from particular countries – Americans are not welcomed everywhere, and white South Africans experience predictable difficulties in gaining access not just to the rest of Africa, but to south Asia as well (though this appears to be changing at the time of writing). In the case of her fieldwork in Iran, Shahrashoub Razavi (Chapter 10) strongly doubts whether a non-national would have been granted research clearance at all.

Many fieldworkers experience long delays while waiting for their visa applications to be processed. As Razavi points out, 'Third World governments are frequently suspicious of Western researchers'; or at best they are indifferent, so that applications for research clearance receive low priority. Although this lack of interest can be extremely frustrating it is, to some extent, understandable. Fieldworkers (especially if they are students) bring no direct benefit to the government of the country concerned, nor does their research tangibly assist the community they study, except in rare cases. Often governments suspect that a fieldworker's reports will be critical, blaming rural poverty on neglect of agriculture, or the failure of development projects on bureaucratic corruption. A government which is unstable and lacking popular support is hardly likely to encourage outsiders to subject its policies to detailed empirical scrutiny.

Although it goes against the grain for some fieldworkers, there is often no substitute for using personal contacts to facilitate the process of gaining permission to undertake research in a foreign country. Having an institutional affiliation – with a local research institute or, as in Garry Christensen's case (Chapter 8), with a World Bank mission – can be invaluable, as can letters of support from a university or employer. Many governments insist that academic affiliation with a local university is obtained before they will grant research clearance. This affiliation can be secured either in a preliminary visit – as was done by Lucia da Corta in India (Chapter 7) and by John Hoddinott in Kenya (Chapter 5) – or by asking people who have links with the university to write letters of introduction.

As with securing financial support, the process of obtaining research clearance should be set in motion well in advance. The average waiting time is probably six to eight months, while delays of a year or longer are not uncommon. Even the most disciplined and patient researcher can find this period of uncertainty unnerving – not knowing how frequently and how aggressively to nag the Embassy or High Commission, being unable to get seriously involved in other work projects, having to put the research 'on hold' for an indefinite period. The only logical advice here is also the most obvious – to be patient, and flexible. Those vital bits of paper usually do come through in the end.

1.1.3 *Choosing where to go*

> 'Of all the millions of villages in the Third World, how did I end up in this one?'
> (The bewildered cry of the hypothetical fieldworker)

For some fieldworkers, such as those involved in project evaluation, the location of the research site is predetermined. Also, certain phenomena (for example, the Indian caste system) are found only in well-defined geographical areas. Similarly, existing literature might suggest a specific location as ideal to test particular theories, or to follow up studies by earlier fieldworkers. (But academic sensitivity can rear its head here – some researchers have a proprietorial 'my village' or 'my peasants' attitude toward their fieldwork sites.)

By contrast, students and academics who begin with hypotheses derived purely from theoretical literature rarely know at the outset precisely where their ideas will be tested. When the choice is completely open, one way of deciding where to do research is to focus in from the general to the specific. A typical pattern is to choose the continent and country, and sometimes a region within the country, from an institutional base in Europe or North America, then to narrow the focus to a district or province after arriving in the national or regional capital, and finally to select the community or village itself by travelling around and talking to local residents, academics and bureaucrats. It is important to take as much time as necessary to consider alternative sites. Even though the desire to get started with the 'real work' immediately will inevitably be strong, this is a decision which should not be rushed.

A very real worry is that the chosen locality might not be interesting in terms of the theoretical phenomena addressed by the research proposal. Even within small geographical areas, communities can differ greatly – in terms of their ecology and climate, ethnic composition and religious affiliations, economic circumstances and local politics. On the other hand, every area has its own interesting features, so there will always be something worth exploring, and it is often feasible to 'try out' two or three sites before deciding finally on one. Besides, in all good fieldwork, the environment itself will suggest modifications to the research questions as the work proceeds.

Apart from theoretical considerations, it is also important to investigate in advance such features as community health conditions and services (availability and quality), support for the research from local authorities, political divisions within the community, and logistical factors (accommodation and transport). A community which seems ideal from the academic perspective could prove impossible to work in because of logistical or political problems.

Finally, though, we should emphasise that, while it is important that the right *kind* of village is chosen (or district or market town), there is no such thing as 'the right village' *per se*. Of the fifteen or more fieldwork experiences shared by the contributors to this book, only once was 'the wrong village' chosen, requiring a change of research site – and that case was one of unusually bad luck.

1.1.4 *Theoretical and methodological preparation*

A problem most researchers face when preparing for fieldwork is not knowing precisely what to prepare for. Uncertainty about what is largely an unpredictable life event can lead to anxiety over minor details. As one contributor to this book put it: 'The major problem I confronted prior to beginning my field study was simply a constant bald fear of the unknown. I had very little idea of what I was going to face, thus my imagination ran wild.'

This suggests that one dimension of preparation is to reduce the unknown. An obvious place to start, for fieldworkers travelling abroad, is to read up on the country – historical accounts, novels by local authors, newspaper reports and magazines. Traveller's guide books, such as *The Rough Guide* series and *Africa on a Shoestring*, contain important and up-to-date information on practical matters. Learning the *lingua franca* before going can save valuable time later, and provide insights into the people and culture. Other useful sources of both logistical and professional advice are aid workers and researchers in related disciplines who have worked recently in the country. As for more general background on fieldwork, accounts by other fieldworkers will provide insights into the experiences of predecessors in similar situations. Finally, there remains the option of a preparatory trip (see below).

On the data collection side, fieldworkers whose preparation focuses on developing theoretical models are sometimes dismayed to discover how rapidly these need to be modified or even discarded when faced with the realities of life in the field. Others, lacking well-defined hypotheses to test or being under-prepared on methodological matters, can find themselves intellectually stranded, with no clear notion of how to proceed. A more sensible approach is to identify a general area of inquiry and to develop several tentative hypotheses, rather than being overly committed to specific theoretical constructs and arriving in the research site with piles of pre-written questionnaire forms in order to 'prove' these ideas. From this flexible beginning a schema can be developed indicating what data are required (and in what order of priority), for which well-focused sets of questions and research instruments can be derived. In any event, precise methodological questions can only be resolved with the local knowledge which is rapidly accumulated from living in the community.

Fieldwork is always full of surprises. The 'perfect' questionnaire and most elegant model, as developed in an office or ivory tower, may be completely inappropriate in the village. None the less, time spent in preparation is never wasted – unless it results in an inflexible commitment to unrealistic goals and methods. Even if much advance reading and writing about theory seems redundant in the field, this intellectual work is important in its own right. As Ludwig Wittgenstein once observed (not, admittedly, referring to fieldwork!): 'Thinking, too, has a time for ploughing and a time for gathering the harvest.'

Preliminary visits

For non-resident fieldworkers, a preliminary visit to the intended country has many practical and methodological advantages. Personal contact can be made with relevant bureaucrats and academics, which often expedites research clearance. This is particularly important where affiliation to a local university or research institute is a prerequisite, and is difficult to obtain from abroad. The preparatory trip also provides an opportunity to clarify the research site. If things go really well, the actual village or community might be selected, and potential research assistants might be primed in anticipation of the fieldwork itself.

A further advantage of a preparatory trip is psychological – reducing the fear of the unknown noted above, by eliminating some uncertainties. In many respects, a preparatory trip achieves little more than what would be done in the first few weeks of fieldwork anyway. But one major anxiety all fieldworkers feel is the urge to get the research under way as soon after arrival as possible (to 'hit the ground running'), and the temptation to rush things is that much greater if the ground has not been cleared in advance.

Most fieldworkers feel a curious gap between the pre-fieldwork period spent writing up hypotheses in libraries and offices, and the exponential leap in understanding they gain after just a few weeks in the field. A preliminary visit can also feed back into theoretical preparation, allowing ideas and research proposals to be sharpened and refined. Garry Christensen, who was not able to make a preliminary visit, believes with hindsight that 'it would have been very valuable in helping me move my proposal away from a preoccupation with theory and methodology, and to focus it more effectively on real issues'.

At the practical level, the case for investing in a preparatory visit is stronger the less the fieldworker knows about the country. Some important questions are best answered with first-hand knowledge. What personal effects and stationery are available in the stores, and what must be brought over from abroad? (At various times, many countries experience shortages of basic consumer goods, and up-to-date information on whether such essential items as typewriter ribbons and carbon paper are available can be difficult to obtain from secondary sources.) Are photocopiers or roneo machines readily accessible, for duplicating questionnaire forms? What about bringing over and changing money? How much does it cost to buy food and travel around? What is the postal service like?

An obvious disadvantage of making two trips rather than one is the cost. A second return air fare adds substantially to the research budget, and most fieldworkers are financially constrained. Besides, during extended fieldwork of a year or longer, a strong case can be made for coming home halfway through, for a break and to consult with colleagues, and the second air fare might be preferred for this purpose instead.

1.2 Being there

The context of fieldwork reflects the conjunction of two sets of decisions – about what lifestyle to adopt ('Living in the field'), and how to interact with people encountered ('Living with others'). These personal and inter-personal dimensions of fieldwork can pose practical and ethical dilemmas on several levels, as Wendy Olsen discovered:

> Some of my stress was inevitable, arising from my unclear social role and my attempt to ally myself with all classes and communities at once. Should I lend money to friends in the village? Should I employ a servant? Should I keep walking to distant villages, even in the hottest season, as opposed to buying a vehicle? I did none of these but in each case I felt a moral dilemma faced me.

Given the uniqueness of each fieldwork situation, and of each fieldworker, questions such as these can rarely be reduced to universally applicable solutions. Accordingly, this section simply draws on the experiences of ourselves and our fellow contributors, in terms of living and relating to others in the field, and identifies common findings.

1.2.1 *Living in the field*

Here we consider four practical aspects of life in the field – living arrangements, managing time, health problems and precautions, and 'fieldwork blues'.

Living arrangements

In terms of both the ideology and methodology of social anthropology, it is considered imperative for the fieldworker to live as closely as possible to the community being studied – in order not just to observe, but to participate actively in community life. The argument applies to any social scientist, and probably to researchers from any discipline, simply because involvement adds a dimension to understanding which living apart can never provide. In any event, if the community is relatively isolated there may be little alternative to finding accommodation locally, given that commuting from a town some miles away is bound to be impractical, time-consuming and tiring.

Showing a willingness to live among the community also breaks down barriers and reduces the extent to which the fieldworker is perceived as an outsider. Living with a local family, if this is possible, provides unrivalled opportunities for 'participant observation' – by picking up vernacular speech, gaining insights into how people relate to each other across the genders and generations, participating in domestic tasks and farming, and so on. In such cases, fieldworkers are often accepted as, effectively, members of the family, and they might even be given caste or kinship identities.

At a practical level, the family will usually offer to cook meals for their guest, and children will help with chores like fetching water and sweeping the verandah. (Incidentally, since households and communities in the Third World exist and function in complex webs of inter-dependence, we would argue that an ideological commitment by fieldworkers to 'self-sufficiency' is misguided. Living with a family means accepting the benefits of incorporation, as well as the obligations, without feeling guilty about 'exploiting' them.)

One methodological drawback to living in the research community is that this compromised relationship with the host family usually requires excluding them from any random sample. For example, if the research includes studying sources of income and the fieldworker pays rent to the landlord, or even buys food for the family, these income data are already prejudiced. (The same is true with respect to paid assistants drawn from the community.) In a wider context, the host family will be engaged in a network of relationships with neighbouring households, and this inevitably influences how those people perceive and respond to the fieldworker, for better or worse. Elizabeth Francis (see Chapter 6) found that living with a respected family in rural Kenya provided a useful entrée into a community wary of outsiders. In other cases, some people may refuse to be interviewed, because they see the fieldworker as being aligned with a family with whom they are feuding, or to whom they are in debt. It is impossible to foresee all the consequences of living with a particular family, but this factor should not be underestimated in terms of shaping relationships with other local respondents.

If the price of living alone is loneliness, the price of living with a family can be loss of privacy. A strong need for 'personal space' is not always shared by residents of Third World communities, and fieldworkers sometimes find that they do not have enough time and privacy to work in the evenings, or just to potter about on their days off. In many African and Asian societies, it is considered bad manners for a person to be left on his or her own. One Western researcher who worked among the untouchables in India had people sleeping in his room, against his wishes, because it was unthinkable for him to be alone, even at night.

Fieldworkers who are accompanied by their partners, or are members of a research team that lives together, are better protected against such intrusions. (Although fieldwork is usually seen as a solitary undertaking – which partly explains the *rite de passage* mythologising which often surrounds it – this is certainly not a rule, and there is no reason why partners and even children should not accompany researchers to the field.) But the question of personal space is a matter for diplomacy and tact. Often fieldworkers are too intimidated by their desire to 'fit in' to try to negotiate this particular cultural difference with their hosts. However, if the matter is approached in the right way, it should be possible to achieve a compromise which is acceptable to both the fieldworker and the host family.

Managing time

One of the many paradoxes of fieldwork concerns time. On the one hand, following the principle that 'more is better than less', there is a temptation to dash about like crazy, meeting and greeting everyone in sight, learning the language, getting deeply involved in community life, collecting as much data as possible. Everyone we know who has done fieldwork works incredibly hard while in the field. This is a natural consequence of the stimulation (when things are going well) of getting up at dawn and being outdoors in the sun all day, doing interesting research with (generally) nice people. Juxtaposed with this are the long hours travelling from place to place, sitting in bureaucrats' offices, finding respondents and waiting to do interviews. One way to manage this paradox is to put waiting time to constructive use, as Olsen found:

> You must accept the inevitability of some wasted time – waiting for buses, being ill, getting stuck in town due to flooded roads, waiting for printing of questionnaires, etc. I tried to use my 'wasted' time wisely by resting, reading, writing, and talking (in Telugu) to pass the time and prepare for the next series of interviews.

A second practical step is to build breaks for rest and relaxation into the work routine. This is especially important if living arrangements preclude having much privacy. One solution is to have a retreat outside the community, where solitude can be guaranteed when work or social pressures threaten to become overwhelming. This might take the form of a room in a government rest-house or cheap hotel in a nearby town, which is rented at weekends. An alternative is a monthly trip to the capital city. In any case, regular breaks from the punishing work schedule most fieldworkers impose on themselves are certainly advisable, if not essential. Time off should be spent doing anything but work – listening to the radio, reading novels, writing letters, pursuing hobbies, travelling. Keeping a personal diary, or writing letters home in diary form, also helps many fieldworkers to record and analyse new experiences and stimulating conversations as they happen, before they are forgotten or reinterpreted with hindsight.

Health problems and precautions

Fieldwork can be an unhealthy occupation. Every contributor to this volume was ill at least once during his or her fieldwork. The enormous differences in climate, diet and lifestyle between, for instance, an urban Western environment and a rural village in the tropics mean that anyone who makes this move will be exposed to new and strange illnesses, no matter what precautions are taken. Diarrhoea and malaria, especially, are occupational hazards of fieldwork.

There are two dimensions to addressing health issues: being well prepared before going, and taking precautions once there. Good preparation includes: getting all the necessary vaccinations and pills; finding out about diseases endemic to the region (some areas – and seasons – within a country are more unhealthy than others, and this can influence the choice of a research site); getting good medical insurance, including the possibility of rapid evacuation (such as a subscription to AMREF, for Africanists); taking a first aid kit (including syringes where AIDS is widespread); and packing a book on first aid, or – the fieldworker's medical Bible – David Werner's *Where There Is No Doctor*.

Soon after arriving in the field, it is advisable to check out the local health facilities – clinics, hospitals, doctors and dentists – to get some idea about the level and quality of services provided, and to ensure ready access to them if required. As far as health and daily life in the field is concerned, many basic points bear repeating – about boiling or purifying drinking water, remembering to take malaria tablets, and so on – but one issue which is not stressed in most 'guidelines for fieldworkers' is that of getting enough rest, as suggested above. The downside of overworking is the danger of becoming run down or exhausted, which is a good way of raising vulnerability to all sorts of diseases.

Without wishing to be alarmist, we suggest that prospective fieldworkers build into their work schedules an allowance for being sick. It is better to plan for illness than to hope not to be affected. This need not be an argument against adopting a fairly rigid work schedule, such as repeat interviewing at regular intervals, but it does at least suggest the need for flexibility and contingency planning.

These points are obvious enough, but there is a more complex issue here too, concerning lifestyle and cultural adaptation. Every fieldworker has to tread a fine line between precaution and paranoia. The dilemma usually rears its head when someone first offers you food or a drink. What to do? Accept out of courtesy (recognising that sharing food can be a very important social gesture) and risk the consequences, or decline and risk causing offence? Barbara Harriss writes that: 'Taking risks with food and drink means paying certain penalties with health', but, like most of us, she felt that some chances were worth taking. If, on the other hand, your health is fragile and you are particularly alarmed about the possibility of contracting dysentery or hepatitis, then try to decline offers to share a meal or a drink as sensitively as possible. (Since even very poor people often offer meat to visitors, being a vegetarian is one good excuse – and can provoke a lively conversation following the stunned disbelief of your hosts!)

On the positive side, most researchers find illness no more than an annoying disruption to their life and work in the field. Every researcher has heard about somebody who came down with some nasty virus and had to abandon their fieldwork, temporarily or for good, but these stories are often apocryphal. And (in retrospect at least) one of the great pleasures of fieldwork is sitting around with other initiates after the event, swapping 'You think *you* were sick!' anecdotes.

'Fieldwork blues'

Depression during fieldwork can occur for a number of reasons, and it is unusual for someone engaged in long-term fieldwork abroad, particularly if unaccompanied, not to feel depressed occasionally, even if the experience overall is generally positive and rewarding. Feelings of isolation and cultural alienation can induce loneliness, which may or may not be alleviated by making contact with local expatriates (doctors, missionaries and aid workers). The desire to see a good movie or have a meal at a favourite restaurant can become overpowering some evenings, but these feelings should be more than compensated for by the excitement of living in a completely different way. More painful is the protracted separation from family and friends, and there is no antidote to this except keeping in contact through letter-writing and other means.

Health problems can also bring on 'fieldwork blues'. There is a strong connection between physical debilitation and emotional vulnerability, and few experiences are more depressing than sweating out a fever on a bed thousands of miles from home. Having said that, it is not an exaggeration to state that African, Asian and Latin American people are generally very caring and sensitive towards the sick, so that fieldworkers who are attacked by malaria or dysentery or something equally unpleasant will probably be well looked after by their hosts.

Work anxiety is potentially the biggest source of stress during fieldwork, and this is aggravated when illness prevents work. Fieldworkers are notoriously insecure about how their research is going, and perpetually worried about what they are missing – which vital questions they have not asked, what is going on under the surface of village life that they have failed to tap into, whether their methodology is rigorous enough. One piece of advice here is to think positive: to count the completed questionnaires and filled notebooks piling up in the corner of the room, rather than agonising over questions unasked and interviews which did not go well. At the end of it all, most fieldworkers return home with far more data than they can ever analyse.

1.2.2 *Living with others*

Fieldwork necessarily involves relationships with several groups of people – respondents, research assistants, the host family and local officials. Here we consider the following dimensions of these relationships: learning the language; encounters with bureaucrats; being given a role by respondents; social and political involvement in the community; and compensating people for their assistance.

Learning the language

As stated above, great emphasis is laid in both the theory and ideology of village-level fieldwork on close involvement with the local community, and a key element is the ability to communicate directly with people on their own terms – in their own language. Although the textbooks concentrate on methodological advantages (such as the fact that fluency allows the researcher to conduct interviews without interpreters), the personal benefits are as important as the professional. Without some command of the local language, all social and professional interactions will be restricted to those people – often a small minority – who speak *your* language. This provides a limited insight into the community, as well as exacerbating feelings of loneliness and alienation.

As with every aspect of fieldwork, though, there are pros and cons to learning the local language. As Devereux argues in Chapter 3, a major drawback is the investment of time and energy required, which can amount to trade-offs being made against other, more pressing demands. Foreign researchers need to know the language very well indeed before conducting interviews unaided. The primary objective of fieldwork is to collect data, and learning the language is only one means to that end. It follows that the degree of expertise or fluency acquired should be a matter of personal choice – this decision being based on such factors as length of time in the field and the type of interviewing to be undertaken – rather than a universal imperative.

Relations with bureaucrats

All fieldwork, unless it is covert, is conducted inside an official (political and bureaucratic) framework. Once research clearance is granted, the fieldwork has been 'legitimised' at a national or Ministerial level, but contact will continue with government officials (Ministry employees, police), the parallel political hierarchy – 'traditional authorities' (village chiefs or headmen) – and technical people (experts in research institutes, parastatal managers). Field research in any given locality must be cleared with local politicians or administrators, and permission should also be sought from local chiefs, where these exist. The third category, technical experts, are people whom the field-worker usually approaches on research-related, rather than administrative, matters.

So much depends on the personalities of individual officials that generalising about the role of bureaucracy in fieldwork is inadvisable. Approaching all bureaucrats with the presumption that they are genetically programmed to be antagonistic is unfair. Our experience suggests that relationships with technical experts are usually straightforward, and often very cooperative and mutually supportive. This is partly because these interactions tend to be conducted on a basis of relative equality at the professional or academic level, and partly because these people wield less power than government officials. Similarly, village chiefs and headmen are often flattered by signs of interest in their district, being hopeful perhaps that development projects and other benefits will follow from the research. If treated with due deference and respect (paying courtesy calls as frequently as local custom demands, for instance), they rarely seem to resent fieldworkers or to hinder fieldwork.

On the other hand, many fieldworkers have experienced difficulties with local government officials. Where the researcher represents an additional burden on overworked staff, this is understandable. In these cases, as the fieldworker gets to be a familiar face, and provided he or she is not too demanding and is demonstrably grateful for any assistance given, suspicions often subside and relations improve. Access to local administration files and records might even be granted where it was initially denied. However, there are instances where a bureaucrat is deliberately unhelpful and persistently obstructive, or demands 'compensation' for cooperation. Local residents and other researchers can advise fieldworkers on what constitutes 'normal behaviour' and what amounts to unacceptable abuses of power by bureaucrats, and on how best to deal with difficult individuals. The best strategy generally seems to be to remain assertive but friendly at all times – *never* aggressive.

Finally, in countries or districts with a strong police or military presence, interactions with these groups are best kept to a minimum. They may well perceive fieldworkers as 'awkward' in some unidentifiable sense, or as intruders on their territory, even when permission to work in the area has been granted by the relevant authorities. Consequently, it is important to keep a low profile, and to ensure that important documents such as research clearance and police registration are in order and renewed when necessary.

Perceptions of fieldworkers by respondents

Elizabeth Francis emphasises in Chapter 6 that fieldwork entails personal and social as well as 'professional' relationships between fieldworkers and respondents (also see discussions in the chapters by Harriss, Razavi and Heyer). Where personal interactions are limited, as when all interviewing is delegated to research assistants, fieldwork becomes a sterile exercise in data gathering – and a more unreliable exercise at that. If there is one essential qualification for successful fieldwork it is a demonstrable and genuine interest in other people. The form these relationships take is also strongly determined by local perceptions of 'strangers' and the 'role' local people give to 'outsiders'. This may be modified by the lifestyle fieldworkers adopt (their attitudes and behaviour) and by their unique personal characteristics (age, gender, nationality and cultural background). How much these factors affect the conduct of fieldwork depends on the extent to which they either create or break down barriers between fieldworkers and respondents.

Older researchers tend to be treated with more respect, and respondents might choose to discuss certain issues only with older fieldworkers. But being middle-aged rather than young is also associated with higher status and greater power and influence. This factor might raise expectations that something tangible will come out of the study – a perception which is less likely to affect younger fieldworkers who present themselves as students.

Gender can be both advantageous and limiting. Harriss argues that female researchers are typically regarded as dissociated from the state, which tends to be male dominated. Women are often perceived as being less threatening than men. But they may find it more difficult to be taken seriously. For example, Francis and Hoddinott undertook research on the same ethnic group in Kenya. They were approximately the same age, and were undertaking research for the same purpose. Hoddinott, as a married man, found it straightforward to speak with older men and women, but problematic to interview young married women if their husbands were not present. As a single woman, Francis had ready access to female respondents, but found initially that older men did not take her seriously.

Some people will refuse to talk with women at all, because they carry less status than men. In general, researchers seem to find it easier to interview respondents of their own gender. But restricted access to certain people or topics is rarely an absolute taboo. Much depends on the individual's personality and style of approach.

Nationality and background can work both for and against fieldworkers. Indigenous researchers avoid many of the adaptation problems (such as learning the language) faced by expatriates. Razavi found that as an Iranian working in Iran, she picked up on subtleties an outsider could easily have missed. But being a national also raised the possibility that she might overlook important features that respondents assumed she already knew.

There are other advantages to being a 'stranger'. Respondents are as curious about the outside world as researchers are about the communities they are studying, so that interviews can become mutually informative dialogues. But foreign fieldworkers are also more likely to be perceived as representatives of international donors or other agencies, and respondents may participate in the research because of their (usually mistaken) belief that the researcher will bring tangible benefits to their community. For this reason, once expectations have been dampened, lone doctoral students may be given less time and status than project researchers or aid workers. However, the overwhelmingly positive experiences of the contributors to this volume do not bear this out.

Social and political involvement

More involvement in the social life of the community is invariably better than less. Putting local people at their ease and being accepted by them can be achieved by accepting invitations to social events, festivals, religious services and (preferably non-partisan) political meetings. Conversely, fieldworkers who lock themselves in their rooms and only venture out to do interviews are bound to set up a wall of distrust which leaves them appearing isolated and aloof. Besides, social occasions offer opportunities to observe interactions and relationships within the village, which add greatly to any outsider's understanding of how the community operates. Interviewing individuals at their homes provides a limited insight into how they live; seeing them in a group exposes nuances of status, interactions between rich and poor, and so on which cannot be discovered only through face-to-face questioning.

A more vexing matter is that of revealing emotions. Researchers who are concerned about appearing judgemental or ethnocentric tend to present themselves as bland, pleasant individuals who never disagree with anyone. Yet, in many social contexts at least, there is surely no harm in revealing one's true feelings and opinions. Unless fieldworkers open up to people, which includes expressing emotions and debating over conflicting views, that level of honesty will not be offered in return, and social interactions will never develop beyond polite formality.

There is also a deeper issue here. All fieldworkers find themselves facing moral dilemmas which arise from their distinctly odd (and temporary) relationship with the local community. How should they respond to the discovery that someone in the village is beating his wife? Do outsiders have the right to interfere, or should they ignore what goes on? As Ken Wilson notes in Chapter 12, living in another community does not require the suspension of a personal moral code. Fieldworkers have as much right (indeed, as much *obligation*) to redress injustices in their host community as anyone else. Their status as outsiders may even give them the freedom to intervene where local people would find doing so dangerous. But any intervention must be well informed and appropriate.

These questions highlight the complex relationship in fieldwork between research and political action – how to resolve the tension between the urge 'to do something useful' (which impels involvement) against the methodological imperative for 'academic objectivity' (which demands detachment). This subject provoked the only heated debate during the workshop out of which this book was born. Doctoral students who argued on behalf of active involvement noted that: 'The process is essentially parasitic. We're all in it for Ph.D's.' Recognising this creates an imperative to put something back, either by direct activism or by advocacy – observing and recording poverty and injustice simply are not enough. Other participants argued that fieldwork is a legitimate form of political involvement in its own right. Successful and rewarding fieldwork requires that the researcher recognises inequalities, decides what to do about them, and gets on with living and working in the community. If political involvement antagonises powerful people within the village, or local officials, then activism and research are in conflict, and the professional objectives of the project may be jeopardised.

Paying for assistance and dealing with expectations

A further set of ethical questions arises out of the evident economic inequality between comparatively affluent researchers and the relatively poor (or absolutely destitute) communities in which most choose to live and work. The problem has to be faced at several levels, including the following:

- Paying or otherwise remunerating interpreters and assistants.
- Compensating the host family.
- Recompensing respondents (and officials?) for their cooperation.
- Meeting the expectations of the community at large.

There are no obvious rules for paying research assistants, which is usually a matter for negotiation in each case. Sometimes fixed norms or salary scales exist (where assistants are hired from research institutes, say), but in the absence of set rates of pay, it is necessary to take advice. A useful yardstick is local salaries in formal sector employment – what do teachers and local government employees earn? Often these rates will seem very low, especially by Western standards, but such comparisons are inappropriate: £200 or $300 per month may seem a derisory sum in Britain or the United States, but might be a huge sum to a research assistant. Besides, a salary paid monthly or by round of interviews is unlikely to constitute the only transfer between fieldworker and assistant. Typically, this relationship will also involve gifts and assistance of various kinds – on both sides.

A similar logic applies to the family the fieldworker stays with. Often local people will be extraordinarily generous in offering accommodation and meals, possibly even refusing to take payment in return. But even if no rent is asked for, this generosity must be reciprocated somehow. Being taken into a family entails accepting certain domestic obligations and financial responsibilities, often unspoken, sometimes articulated as expectations about help with teaching the children or paying their school fees.

Fieldworkers do not like to pay respondents in cash for interviews, nor is payment (generally) expected. But interviewing does take time, and can cost respondents money in terms of lost income. When interviews imply a financial sacrifice, then compensation seems appropriate. In Iran, for example, Razavi paid some of her respondents the equivalent of a daily wage, in recognition of the fact that they were giving up a day's labour. An alternative to cash payment is to offer small gifts as a tangible expression of thanks. This can take a number of forms – food, photographs, medicines, writing letters to relatives or officials, even interceding on the respondent's behalf with local bureaucrats or hospitals.

But compensation might create friction between respondents as well. If significant inequalities exist within the community, equal payments are inadvisable – a sizeable sum to a landless labourer will be an insulting pittance to a wealthy merchant. Yet paying wealthy respondents more than the poor only exacerbates existing inequalities, whereas offering payment or gifts only to the poor appears to favour some people at the expense of others. (How to draw the line between 'poor' and 'non-poor' interviewees?) Besides, cash compensation can interfere with the data collection exercise, particularly if it is more than nominal, and if it relates (directly or indirectly) to the research issues. Conversely, if no payment is offered, non-respondents may ridicule participants for being 'used' for nothing. Others who are excluded from the sampling frame may want to be interviewed (and may resent being excluded, believing that those selected for interviews will benefit somehow), while some who are selected may complain that they have been picked on to answer interminable boring questions.

As soon as fieldworkers give gifts, pay informants in cash or lend money, a precedent is set which inevitably fuels escalating expectations. Failing to meet these may compromise both the current fieldwork and subsequent research projects. Faced with these dilemmas, the researcher may prefer to offer a single, sizeable contribution to the wider community as a whole. This, too, can take a number of forms – such as a party, contributions to community events, a well or health centre, or trips to crop research centres. But this must be handled delicately. It is important to donate something to which all members of the community will have equal access. Again, the gift might distort the research in some way, unless its presentation is deferred until departure.

More generally, Bleek (1978) has pointed out that all transfers between fieldworkers and the community they observe are based on an inherent and irreversible inequality. At one level, therefore, compensation must be seen as a token gesture because (typically) it requires no significant sacrifice by the researcher and does nothing to diminish the inequality between donor and recipient. It also sidesteps the deeper moral issues which serious political involvement can address. While recognising the legitimacy of this view, we believe that compensation can also act as a tangible and legitimate expression of appreciation.

In conclusion, the issue of compensation is as complex as any in fieldwork. On a personal level, it is difficult to refuse to assist people who are demonstrably worse off, particularly when they have been generous and welcoming. At the same time, expectations and demands may rise to levels that leave the fieldworker feeling pressured and manipulated. Researchers sometimes cannot disentangle the feeling that they are 'liked' from the suspicion that they are being 'used'. (Of course, their role in the community must seem equally confusing and double-edged to the local population!) The way this contradiction is resolved can have a significant bearing on both the personal and professional success of fieldwork. Trying to stay relaxed and easy-going is advisable, as is striving to see relationships with respondents and assistants from their perspective.

1.3 Coming home

Strictly speaking, what happens after the last questionnaire has been filled out has little to with 'the context of fieldwork'. But this chapter would be incomplete if it stopped at this point. Here we give brief attention to the nature of post-fieldwork obligations to the researched community, and to 'post-fieldwork adjustment'.

1.3.1 *Post-fieldwork obligations*

Fieldwork does not end with the completion of the final interview. Researchers have responsibilities to their host communities. A primary obligation is to tell respondents' stories truthfully. In Chapter 12, Wilson suggests that researchers should consider how people wish to be represented while still in the field: 'Responding to the challenge of "writing for the people studied", before you are obliged to write anything, can give foundation to ethical concerns of how to represent others accurately, yet sympathetically.'

Before disseminating the results of the research, it is important to consider how this will affect respondents, particularly when working through non-academic channels or taking on an advocacy role. Being absolutely sure of the facts is essential. Failing to understand fully the context of a given situation, and the effects pronouncements or lobbying may have, will lead to misunderstandings at best and physical harm at worst. It is also possible that particular individuals, or institutions, will distort fieldworkers' findings to suit their own interests. In such an environment, it is important to maintain respondents' anonymity. No-one wants his or her research to be used against individuals on whose goodwill the researcher has relied.

Finally, expatriate fieldworkers should leave as much information as they can in the host country. This can be accomplished by depositing a copy of fieldnotes in the national library or relevant university department, or leaving them with colleagues. Not only is this a courtesy, but it provides a potentially valuable source of information for resident academics, development agencies and future fieldworkers. Sending back photocopies of published articles or reports also helps in this way.

1.3.2 *Post-fieldwork adjustment*

As far as we know, the phenomenon of 'post-fieldwork blues' has not been commented on in the fieldwork literature. Yet once they return home, many researchers feel distinctly peculiar. Their once familiar professional and domestic routines now seem small, cut off and unreal. Work colleagues, as well as family and friends, seem unable to comprehend how profound the fieldwork was as a life experience (even if they have done fieldwork themselves, because they have 're-adapted'). The seminars, lectures and conferences, the obligatory number-crunching and report writing, the elaborate theoretical models, the recently published papers, journals and books – all seem not just meaningless, but positively bizarre, next to the stark realities of life in a Third World community.

For some expatriate fieldworkers, reintegration is relatively swift. For others, the social pressures, professional competitiveness and different rhythm of life make adjusting back to their previous lifestyles even more difficult than the move to the fieldwork village. Researchers who go abroad to study an exotic culture *expect* it to be different. It is doubly alienating to come back and yet fail to feel 'at home', for reasons that cannot easily be articulated. Ironically, these feelings tend to be stronger the more stimulating, enjoyable and rewarding the fieldwork is. The deeper researchers crawled beneath the skin of the community, the more closely they lived like the villagers, the more personal and intimate were their relationships with assistants and respondents – the greater the wrench of pulling suddenly away from that life and returning unceremoniously to a new relationship with the old.

There is no advice anyone can offer for dealing with 'post-fieldwork blues', except to expect this and sit it out. It certainly is not a significant enough factor to put people off doing fieldwork altogether – on the contrary, as suggested above, a healthy dose of disorientation and nostalgia is surely the sign of a *successful* fieldwork experience.

Notes

1. We would like to thank our fellow contributors for sharing their thoughts and experiences on the issues raised in this and the following chapter. Some of their

written comments are quoted here; other quotes are extracts from their individual chapters.

2. *The Grants Register 1991–1993* (Basingstoke: Macmillan, 1990); *Directory of Grant-Making Trusts 1989* (Tonbridge: Charities Aid Foundation, 1989). See also the *Scholarships Guide for Commonwealth Postgraduate Students, 1989–1991* (London: Association of Commonwealth Universities, 1988); and *The Directory of Work and Study in Developing Countries* (Oxford: Vacation Work, 1990).

2

Issues in data collection

Stephen Devereux and John Hoddinott

Introduction

As we have already stressed, this is not a textbook on fieldwork methodology. Instead, it tries to illustrate how community-level research occurs in practice, through the experiences of several fieldworkers. But the case studies presented in Part 2 also have a good deal to say about data collection, and it is appropriate to see this book as complementary to standard texts in this respect. We address issues not addressed in those books, as well as commenting on real situations where circumstances made it difficult to implement a 'standard' approach, forcing us to develop our own solutions.

The purpose of this chapter is to provide an overview of these issues in data collection. Our intention is not to be comprehensive but rather to introduce and synthesise key points and conclusions drawn in later chapters. We have grouped the issues into three categories – interpreters and assistants, interviewing, and broader methodological matters.

2.1 Research assistance

One of the strengths of primary over secondary research is that analysis can be undertaken by the people who actually collected the data.[1] The closer the fieldworker is to the data (and the data sources – people!), the better her or his understanding of its strengths and limitations. The choice of whether to work alone, or with an interpreter, or to delegate interviewing responsibilities to research assistants and enumerators, becomes important for this reason.

2.1.1 *Enumerators, interpreters or research assistants?*

The choice between a team of enumerators, a research assistant or an interpreter will depend in the first instance on the scale and nature of the research. Delegating data collection is necessary when a larger survey is undertaken – as in Christensen's study of 150 households in 6 widely dispersed villages. While this approach limits the fieldworker's all-important 'feel' for individual respondents, it has the advantage of exposing her or him to a wider range of physical and social conditions.[2]

Working entirely without help is not feasible unless the fieldworker fully comprehends the local language, and has a good understanding of the local culture. (This was the case in Razavi's fieldwork, since she returned to her home country.) Also, doing all interviews personally limits the sample that the fieldworker can conceivably work with, even if it adds depth and colour to the data collected. Finding the right balance between comprehensiveness and manageability is not straightforward, and some fieldworkers end up struggling with a sample that is too large to handle, while refusing to delegate work to anyone else. Between these two extremes lie several intermediate possibilities, including using an interpreter and a research assistant.

The main advantage of working with an interpreter – someone whose responsibilities are confined to translating – is that the fieldworker enjoys fairly direct contact with respondents, while retaining some flexibility (to write and think) during interviews. The drawback is that information is received second hand, rather than directly from respondents. Having at least a rudimentary understanding of the language helps the fieldworker to pick up obvious mistranslations and to detect when words are being put into the respondent's mouth. Some interpreters may hide facts, perhaps out of embarrassment or loyalty to their relatives and friends, or because they believe the researcher does not want to be bothered with details.

A second option is to employ a research assistant. This is someone who works closely with the fieldworker and knows what sort of follow-up and supplementary questions to ask. In Hoddinott's case, he and his research assistant conducted the first two rounds of interviews together, but worked separately during the final round in order to complete the interviewing more quickly. Having effectively an extra fieldworker collecting data can greatly increase productivity – when the researcher is sick, for instance, an assistant might be able to continue interviewing alone.

Most people who feel their fieldwork was 'successful' comment that research assistants were indispensable to that success. A good assistant fulfils a number of useful functions beyond translating. One is to provide vital contextual information – about the village, local culture or subtleties of language – that might otherwise be missed altogether, or be acquired through making painful mistakes. Assistants can provide a guide to the sensitivity of different topics, and screen questions that respondents might object to or resent. They act as ambassadors at large, introducing fieldworkers to the local community and discreetly explaining their presence to people who might be too shy or suspicious to ask directly. In interviews, as Harriss describes, they permit a useful division of labour. If an assistant does all the talking, the researcher can concentrate on writing down responses, taking comprehensive notes, and thinking about further areas to probe.

2.1.2 *Characteristics of good assistants*

A job description for the ideal research assistant would probably include: communication skills, good knowledge of English (or French, or Spanish) as well as the local language(s), a perceptive intelligence, inexhaustible patience, unfailing dependability, and an ability to get along with all elements of the local population. Educated applicants (such as teachers or local government employees) are likely to have a better understanding of the nature and purpose of research than someone whose only obvious qualification is an ability to translate. On the other hand, well-educated young assistants may be looking for better jobs and can quickly get bored if they are not given responsibilities commensurate with their skills.

A research assistant's gender can also be significant. Someone who seems perfect in all respects may be excluded from working with half the population (in Muslim societies, for instance, men might be barred from interviewing women). Christensen found that female enumerators in Burkina Faso could not ask male respondents about cattle ownership and credit, while Razavi observed that female respondents in rural Iran were far less communicative when her (male) assistant was present. Other researchers have found it advantageous to work with an enumerator of the opposite gender. In Tanzania, Lockwood employed a young local woman to obtain reported ages of women from women themselves – with significantly different results to ages reported for the same women by older men in their households. Heyer chose male assistants to provide both protection and a 'counterweight' to her being a woman.

An important consideration is whether assistants should be drawn from the community itself or brought in from outside. Local people have local knowledge, but they also have local affiliations and interests to protect, of which the fieldworker, as an outsider, will be unaware. These may compromise the quality of certain data, inhibiting or even prohibiting interviews with hostile individuals. Villagers may be more suspicious of an assistant whom they do not know, at least initially, but they may also talk to her or him more freely than they would to a local person. More generally, an important characteristic of any research assistant, whether local or an outsider, is an ability to get on well with respondents. However, it is rarely clear in advance whether the person chosen has this quality.

In some circumstances the choice of potential assistants is strictly limited, and the decision is made more by default than a process of elimination. Heyer's experiences of fieldwork in both Kenya and India suggest that there may generally be a larger pool of educated people willing to work as assistants in south Asian than in African rural communities. Another constraint is that it can be difficult to find qualified (literate) female assistants, due to gender bias against girls in education. Husbands and parents may also object to their wives or daughters working with a male outsider.

In the end, though, basic literacy aside, perhaps the most important characteristic in a good research assistant (and in a good fieldworker!) is that both parties get on well with each other. The nature of long-term fieldwork requires the researcher and the assistant to be together almost every day for a year or more, often working unsocial hours in physically uncomfortable settings. Together with radically different cultural, social and economic backgrounds, these factors produce scope for tension at both the personal and professional levels. Given the conditions in which most fieldworkers live, it is highly desirable to work with an assistant in an atmosphere of mutual respect and friendship.

2.2 Interviewing

The basic methodological technique in most social science fieldwork is the one-to-one interview, supplemented by other methods such as group discussions, collection of market prices, anthropometric measurement and participant observation. Interviewing raises such a range of issues that entire books have been devoted to it. In this section, we consider five sets of questions: selecting respondents, alternative types of interview, where and when to conduct interviews, confidentiality and sensitive issues, and cross-checking responses for consistency and accuracy.

2.2.1 *Choosing respondents*

In all fieldwork based on sampling (rather than case studies), two stages are involved in the selection of respondents – identifying a sampling frame or survey area, and choosing individuals or households from within that sampling frame. The delineation of a survey area can present immediate problems. In rural areas, village boundaries may not be clearly defined, or kin relationships represent more important connections between households than geographical proximity. Sometimes part of a village is virtually inaccessible (lying beyond a river, say), but there is no reason why such areas must necessarily be covered – there is nothing sacred about the village as a bounded unit for sampling purposes. Similar problems arise when working in urban centres (Chapter 9 discusses some of these). A cursory understanding of the area will help to determine how important the inclusion or exclusion of remote sections will be. Crucial to the selection of a sampling frame is whether clusters of households are distinct from others in ways which matter to the research. For example, a study of rural out-migration might well consider migrants from the village, now living in urban areas, as part of its logical sampling frame (even if tracking down these people is difficult and time-consuming).

A useful method for improving the representativeness of a sample, or of ensuring that specific categories of households are included, is sample stratification. Households or individuals can be classified in various ways – by relative wealth, ethnicity, gender, occupation, age and so on. For sampling purposes, the choice of stratifying criteria should reflect the research interests (female-headed v. male-headed households; farmers v. traders). Olsen's fieldwork in south India provides an instructive case study of stratification in practice.

Although sampling is often conducted in terms of households, interviews are not. Defining the unit of analysis is important at the outset, since it influences the composition of the sample. In much of west Africa, the residential unit (the compound) can include several households, and a single household (as locally conceptualised) can include several 'nuclear families' (see Chapter 3). Whether the compound, household, nuclear family or individual is preferred as the sampling unit will depend on the focus of the research. As Deane (1949, p. 47) noted, writing on Zambia in the late 1940s:

> the sleeping household, the eating household, the cash-earning household, the cash-spending household, and the producing household all represent different combinations and permutations within one wide group of relatives. . . It is usually necessary to place these persons in households for the purposes of analysis on the basis of arbitrary decisions. The decisions will depend largely on the form of the analysis.

Finally, as with any other aspect of fieldwork, the more time is spent creating a sample, the less time is available for the research itself. This is particularly important when the fieldworker's time in the field is limited. Harriss and Hoddinott describe some methods for shortening the period required to create a sampling frame.

2.2.2 *Types of interview*

Our focus in this volume is on one-to-one interviewing situations, and on individual relationships with respondents. This largely reflects our own experiences, which in turn reflect the kinds of data social scientists doing fieldwork typically collect: information gathered from individuals about themselves, their households and the environment in which they operate.

These encounters can take two forms: that of a structured interview (typically with a set questionnaire), or a more unstructured setting, with information written down as it emerges.

In an unstructured interview, there is no formal questionnaire. Rather, a series of topics is introduced from a checklist, and discussed in any order that seems natural. Instead of extracting identical bits of data from everyone, the interviewer encourages respondents to talk on topics about which they have most to say. They may also find an unstructured approach more friendly and less intimidating than a formal interview. Responses can be copied down in a notebook and scrutinised after the interview. (Unless respondents feel inhibited by the tape recorder, it can be useful to record these interviews, though there is a danger of being swamped with tapes which take more time to transcribe than they did to record!)

This method is especially useful at an early stage in fieldwork, to reveal important background information and the concerns of local people; and in certain types of questioning – life histories, local history, group discussions and the like. Iterative unstructured interviews can be used to build a qualitative profile of an individual, firm, family or kin group. Harriss outlines this in relation to her fieldwork on traders, and Francis further discusses this method in the context of collecting life histories.

The obvious drawback to the unstructured interview and case study approach is their unrepresentativeness. For example, collecting life histories only from old people risks losing perspective on how younger people view processes of social change. Unstructured interviews generally produce good case studies and quotations, not statistical aggregates. Responses are difficult to compare where each individual is asked different questions, or leads the discussion towards his or her own interests. Even when specific quantitative information is asked for, important details might be missed because the fieldworker does not have the memory prompt of a coded questionnaire form on her or his lap.

A structured questionnaire constitutes a means of obtaining a large number of quantitative data relatively quickly, in a form amenable to relatively rapid analysis.[3] The danger here is that the research becomes driven by the obsession with filling in the cells on the questionnaires, to the exclusion of the interesting stories and relevant comments respondents might wish to add. Also, the numbers can acquire a spurious validity that fails to reflect the conditions under which they were collected. Lockwood critically explores this issue – the nature and interpretation of fieldwork data – in Chapter 11.

The type of interviewing also dictates what kind of assistance is needed. Experienced research assistants will usually be more comfortable doing unstructured and in-depth interviewing (such as life histories) than less qualified assistants or interpreters, who typically prefer to ask direct questions which produce unambiguous (especially quantitative) responses.

There is a temptation to squeeze as many questions as possible into each interview. This should be resisted. Lengthy questioning is hard on respondents; they understandably get bored or tired and may give incomplete answers to shorten the interview. If they get terminally irritated, they might refuse to participate, and a valuable respondent will have been lost for the sake of a few (often irrelevant) questions. Each inquiry should be justified in terms of the aims of the research; otherwise it should be dropped. If a long questionnaire is unavoidable, it may be better to implement it over two or three interviews.

The sequencing of questions also affects the nature of the interview and the quality of the data collected. As discussed below, many fieldworkers choose to introduce sensitive topics towards the end of the interview, or on a second visit, once a feeling of trust has been established. From a practical point of view, the physical layout of the questionnaire is important for the fieldworker or research assistant. It should be easy to follow (particularly if 'skip' questions are used: 'If NO, go to page 12'), there should be plenty of room to enter both answers and comments, and it should be easily portable.

Structured and unstructured interviews can be either one-off, multiple visits (more than one visit, different topics each time) or repeat interviews (multiple visits, same topics or core set of questions repeated). There are advantages and disadvantages to each, as discussed by Olsen in Chapter 4.

One-to-one interviews, whether structured or unstructured, should not be regarded as the only means of eliciting information from respondents. Group interviews are very useful as a kind of brainstorming, which fills in background information. With women, for instance, a frank discussion of gender issues might be easier to achieve in a group context than on a one-to-one basis. Group discussions with old men or women are often useful for recall of historical information – and for cross-checking names, dates and events (see da Corta and Venkateshwarlu, Chapter 7, on this).[4]

Another approach is participant observation. Eating, living and conversing with a community is part of the process of participating and observing. In this sense, as McCall and Simmons (1969, p. 1) note, participant observation is less a single method and more:

> a characteristic blend or combination of methods and techniques that . . . involves some amount of genuinely social interaction in the field with the subjects of the study, some direct observations of relevant events, some formal and a great deal of informal interviewing, some systematic counting, some collection of documents and artifacts, and open-endedness in the direction the study takes.

A well-developed literature in social anthropology discusses the methods, techniques, and ethics of participant observation, as well as the process of analysing data obtained in this way.[5] The use of participant observation, rather than formal interviews and questionnaires, will depend largely on the research topic and particular fieldwork circumstances. For example, as Bernard (1988) notes, long-term participant observation can reduce problems associated with respondents changing their behaviour when studied.

In our fieldwork, we have used participant observation to inform our understanding of processes rather than as a principal method of data collection, but this was largely a consequence of the topics we were researching. (It is difficult, for example, to 'participate' in long-term rural differentiation!) But even in this limited way, we found it providing insights into events or activities that would not have been understood had we remained outsiders. To quote Heyer: 'I learned a great deal from going to weed finger millet with a group of Kipsigis women one day – it gave me a completely new attitude to recorded "hours of work".'

2.2.3 *The interview setting*

Two issues here are where to conduct an interview, and when. The principal decision with respect to interview location is the relative merits of a private versus a public encounter. A public encounter may encourage a more general discussion of the issues; and where information is in the public domain, onlookers may assist or correct respondents with particular questions (although there is no guarantee that they will, especially if there are differences in status between respondent and onlookers). When the research deals with matters that are personally sensitive, the presence of outsiders or other family members may inhibit respondents, embarrassing them into evasion or silence. Onlookers may even encourage respondents to answer untruthfully. For example, working during food crises is problematic (apart from posing moral dilemmas) because respondents have an incentive to understate their stocks of grain, and their general wealth, in the expectation that food aid will be brought into the community. This tendency will be exacerbated in a public interview, since the respondent who admits to being wealthy may face demands for help from poorer neighbours.

In general, therefore, the more sensitive the topic, the stronger the case for conducting the interview in private. However, often there is no choice. In some societies, it may be impossible to keep neighbours and visitors away. But ways can be found around this problem. One researcher simply stopped interviewing when visitors arrived, until they were embarrassed into leaving. Others changed the subject of the interview to avoid sensitive topics while other people were around. Another solution is to catch people alone – in the fields working, or on their way to market.[6]

The second issue is when to conduct interviews, bearing in mind that they can be a real imposition on respondents' time. It is important to meet on days and at times convenient to respondents. For example, women may be busy on market days and when preparing meals. One way of ensuring that interviews are not too intrusive is to make appointments to see people. Francis did this in western Kenya, and left a 'calling card' saying when she would return. However, the agreed time may still prove inconvenient and it may be necessary to reschedule the interview.

A related matter is finding the best time of year to conduct interviews. In semi-arid areas, it may be easier to work mainly during the dry season (unless the research demands close monitoring of agricultural activities), when people who are actively engaged in farming have time to spare.[7] Where farm plots are very dispersed, it can be difficult even finding people who may be farming several miles from their homes. At a practical level, travelling around a community may be debilitating during the heat of the dry season, but can become virtually impossible during the rains.

On the other hand, farmers in semi-arid areas do not work on their farms for half the year and sit around under trees waiting to be interviewed by researchers for the other half! Seasonal out-migration is common in such communities, notably among young men, and it would be myopic to defer interviewing until after the harvest if a large number of respondents then disappear from the village. All we are suggesting is that interviewing schedules should be built around the seasonal, weekly and daily patterns of domestic and economic activities.

2.2.4 *Confidentiality and sensitive issues*

Data that are sensitive, for whatever reason, are the most difficult to collect – and also, frequently, among the most interesting to the researcher. While there is a big difference between reluctance to discuss a subject out of mild personal embarrassment, and recalcitrance caused by real fears of criminal prosecution for breaking the law, the problem of overcoming this recalcitrance and obtaining accurate information is the same in both cases. Techniques relating to the collection of sensitive data are discussed by Christensen (credit and livestock) and Harriss (trade). Here, we note some general points.

The first problem is how to determine what is sensitive and what is not. Individuals and cultures do not all share the same sensitivities, and different information is public and private in different societies. Topics that Westerners feel are private (such as personal incomes) might be common knowledge in an African village, whereas apparently innocuous questions ('How many children do you have?') could produce an evasive or hostile response where counting children or animals is believed to bring bad luck. As Christensen observes, sensitivity usually relates to the fear that information divulged will be used in a manner contrary to the respondent's wishes or interests. If the researcher is perceived as being associated with the state, for example, respondents may suspect that details of their incomes, assets and numbers of children will be used for purposes of tax assessment. It follows that the best way to obtain such information is to reassure respondents that this fear is groundless, and this in turn is best achieved by establishing relationships of trust.

One strategy is to persuade respondents that any information they provide will be treated confidentially, or to convince them that the interview is anonymous. Curiously, though, this tactic seems of limited use. As Olsen and Harriss found, people simply do not believe that their anonymity will be protected, when they see the researcher writing down everything they say! Besides, as Wilson observes, people often *want* their stories and living conditions to be publicised, and in such cases doing so becomes part of the fieldworker's obligations to the community.

A popular technique in addressing sensitive topics is to introduce them gently, either indirectly or after one or two previous interviews, once a degree of trust has been built up. But being indirect can raise rather than dispel suspicions, as Devereux discovered in his exploration of the nature of credit transactions in northern Ghana:

> I asked whether the lender was a farmer or trader, man or woman, local resident or not, and relative or friend. My respondents either thought I was tricking them into revealing the lender's identity, in which case they often lied (I think); or else they simply told me the person's name straight away, and seemed amused by my 'deviousness' in not asking for names directly!

An alternative strategy is recommended by Christensen, who argues that sensitive topics should be introduced *generally* rather than *indirectly*. Invite the respondent to talk about village norms and practices in a way that does not require revelation of personal details. Then shift the focus of enquiry to the respondent's own situation, in a way which is completely transparent. By now they should feel relaxed enough to talk openly about the subject, without feeling manipulated or deceived.

Finally, as discussed previously, respondents' willingness to discuss confidential topics may be affected by the presence and characteristics of the research assistant. In Tamil Nadu, Heyer found that people would talk more freely about sensitive subjects when questioned by someone with a professional interest in and technical knowledge of the subject (such as a university staff member).

2.2.5 *Cross-checking data for consistency and accuracy*

'Getting at the truth' involves separating out lies and evasions from genuine errors and from imagery or cultural projections. Inaccuracy is more often related to poor recall than to deliberate dishonesty, but the imagery is part of the truth, and is important to understand in its own right. Lockwood discusses this in detail. Specific techniques for cross-checking data are suggested by Christensen (livestock and credit), Harriss (trade), Hoddinott (household income), Lockwood (age), da Corta and Venkateshwarlu (long-term recall data) and Francis (life histories). In addition, Gregory and Altman's *Observing the Economy* (1989) provides a great deal of useful information on cross-checking data on a variety of topics, including labour, time allocation, measuring output and productivity, and expenditures.

Given this coverage, we restrict ourselves here to making one general recommendation. By and large, the best way of cross-checking data is to adopt a variety of approaches to the same issues: different questions, similar questions asked at different times, different respondents and different methodological tools. In cases of deliberate deception, there is little to be gained by becoming angry – a more positive approach is to suggest there may be a misunderstanding. Operating in good faith is more likely to produce accurate data than interrogating respondents. At the very least, this may give insights into the reasons behind the deception, and these can be illuminating.

2.3 Broader methodological matters

A number of questions arise during fieldwork that are rarely considered by texts or courses on fieldwork methodology. Finding the right balance between 'numerical' (quantitative) and 'anecdotal' (qualitative) data is one such issue. A second is how to contextualise a community-level research site in its wider (regional or national) environment. Two further questions considered here are the 'ideal' length of time fieldworkers should spend in the field, and their relationships with colleagues and supervisors while there. Finally, this section (and chapter) closes with a brief discussion about the prospects for doing fieldwork more than once.

2.3.1 *Integrating quantitative and qualitative data*

Fieldwork necessarily involves the acquisition of both quantitative and qualitative data. For researchers who are more comfortable with the collection of numbers than case studies – statistical analysis rather than verbal description – life stories and other 'facts' which modify the numerical data can seem nebulous and confusing. Confronted with the reality of village (or urban) life in a developing country, many fieldworkers take refuge by 'counting things' as a way of doing something demonstrably productive. As Barley (1983, p. 55) commented:

> In those first three weeks all I knew was that I had undertaken to learn an impossible language, that there were no Dowayos in the village, that it was pouring with rain, and that I felt weak and terribly lonely. Like most anthropologists in this situation, I sought refuge in collecting facts. The prevalence of factual data in anthropological monographs stems, I am sure, not from the inherent value or interest of the facts but from an attitude of 'when in doubt, collect facts' . . . So off I went every day, armed with my tobacco and notebooks and paced out the fields, calculated the yields, counted the goats in a flurry of irrelevant activity.

The collection of quantitative data is necessary for many types of analysis. Even in cases where the emphasis is on other forms of data, 'numbers' can provide useful background information. But the problem with collecting only quantitative data is that a number 'calcifies' at each stage – from questionnaire to coding sheet to analysis – until it is one of several hundred numbers contributing to the production of a percentage, in which uncertainty over the accuracy of each individual number is buried forever. Also, qualitative data are often necessary to 'tell the story' that the numbers suggest. Quantitative data are not always suited to explaining processes, particularly those relating to changes over time – indeed, they can be misleading in this regard. Da Corta and Venkateshwarlu provide an example of this in their discussion of land sales in south India.

These considerations provide good reasons for collecting a mix of qualitative and quantitative data. In our own work, we have found it helpful to ask 'Why?' as well as 'What?' and 'How many?', and to do so in a variety of settings (such as group interviews, unstructured discussions, at social occasions, even while waiting to catch a bus). As with all research methods, it is important to be aware of the biases and background of the respondent. One person's story might well contradict another's. But even these differences can be illuminating. At the very least, they are helpful in terms of making written work more 'transparent' – that is, as Lockwood argues, in explaining the context in which the data were collected.

2.3.2 *Understanding neighbouring districts*

Village studies are often criticised for their 'micro-level' focus, which makes generalisations drawn about 'south Asia' or 'east Africa' (or even 'southern India' or 'western Kenya') at best tentative, and at worst highly misleading. Though the legitimacy of this criticism can be questioned (see Chapter 13), it is often true that analysis of fieldwork is written in an uneasy style which flips between extremely detailed household-level data and excessively aggregated regional or national statistics. As Olsen explains (Chapter 4), this problem arises partly from the process of selecting a particular sampling frame (such as a village) out of a larger population. No matter how random a choice of research site seems to be, it is never either 'typical' or 'representative', just as neither Cambridge nor Las Vegas is a representative microcosm of Britain or the United States. There is a real danger of getting so immersed in one village or community that it becomes difficult to draw comparisons or wider conclusions (this is true even if an entirely random sample is taken from the sampling frame).

It is important to contextualise fieldwork by developing an understanding, no matter how superficial, of neighbouring villages or districts. One option is to do a 'less serious study' of a secondary site while conducting the main work in the primary site. This can illuminate the research in surprising and useful ways, and give the analysis some degree of wider applicability. Lockwood, for one, spent 2–3 months working in several villages and towns up to 30 miles away from his primary research site in Tanzania. Partly this was to follow up migrants and visitors who were moving from one area to another, but he also carried out surveys in different villages which clearly revealed both the uniqueness of each village and similarities between them. On a larger scale, Christensen's 6-village survey in Burkina Faso was deliberately structured to provide inter-regional comparability.

Of course, it is easy to assert the importance of this complementary level of analysis, but difficult to do it in practice. Not surprisingly, most fieldworkers find getting to grips with one community a full-time job, without trying to understand others in their 'spare time'. Less demanding ideas are to maintain close contacts with other researchers working concurrently nearby, to read up on published reports about the area, and to talk to people in local universities or institutes who have done research in the region, even if their theoretical interests are different. At the very least, it is well worth travelling to neighbouring areas or other regions (perhaps as part of a break period) to get some sense, however crude, of the variety of environmental and economic patterns within which the primary research site is situated.

2.3.3 *What is the minimum time necessary in the field?*

Hoddinott argues in Chapter 5 that there is no 'correct' or 'ideal' length of time for undertaking fieldwork, but that this should be determined by the aims of the research. A 'rapid rural appraisal' can be accomplished in a few weeks,[8] while a detailed study of religious ceremonies may require two years or more. Other factors include the necessity of learning the local language, the degree of intimacy required with respondents, and practical factors such as the accessibility (in terms of transport) of the research site.

Other things being equal, the longer the time spent in the field the better. This permits greater flexibility in the research schedule, more time to investigate topics and get close to respondents, and more opportunities to cross-check information. It also allows more time to correct things that go wrong. Furthermore, where agricultural seasonality is an important factor, monitoring a full annual cycle is desirable if meaningful and non-misleading data are to be collected.

Fieldworkers are often constrained, for financial or personal reasons, from living in the field for as long as they would like. But this does not mean that there are no advantages to shorter stints of fieldwork. Doing research for just a few months maintains a healthy tension and pressure, whereas staying too long may breed complacency. There can be diminishing returns to fieldwork (in the sense that less is learned in the second year than in the first). Also, 'post-fieldwork adjustment' is easier after a period of, say, six months abroad than after one of two or three years. Of course, a shorter period requires compromises to be made in both method and scope of the research, but there are ways in which corners can be cut without invalidating the data collected (see Chapter 5). Finally, the disadvantages of shorter periods of fieldwork can be mitigated through repeated visits, as exemplified by Harriss' work on traders in India.

2.3.4 *Relationships with colleagues and supervisors*

Despite being surrounded by people, fieldworkers are more alone in the field than they sometimes anticipate. Time-lags in communication (postal delays and distance from telephones) mean that relationships with colleagues back home tend to recede into the background. Fieldworkers who are doctoral students also have to accept that their academic supervisors have many other commitments, so they may not provide the amount of support and direction the student would like. Basically, problems that come up must be faced and solved by the fieldworker, with little if any outside assistance. There is no time to write home for advice on stratifying the sample when the first round of interviews starts next week. This may be a good thing in the end, even if it does not feel like it at the time! It also highlights the importance of solid preparation in the technical aspects of methodology.

A partial antidote to professional (and personal) isolation is the mid-fieldwork trip home. If finances permit, expatriate researchers should consider returning to their institutional bases for a week or two half-way through the fieldwork. This provides an opportunity to consult colleagues, assess how things are going, perhaps catch up on relevant new literature, and generally get some perspective on the research. If this is not practical, just writing letters and sending home fieldnotes can be very useful, in terms of clarifying and articulating thoughts, ideas and preliminary findings.[9]

2.3.5 *Doing fieldwork more than once*

Harriss concludes Chapter 9 by noting that at the completion of one stretch of fieldwork, the subject of further research is obvious. During data analysis and writing up, everybody thinks of questions he or she should have asked, or becomes interested in spin-off issues. Not every fieldworker will be able to undertake a second stint, but the majority of contributors to this volume have either done fieldwork more than once, or are planning to do so. Here, we note several issues that doing further fieldwork raises. Heyer's comparison of her experiences in Kenya and south India develops these ideas, and addresses a number of additional points.

One issue is the choice of returning to the first fieldwork site, or picking a new area within the same region, or in another district of the same country, or even a different country or continent altogether. The principal consideration will be the research issues to be pursued. Beyond this, learning costs are associated with becoming familiar with any new site, and these are not incurred when returning to the original village or region (though changes may have to be adapted to). A completely new area gives fresh perspectives on economic and social processes and allows scope for comparative work, whereas visiting the same research site over a period of years permits first-hand observation of processes of change. On a personal level, it allows the re-establishment of some rewarding relationships. But it also requires addressing respondent expectations – gifts to them as individuals, projects and aid for their community – which might increase over time.

A related point is that relationships with respondents will be different. A researcher who first went out when young and single may return as a parent with children, and the role assigned to her or him may be altered accordingly. Fieldworkers revisiting the same village will find that their respondents have changed in life-cycle position and status (as they themselves have). Broader processes of change will also influence these relationships – for example, people may become less suspicious of outsiders; or they may be more hostile to Westerners.

The principal advantage of having done fieldwork before is that it reduces the fear of the unknown. Researchers undertaking their second, or subsequent, round of fieldwork have some idea what to expect – though fresh problems will certainly arise, while other, anticipated obstacles will not recur at all. At the very least, returning fieldworkers have the confidence associated with having survived and enjoyed the experience once, and the wisdom that supposedly comes with being older. Set against this is the danger of being complacent, of believing that fieldwork is simply a skill which, once 'learnt', becomes easy. Good fieldwork is always challenging and unpredictable – which is why it is also so stimulating and rewarding.

Notes

1. Primary research refers to the collection of data at source (through interviews, participant observation and so on), while secondary data are gathered from institutions such as libraries and archives, and from other published materials.
2. This type of study often requires a team of enumerators. Casley and Lury (1987) provide a useful discussion of the problems associated with their use.
3. Casley and Lury (1987) include a good discussion on designing and implementing a structured questionnaire.
4. For a useful discussion of the biases inherent in group discussions, see Vierich (1984).
5. Examples include McCall and Simmons (1969), Spradley (1980), Burgess (1982), Ellen (1984), Bernard (1988) and Gregory and Altman (1989).
6. Heyer used this approach, as has Rudra (1989).

7. See Harriss (1984a) on this and many other practical aspects of fieldwork in rural areas.
8. See the 1981 *IDS Bulletin* on techniques for 'Rapid Rural Appraisal'; also Longhurst (1981) and Carruthers and Chambers (1981).
9. Sending home duplicates or carbons of fieldnotes and completed questionnaires also provides insurance against loss of these vital materials. The famous case of M.N. Srinivas, while not entirely analogous, is instructive. An anthropologist, his data and fieldnotes were destroyed when a fire at Stanford University burnt down his office. Incredibly, he managed to write up his research out of his head – aptly titled *A Remembered Village* – without the aid of a single note or datum! The book subsequently became a classic, despite the absence of direct quotations or statistics, because of the quality of the writing. (Impressive though this achievement is, we do not recommend that anybody sets out to emulate it.)

PART 2

Case studies: fieldwork experiences in Africa and Asia

3

'Observers are worried': learning the language and counting the people in northeast Ghana

Stephen Devereux

Introduction[1]

From July 1988 to August 1989, my wife and I carried out village-level research in Upper East Region, northern Ghana. We lived and worked in a semi-arid farming area characterised by climatic seasonality, declining crop yields and, consequently, chronic food insecurity for many households. The focus of my research was the economics of hunger – how the poor respond to seasonality, drought and famine in terms of liquidating their assets or borrowing to buy grain, migrating in search of work, rationing consumption, and other 'coping strategies'.

I first saw the phrase 'Observers are worried' painted on a market lorry in Accra, shortly after we arrived in Ghana. It struck me that this was an apt slogan for researchers everywhere, and particularly for fieldworkers. Like most academic observers of foreign communities, I worried incessantly during my year in the village – about my methodology, personality and morality, to mention a few. (But we also had a marvellous time, as most fieldworkers do, which more than compensated for the work crises and occasional bouts of 'fieldwork blues'.)

This chapter addresses two issues which worried me in the early weeks of my fieldwork: learning the local language, and enumerating the local population for purposes of selecting a sample. The first issue might be described as only indirectly methodological, while the second is usually regarded as a methodological prerequisite. In this chapter I challenge the golden rule which insists that learning the local language is essential for successful fieldwork. I do not question the need, in most cases, to enumerate the local population. Instead, I describe a situation where doing so was problematic, from my own experience.

3.1 Learning the local language

> The need to learn the local language . . . is so well accepted that no elaboration is needed.
>
> (Gregory and Altman 1989, p. 12)

3.1.1 *A little elaboration*

The costs and benefits of learning the local language should be spelt out and clearly understood at the outset. Instead of arriving in the chosen village and immediately hiring a schoolteacher to provide instruction in Hausa or Swahili or Tamil, fieldworkers should ask themselves these questions: What will I gain from fluency (socially as well as professionally)? What will it cost me to become fluent (in terms of lost time and energy)? Is hiring a teacher the best way to learn or should I simply pick up basic vocabulary as I go along?

As suggested parenthetically above, language impinges on both major components of fieldwork – the research exercise and the social or personal aspect. From both points of view, there can be little doubt that fluency is preferable to total incomprehension. The ability to conduct interviews on your own adds texture and depth to the data you collect, while the enjoyment of social conversations with local people adds a rich dimension to life in the field which is denied to those who are cut off from everyone around them by the language barrier. If acquiring fluency were an entirely costless procedure, therefore, there might be a case for insisting that this should be a prerequisite for every fieldworker.

But learning the language is a 'data collection exercise' in its own right, and the investment of valuable time and intellectual energy in acquiring this knowledge should be assessed alongside the imperative to collect other types of data. Even if the benefits of fluency are sizeable, this time and energy might be better employed doing other things.

This dilemma was resolved in contrasting ways by two other contributors to this volume. Francis, who became fluent enough to conduct interviews in western Kenya without an interpreter, commented that learning Dholuo 'was taken as a sign of respect and a desire to become a fuller member of the community, which it did promote'. On the other hand, da Corta 'found it extremely difficult to actually "study" the language and at the same time get my survey going. More specifically, given the choice between mastering the language or obtaining good (rather than superficial) data, I chose the latter.'

Another complicating factor is that there may be several local languages rather than one. Christensen's research project in Burkina Faso covered such a wide area that his sampling frame included members of five different ethnic groups, each with their own language or dialect, none of which was common to all. (The official language, French, is spoken by a small minority in rural areas.) This made learning 'the' local language impossible. However, the scale of the project was such that most of the interviews were conducted by a team of enumerators, so the language issue was not crucial in this case.

Even where one language or dialect predominates, it is important to recognise that no language is a linear, static set of words and rules – it is dynamic and constantly evolving, and has a social context. The same vocabulary may be used differently in urban and rural areas, by old and young people, or by men and women. So understanding the structure of communication and colloquial usage is more important than merely 'learning the language' – *knowledge* of vocabulary is not *understanding* of meaning.

The naming of famines provides a pertinent illustration. A famine occurred in my research area in 1946 which is known locally as '*Poyanglal*' – a contraction of the phrase '*Apoyanga Alale*'. Literally, a schoolteacher explained to me, this composite word means 'an old lady called Alale', or 'the widow Alale'. But he could not tell me *why* this name should be given to the famine. 'Perhaps only old women died', he shrugged. In fact, according to old men in the affected villages, the explanation has two components, like the phrase itself. First, widows are generally thought of as tiresome and demanding, a burden to their families. Secondly, the name *Alale* is given to any child whose mother was unlucky enough to see a bush rat ('*lal*') during her pregnancy. It is believed that the child will die if it is not named after the bush rat, and that even if it lives, it will grow up to be sickly and complaining. A literal translation of '*Poyanglal*' gives no hint of these colloquial subtleties. Perhaps the closest English equivalent is the equally colloquial phrase 'double trouble'.

This example suggests that employing trained teachers may not be the most appropriate way of learning the language; they often teach in a dry, technical way which has little relevance to day-to-day communication. (In the south Asian context, Harriss' phrase 'Chaucerian Tamil' exemplifies this phenomenon.) It may be better to learn from the people you will be working with – they will know the relevant vocabulary. If you are studying agriculture and living in an agrarian community, for instance, it seems sensible and logical to learn the names of crops, seasons, farming tools and so on from the farmers themselves.

In any event, the issue of whether or not to learn the local language is not an 'either–or' decision; the notion of fluency is one of degree. Local people will always be better at handling their language than outsiders. On the other hand, it is impossible *not* to pick up the rudiments of social interaction (especially standard greetings) simply by living in a village for a period of some months. How much further the researcher chooses to take that understanding is a matter of choice. It would be wrong to prescribe fixed rules here. If you find it easy and stimulating to pick up new languages, why not study the local dialect fairly intensely? If, on the other hand, you struggle to learn languages, there seems little reason why you should spend long hours toiling away for relatively little reward.

Another point to consider is the nature of the research – not just what kinds of data are to be collected, but how interactions with respondents will be conducted. If you become fluent you can interview without interpreters. So the decision about learning the local language is intricately connected with broader methodological decisions. Three general cases are possible, as follows:

- The researcher is fluent in the local language and conducts all interviews alone, without interpreters or assistants.
- The researcher partly understands the local language and sits in on interviews, but employs an interpreter to ask the questions.
- The researcher has a poor understanding of the language, in which case interviewing might be delegated to research assistants, and the researcher may or may not attend the interviews personally.

It might be argued that these choices depend on the type of data being collected. If the information gathered is purely quantitative (market prices, annual production, or numbers of animals owned), there might be little need to learn more than the local counting system, names of crops and assets, and a few key verbs such as 'buy' and 'sell'. Where qualitative data are being collected, and/or where interviews take the form of conversations rather than entering numbers into cells on coded questionnaire forms, the benefits of understanding the nuances of what respondents are saying are appreciably greater. Even with quantitative data, though, fluency at least offers the researcher some insurance against partial translation or mistranslation. There can be few more frustrating experiences in fieldwork than asking a question, listening to an animated but unintelligible exchange between interpreter and respondent, and then being told simply: 'He says "No".'

Of course, as mentioned earlier, the decision also has consequences for other aspects of fieldwork. Socially as well as professionally, you gain enormously from understanding what people are saying in the market, in the bars and in the fields. At the personal level, there is no better way to feel at least partly integrated into your community than to speak the language fluently – and conversely, no starker sign of your alienation and 'otherness' than an inability to comprehend what is going on around you.

An example which applied on both levels occurred two months after I arrived in Pusiga (my fieldwork village). One evening – just a few hours after I had interviewed him – a wealthy, influential old man and his youngest wife (of five) died dramatically of poisoning after drinking some insecticide they had mistaken for Guinness beer. Rumours flew around the village: they had been poisoned by a senior wife who was jealous of her young rival; he had committed suicide in remorse after his wife was poisoned by the senior wife; they had died in a suicide pact because of tensions in the household. I have no idea what the truth of the matter was, nor even of the consensus opinion within the village. The four variants on murder, suicide and accidental death were told to me by the only four English speakers in the vicinity.

In the end, no charges were brought against anyone, and the rumours slowly subsided into dark suspicions, but the incident revealed things to me which I would not otherwise have picked up – the intense rivalry between wives in many polygamous households (a general point); and the immense unpopularity in the village of the old man who died (a specific point). He was mean (he hid his beer and pesticides under his bed, which was how he had allegedly confused them when inebriated), and he was a political opportunist, who had taken advantage of a local ethnic conflict to have himself installed as sub-chief in the village, though he had little popular support and no lineage claim to this position. More generally, the way people discussed the old man revealed the high priority attached locally to sharing and being seen to be generous (especially if wealthy, as this man was); and different attitudes to his political career (depending on who was telling me about him) clearly exposed deep factional divides, both between ethnic groups and between certain powerful families within the village.

Information like this, as any researcher working in an alien culture can confirm, is more than mere gossip. It illuminates many aspects of local ideology and social relations which are essential for a deeper understanding of the community being studied – which in turn is vital at least as background material, whatever the specific questions being addressed by the research. How much more I might have picked up as I sat in the beer-houses on market days listening to animated conversations which I could only vaguely comprehend, I will never know.

3.1.2 *Hunger, rationing and famine in northern Ghana*

The Kusasis of northeast Ghana are polygamous polyglots, which presented me with insurmountable obstacles to my 'participant observation' ambitions, since I am a monogamous monoglot. In my research site of just over 200 households, four languages are spoken. (This is a consequence of high rates of migration into the area from Burkina Faso earlier this century. The British colonial administration of the Gold Coast was less unpopular with the indigenous peoples than the French administration of Upper Volta, with the result that the northern borders of Ghana became densely settled during the 1920s and 1930s.)

As the Kusasis are the numerically dominant ethnic group, my wife and I took lessons in *Kusaal* with a local schoolteacher for the first few months after our arrival. But my linguistic abilities are abysmal, and I never progressed beyond being able to greet people, count, and recognise perhaps fifty key words in conversations or interviews. This was my failure; the multiplicity of languages and dialects was no excuse, since *Kusaal* and *Moore* fall within the same language sub-group, and both are spoken by everyone in Pusiga, including settlers from Burkina Faso whose first language may be *Bisa* or *Hausa*.[2] A Kusasi man or woman has no difficulty communicating with a Busanga or Mossi person, even if both use their mother tongue.

The focus of my research was people's responses to hunger; it was therefore important for me to understand how local people conceptualise and talk about hunger. I was surprised, and rather disappointed at first, to discover that the Kusasis have just a single word for hunger (*kom*) which describes a wide range of phenomena, from mild hunger to seasonal food shortages to major famines. The density of meanings contained within this word is confusing to outsiders, particularly since the local people have a much subtler understanding of the differences between various forms and intensities of hunger than is implicit in narrowly defined Western notions such as 'famine'.[3] When Kusasis speak of '*kom*', they can be referring to any of the aspects shown in Table 3.1. The sense in which the word is meant will be conveyed by the context in which it is used. For instance, if you feel mildly hungry, you say: '*Kom m zabid*' (literally, 'I am attacked by hunger'); but if you were starving, you would say: '*Kom m kudum*' ('Hunger is killing me').

In addition, a number of phrases include the word '*kom*' to describe activities or events associated with hunger and poverty. '*Kom tuma*', meaning 'hunger work', refers to low-status activities such as agricultural labouring, which are usually undertaken by poor people. '*Kom win*' means 'hungry season', the months between the first rains and the harvest of early millet each year, when stocks of millet and sorghum in household granaries are at their lowest and market prices are at their highest. '*Kom dib*' refers to 'famine foods' such as wild figs, roots and berries, which are gathered in years of grain shortage.

It is a tribute to my genius as a fieldworker that I discovered the difference between rationing and hunger despite hearing the word '*kom*' being used by my respondents apparently indiscriminately. It is less of a tribute to my perspicacity that it took 180 interviews before this distinction sank in, despite the repeated efforts of my interpreter, Seidu Mumuni, to point it out to me.

Table 3.1 Meanings for the Kusaal word '*kom*'

Alternative meanings	Aspect of hunger referred to
Hunger pains	Hunger as a *biological* phenomenon
Seasonal hunger	Hunger with a *temporal* dimension
'Hunger' meaning 'poverty'	Hunger as an *economic* phenomenon
Rationing of food consumption	A *strategic response* to shortage
Localised food shortage	Hunger as a *geographic* phenomenon
Major famine	Hunger as a *community crisis*

The answer to my rather vague question: 'Was there hunger in your household last year?' was invariably an incredulous '*Aie! Kom be!*' (best translated perhaps as 'Are you kidding?'), but Seidu would always distinguish carefully, in translating this response, between: 'Yes, there was hunger' and 'He says there was rationing.'

The Kusasis have a saying that 'rationing begins as soon as you have to buy grain in the market'. In good years, most households are self-sufficient in terms of their foodgrain needs, but drought and army-worms devastated foodcrop production in Pusiga in 1987 and 1988, so that almost every household depended on the market for grain to get through the 1989 'hungry season'. Although all these households were, therefore, 'rationing' food consumption, the extent to which they rationed depended on their relative wealth. There was a big difference between mild rationing by the rich because of their awareness that food was costing money this year, and serious hunger in the poorest families because there simply was not enough money to buy the food required.

Seidu was well aware of this distinction, either because of variations in the vehemence of the response or because of his personal knowledge of the circumstances of each household, and he took pains to distinguish between rationing as an *economic response* to food shortage and hunger as a *nutritional outcome* of food shortage. The two did not always go together; indeed, the following three distinct categories could be identified:

- Self-sufficient, non-poor households, which had no rationing and no hunger.
- Market-dependent, non-poor households, which had rationing without hunger.
- Market-dependent, poor households, which had rationing and hunger.

There were no 'poor but self-sufficient' households in my sampling frame. It was the middle category above, the intermediate possibility, which eluded me for some time. Given the nature of my research interests, this failure to grasp local conceptualisations of hunger had potentially crucial implications for the success of my fieldwork. The irony is that learning Kusaal by rote would not have helped me to stumble on this any sooner. On the contrary, without a discerning interpreter I would probably have remained blindly oblivious to such subtleties as these, which could *only* be conveyed to me by careful translation into English.

3.2 Enumerating households in northern Ghana

> The frame for a sample is a list of the units in the population (or universe) from which the units that will be enumerated in the sample are selected.
>
> (Casley and Lury 1987, p. 72)

The first methodological step most fieldworkers take after arriving in their fieldwork site is to list or enumerate the population (individuals or households) in the sampling frame. In most cases there is little difficulty at this preliminary stage of the research. It might be a little tricky to determine the boundaries between villages or sections of settlements, but the real methodological problems are not supposed to start until the sampling stage.[4] But what if counting the households is not quite so simple?

There is an ancient monument near Oxford called the Rollright Stones. It is said that every time anyone tries to count the stones in this circle they get a different number. I felt like this when I was struggling to count the households in my village in northern Ghana. As I discovered, the notion that a sampling frame can be easily identified and enumerated (and that all the units will stay put for as long as the researcher needs to observe them) is yet another textbook myth which the reality of fieldwork rudely contradicts.

3.2.1 *Pre-survey enumeration errors*

The Kusasis have a word ('*yim*') which clearly identifies households as discrete production–consumption units.[5] In practice, enumerating individual households is complicated by both the production system and local living arrangements. The residential unit in rural areas is the compound – a connected series of huts or rooms enclosed by a wall with a single entrance – but a compound can be home to anything from one to sixty people, and from a single household to five or six. As a Ghanaian sociologist points out: 'The researcher needs some ingenuity to understand a household unit in a typical rural Ghanaian settlement. It is not easy to define even a household unit' (Twumasi 1986, p. 26). The potential for confusion arises because, although a *compound* is a physical construction, the *household* is a cultural construct. Since the two are not necessarily congruent, counting households is not simply a matter of counting compounds.

In a complex compound there may be several nucleated family groups – say, a man with four wives and several unmarried children, together with three married sons, each having one or more wives with children of their own. Whether this constitutes one household or four (or two, or three) depends on whether the sons are farming with the father or separately.[6] If they all work together as a single household, the men will farm the same fields and store the harvest in joint granaries, from which grain is removed and shared out among everyone living in the compound, on the father's sole authority, at regular intervals. If any of the sons are 'feeding themselves', they have separate plots of land and store their harvests in individual granaries, with each male head of household deciding how and when grain is distributed among his own wives. In either case, the head of the senior household (the father) retains his status as the compound's 'landlord'.[7]

When I first arrived in my chosen village of Pusiga I introduced myself to the sub-chiefs in the two sections, Terago and Tesnatinga (or Teshie), in which I

Table 3.2 Sampling frame, Pusiga: summary of corrections before and changes during the research period

	Number of households			Number of compounds		
	Terago	Teshie	Total	Terago	Teshie	Total
Original household lists:	118	119	237	94	69	163
– Over-reporting errors	–17	–11	–28	–15	–6	–21
+ Under-reporting errors	+3	+3	+6	+2	+3	+5
Corrected totals: July 1988:	104	111	215	81	66	147
Changes during the year:						
+ Increases	+1	+5	+6	+1	+1	+2
– Decreases	–3	–5	–8	–0	–2	–2
Final totals: July 1989:	102	111	213	82	65	147

planned to work. These sub-chiefs had recently compiled lists of households for their sections, which were used by the District Administration to distribute small quantities of government food aid (following the two successive poor harvests mentioned above). Had these lists been compiled for an unpopular purpose such as tax collection, I would have had reservations about their accuracy. But since everybody had an incentive to register for food aid, I decided to use the sub-chiefs' lists as a basis for household enumeration.

None the less, these lists were inaccurate in several respects. Table 3.3 identifies six sources of over-reporting of households involving 28 households living in 21 compounds, and three sources of under-reporting involving 6 households in 5 compounds. Table 3.2 summarises these errors (together with changes during the year), and shows that correcting them reduced the numbers of units in my sampling frame from 237 households to 215.

Over-reporting occurred mainly in large, complex compounds, and typically took the form of young men claiming to be separate households when they were, in fact, still farming with their brothers or father. The explanation for this was simple. When the household lists had been drawn up, local residents were well aware that the purpose was to distribute food aid. People in large compounds reasoned that if each household were to receive free food, it was to their advantage to exaggerate the number of separate households in their compound. When I made my first round of interviews, the expectation that I would be bringing some kind of free or subsidised assistance to the village was high, and over-reporting was standard practice. During the year I gradually discovered which compounds had over-reported household numbers, and simply crossed them off my list. (A clear indicator was when I asked several 'household heads' in a compound about planting, harvests and asset ownership, and received identical or near-identical figures – since they were each listing, in fact, the same (joint) production and assets.)

Several people with strong family connections in Pusiga who were now wealthy traders living in Bawku town (8 miles west of Pusiga) and even in

Table 3.3 Sampling frame, Pusiga: reasons for changes in numbers of households and compounds before and during the research period

	Households involved	Compounds involved
Pre-survey errors:		
Over-reporting:		
– Men farming together reported as separate households	9	–
– Household heads within one compound reported as landlords of separate compounds	–	10
– Two men from a single household reported as landlords of two separate compounds	–	2
– People living in Bawku (8 miles west) and Kumasi (250 miles south) reported as farming in Pusiga	13	7
– Households which had left Pusiga or were away for several years reported as still living and farming in Pusiga	5	1
– Dead people reported as extant households	1	1
Total:	28	21
Under-reporting:		
– Complete households or compounds missed altogether	3	3
– Widows living as single-member household heads in complex compounds included in son's household	1	–
– Widows living alone missed altogether	2	2
Total:	6	5
Changes during the year:		
Decreases:		
– Whole household migration	4	2
– Migration of household head; dependants assimilated into other households	2	0
– Death of household head; migration of dependants or assimilation into other households	1	0
– Incorporation of one household into another	1	0
Total:	8	2
Additions:		
– Return of migrant households or household heads	4	1
– Separation of sons to create new households	2	0
– Building of new compounds	–	1
Total:	6	2

Kumasi (250 miles south) were also registered for food aid purposes if they had once farmed in Pusiga. In the most bizarre case, a woman who had died two years before was added to the list by her relatives so that they could collect an extra allocation of food aid for themselves.

Under-reporting of households occurred most commonly with old women, especially widows. Although most elderly widows are looked after by a son or son-in-law, this is not always the case, and some old women constitute separate households, either because they insist on retaining their independence by farming their own land, or because they have been cast adrift to fend for themselves. In my sampling frame there were three such single-person 'households', one in the first category and two in the second, all of which I missed until it was too late to incorporate them in the lists of households from which my samples were randomly selected.

The reason why these widows were missed is to be found in the local conceptualisation of a household, which corresponds broadly to the Western notion of a 'production-consumption unit'. As discussed above, a man is said to be the head of a distinct household if he is 'farming separately' (from his father and brothers) and 'feeding himself' (plus his wives and children) – that is, the household constitutes both a production entity and a consumption entity. The two widows living on their own were virtually beggars, being too infirm to work and having no-one to help them with farming. In fact, they were dependent on handouts from relatives and neighbours. So they did not strictly qualify as households in terms of the local definition because they were neither 'farming separately' nor 'feeding themselves'. They were also socially stigmatised – one had been abandoned by her family, which migrated to southern Ghana and left her behind, the other ejected from her son's compound because she was 'too troublesome'. For both these reasons, my assistant took pains first to conceal their existence from me and then to argue against the necessity to interview them, describing the first widow as 'mad' (she was not) and insisting that the son of the second was, in fact, 'feeding' her (he was not).

3.2.2 *Household mobility, mortality, assimilation and fission*

During the year there was a significant amount of mobility of both individuals and households. Seasonal migration of young men was the most common reason for leaving the District. In these cases other members of the household usually remained behind and this migration was only temporary, so the number of households in the sampling frame was not affected. (Wives and children were left either fending for themselves or in the care of another man – usually the migrant's brother or father.) Similarly, women often returned to their father's home after giving birth (a customary practice associated with birth spacing), and wives or children in poor households were sometimes sent to wealthier relatives for a time because of hunger and poverty.

Whole household out-migration occurred in four cases. It was always difficult to separate out seasonal from long-term and 'permanent' migration. When people told me of their intention to migrate in advance, they often could not say themselves whether or when they would return. Much depended on what would happen in the destination to which they were migrating, which of course could not be predicted. (Conversely, several men assured me that they had no intention of 'going south' during 1989, then promptly did so. This, I felt, they could have predicted.) In all such cases I adopted a simple rule of thumb: if the household head returned for the new farming season (before July 1989), I classified this as seasonal migration; if not, the man or household concerned was listed as a long-term migrant. For interviewing purposes I either spoke to a wife or son of the household head while a male migrant was away, or waited until his return.

When the head of a household died, either another family member was promoted to this status or the relatives were assimilated into another household. Four of my respondents died during the year – including the old sub-chief who died tragically within a few hours of my interviewing him. In two cases a son of the deceased became the new household head, and in a third the dead man's wife continued as a female-headed household; but in the fourth case the household dissolved, the deceased's wives being absorbed into the household of a son and his assets divided between the relatives.

Household segmentation (or fission) and assimilation during the year further confused the issue. Two sons of a wealthy farmer-trader 'separated' from their father when the new farming season began in July 1989, adding two new households to the list. (This presented me with a complicated analytical question. One wealthy household had sub-divided into a wealthy household plus two apparently poor households, though all three remained as residents of a single compound. However, although the young men had few assets, they were by no means 'poor' in local terms, and they certainly could not be classified as 'food insecure'. How were they to be treated analytically?) Another man who had recently arrived from Burkina Faso with no assets at all built a separate granary outside his brother-in-law's house, where he was staying; but halfway through the year this granary was knocked down and from then on he was treated as a member of his brother-in-law's family. When this happened I stopped interviewing the new arrival separately and treated the compound as comprising one household, not two.

All these changes in my sample population, both before and after I started my research in earnest, adversely affected my work, but never very seriously. Because I had anticipated some sample decay, I started with a sample that was 10–15 per cent larger than I needed, so that just over 100 households were left by the end of the year, even after several had dropped out. I was less confident about how to deal with newly created households, or returnees. Usually I interviewed them anyway, but since I was doing a multiple round survey (working with the same group of households throughout the year), these data were obviously incomplete, and I have subsequently discarded most of these interviews as analytically unusable.[8]

The general point is that fieldworkers must expect a certain degree of mobility among respondents during the period of their research. Even in the remotest rural communities, people migrate for work, visit relatives, move house, leave home, get married and separated, and die. The fluctuating nature of households and household composition is inconvenient for all social research. But fieldwork which depends on repeated contact with the same individuals over a fairly lengthy period is particularly vulnerable to demographic variability. There is no solution to this that I can suggest except pre-emptive 'over-sampling'.

3.3 Two conclusions

Although I have used the articulation of hunger and rationing by the people of northeast Ghana to illustrate how I was handicapped initially by my inadequate grasp of the local language, it might equally be argued that this provides a good example of how learning a language actually occurs. As a cultural and linguistic outsider, the fieldworker moves from ignorance through a rudimentary knowledge of vocabulary to an understanding of how that vocabulary is used in practice. Perhaps the ideal situation, as far as interviewing is concerned, is to be as fluent as possible in the local language, but to employ interpreters and sit in on the interviews anyway. This leaves you free to take comprehensive notes and plan the next question while your assistant does the talking, as well as allowing you to listen to both what respondents are actually saying and how their words are being translated.

As far as enumerating households is concerned, my experience suggests that I was trying to count something that would never sit still. Fieldworkers are usually prepared for the fact that the demographic *composition* of households changes constantly, but not for the possibility that the *number* of households in their sample might change as well.

In conclusion, therefore, concerning the two central questions addressed in this chapter, I would simply offer the following advice:

1. Learn the language. Don't give up your fieldwork if you can't.
2. Count the households. Count them again!

Notes

1. I am indebted to ESCOR-ODA, whose generous grant made my fieldwork possible. My thanks also to Jovito Nunes, my discussant at the workshop, and to the other workshop participants. Many of their insightful comments on my paper have been incorporated into this revision.
2. *Kusaal* is spoken by perhaps half a million people. It is a Gur language of the Oti-Volta (north Ghana) sub-group (Barker 1986, p. 111), as is *Moore*, the language of the Mossi and Yarse peoples, though it originated in Burkina Faso. *Bisa* is a Mande language, with no relatives in northern Ghana, and is spoken by Busangas. *Hausa*, which originates in northern Nigeria, is a trading language throughout west Africa, and is the first language of Fulanis living in Pusiga.
3. This concatenation of meanings is not unusual. De Waal (1989, p. 73) notes that a single word is used in most African languages for both hunger and famine, as well as being a general term to describe poverty and all 'manners of suffering'.
4. On sampling issues, see also Chapters 4 and 5.
5. Because domestic units vary across cultures, there is an extensive sub-literature within recent writings on development about how to define and analyse the 'household'. Rather than address this debate here, I have chosen to stick to the local (northeast Ghana) conceptualisation. (For the western Kenya equivalent, see Chapter 5.)

6. Devereux (1989) discusses this further.
7. The status and responsibilities attached to the label 'landlord' are taken very seriously. I inadvertently offended a man who returned to the village from Ashanti Region *after* I had started interviewing, by treating him for several months as a junior householder when he was, in fact, the senior brother of the man I had regarded as the landlord of their compound.
8. Olsen (in Chapter 4) faced similar problems in south India.

4

Random sampling and repeat surveys in south India

Wendy Olsen

Introduction

In April 1986, after several preliminary visits to India, I started a one-year survey of 90 households in southern Andhra Pradesh, India. It was May before I knew exactly which villages I would be studying, and June before the first monthly survey could be done. It was July before I could start printing the monthly questionnaires (as opposed to xeroxing an ever-changing form). I had an assistant to help me by interviewing (with me alongside) and translating. I lived in the survey village and made a great effort to learn Telugu, though to my chagrin I found that this offended local Muslims whose first language is Urdu.

My study was directed at exchange relations: flows of money and crops within the village in the context of drought, seasonality, growing commercialisation and extreme inequality. I aimed to interview households once a month each for a year in order to obtain a continuous record of their grain transactions and money flows over that period.

This fieldwork project was ambitious. With assistance from several funding agencies for my doctoral studies, I could afford to pay research assistants and to buy my own transport.[1] The personal problems of adjustment to village life loomed large throughout the study, but were specific to my own case so will not be discussed here. But the questions of *sampling methodology* and *repeat survey methods* have relevance for other researchers – particularly economists – and so are discussed below.

4.1 Random sampling and stratification

The fieldworker's objective is to arrive at reasonable, well-substantiated generalisations about a particular set of social phenomena. Part of the process is to avoid the bias that can result from one's own experience being limited by social, ethnic, geographic or other boundaries. It has been argued that it is impossible to understand a village society completely because the researcher naturally finds his or her niche in one class and cannot therefore be an 'impartial' observer.[2] While I accept this claim, I would argue that researchers can recognise and even participate in social conflict, yet still do their best to understand all the various parts of society. A study of social relations must examine both sides of each relationship.

In the sections that follow I discuss how the selection of households wlthin a given community may be done in a way that avoids the worst excesses of selection bias. I do not discuss the problems of gender and age bias. Each researcher must decide who to talk to within each respondent household. My own study took the gender-based division of labour within the household as given (varying, as it did, across social classes and ethnic groups), and simply asked each question of the best-informed person available. Other researchers might prefer to use the individual as the unit of analysis, carefully selecting a random sample of individuals, instead of starting from the 'household' point of view.

4.1.1. *Your study area and its surroundings: the myth of representativeness*

The 'myth of representativeness' goes something like this:

> Enumerate all the households in the area. Write all the names on slips of paper and throw them in a hat. Pick out as many as you can handle and that is your random sample. Since every household has an equal chance of getting in the sample, the random sample will be representative of the population.

The first problem with this procedure is that it presumes a boundary for your study area. What if your chosen village or town has offshoots, suburbs or perhaps a riverside ghetto that was not included in the enumeration? In parts of rural India outlying hamlets have an entirely different composition from central parts of villages and official boundaries sometimes cut through a large village, thereby cutting off one ethnic group from another. The second problem is that you may only have one chance to do your survey, and your chosen locality may not be representative of the area.

There are two steps you can take to deal with these problems. First, if possible, travel widely in your chosen area – walk off the roads and examine for yourself the location of the houses (or farms, or shops, or factories, or whatever your unit of study is). Asking educated rich people will not be much help; by all means ask, but do not be surprised when your own investigations reveal gaps in their knowledge of where and how other people live. Secondly, you can enumerate all the people in this wider area. Later I will give an example that shows how illuminating this can be. Though time-consuming, it allows you to introduce yourself to a lot of people in a relaxed atmosphere.

From the wider area you must choose your *sampling frame* or *population*. Well-funded, large-scale surveys can choose villages in several regions and then select a few study households within each village, but an individual on a small research project may be restricted in the distance she or he can travel on a regular basis in order to conduct interviews. Your census should give you an idea of what is to be gained by setting boundaries 1 km, 2 km, 5 km, or even 30 km from where you plan to live. But in the end setting a boundary, or selecting some clusters of households scattered over a plain, is the most arbitrary and least scientific part of the selection process. Hence 'the myth': even if everything beyond this stage is extremely scientific and 'random', a non-random element has already been introduced. Consequently, care must be taken in interpreting your findings. I found large differences in historical experience, credit and labour relations, prices, and wages over small (1–3 km) distances.

4.1.2. *Random sampling and creative augmentation*

In spite of this rather awkward start, it is worthwhile to proceed by systematically sampling the area you have defined. With your list of households, identified with enough detail so that you can distinguish similar names and relocate the selected households, you are ready for *random sampling*.[3]

Random sampling is based on probability theory. It says that, if 30 per cent of your population lives 'down by the river', then it you drew 100 different samples at random, on average 30 per cent of the sample households would be 'down by the river'. But since you only draw one sample, the probability of exactly 30 per cent of that sample being 'down by the river' may be quite low! For example, if you draw 20 households out of a population of 200 (a 10 per cent sample), there is a high probability of 6 households (30 per cent) being 'down by the river' – but the chances are also high that there will be either 5 or 7 households 'down by the river'.[4] In this example the *sampling fraction* is 10 per cent. The higher the sampling fraction, the more likely your sample is to be representative, but there is a trade-off between sample size and depth of contact with respondents.

Stratified random sampling helps to resolve this conflict in your favour. If you want 30 per cent of your sample to be from the area 'down by the river', then just divide the population (or enumeration list) into two parts ('down by the river' and 'the rest'), work out what a 10 per cent sample would be from each area, and choose the correct number of households randomly from within the sub-populations. You could use this method to stratify the population by landholding, by occupation, by size of house, by ethnic group, or by combinations of these characteristics. Your sample is still random, but you have controlled the proportions falling in these categories. (Always document your procedure, as later on it is amazingly easy to lose track of what you did at this early stage.)

The problem with this approach is that it requires more information than straight random sampling. The best stratifying characteristics are those that are easy to identify, that are not sensitive or controversial for any respondents, and that separate the population into a few, very disparate groups. For many economic surveys, one might wish to stratify by social class or total wealth, or type of farm management, or net labour use. Socio-economic position, landholding and neighbourhood are proxies for these multi-dimensional taxonomies – and in a south Indian context, relatively good proxies, in my view. As discussed below, I stubbornly refused to use these three simple indicators, constructed my own, and later found serious misrepresentation in my sample.

Whatever your sampling method, it is vital to include households from every major group. Social classes differ qualitatively from each other, and some very important groups are quite small in number. In my work, landlords and merchants were crucial. For other researchers, the critical yet small group may be tribals, pawn-shop dealers or families receiving government subsidies. If you cannot ensure that these groups are represented through sample stratification (the characteristic is too sensitive to ask about on a brief census visit), then you should ensure some representation by arbitrarily *augmenting* your sample.[5] Be creative, be friendly: find some cooperative households with the characteristics you are seeking. The most helpful 'augmented' families for a white Western researcher may well turn out to be educated, salaried and perhaps English-speaking, with urban connections and strong economic aspirations. Beware of the bias your experiences with these types may engender in you – but there is no point shunning them either. These people may be your best informants.

At the final stage of analysis, you can deal with your augmented households' data in two ways. You can omit them when quantifying averages across the sample ('representing' the chosen population). Or, on some dimensions, you may wish to include the augmented households but reduce the weight of each household in their class so as to keep the total weight of that class constant. An example of this *reweighting process* is given below. Though it can be complicated, it has the potential for compensating for misrepresentation in the 'random' sample itself.[6]

The only thing you cannot do is reconstruct data for households that were not in your survey at all. Stratified random sampling and creative augmentation allow you to ensure that you have selected people from all relevant groups at the start.

4.1.3 *An example of poor stratification but good augmentation*

Choice of villages

My selection of survey villages was quite arbitrary! It depended on a few suggestions from my town-based assistant and his friends. My only concern was

Table 4.1 Relative populations of the three regions

	Total number of hamlets	Total number of households	(%)	Number of people	(%)
Nimmanapalle*	4	347**	32	1825	34
Tavalam*	6	200	18	1009	19
Hinterland	24	545	50	2556	47
Total:	34	1092	100	5390	100

Notes:
* Nimmanapalle and Tavalam include 3 and 5 nearby hamlets (respectively) as well as the central village.
** In the text, the figure 340 is used. Seven households were discovered after the random sampling had been done.[8]

that there should be no major local project intervening in the general economic situation. This restriction was ignored or not understood by my advisors, who led me to a village only 2 km from an irrigation scheme with a dam and three canals. I did not realise the scheme's importance at the time, because the canals were dry due to drought.

I decided on Nimmanapalle (NPL) and several hamlets attached to it as my base village. Quickly realising how relatively central NPL is, I branched out and chose the smaller village of Tavalam (TVM) 3 km away as a second study village. TVM is not on a major road, as NPL is, but is still a roadside village with a bus service. By including some hamlets of both TVM and NPL that were not along roads, I thought I had a wide, though not random, cross-section of the local area.[7]

I then moved from this arbitrary method of village selection to a 'scientific' method of household selection within the two villages chosen. I started with a one-page enumeration of all households in each central village and their hamlets (Table 4.1).

After a month in the village, I was ready to stratify the census list of 540 households for the purpose of choosing a random sample. A month later I began to understand that remote hamlets are far more numerous than central villages in the area. I then extended the enumeration and discovered that the outlying hamlets ('hinterland' in Table 4.1) had been neglected by my initial choice of roadside villages. As discussed below, this neglect was a great shame and care must be taken in generalising from the resulting data.

Problems in random stratified sampling

I planned to take a random sample of 75 households. I used imaginary geographical boundaries delimiting the two villages NPL and TVM to get the base population of 540 households. I then had to decide how to stratify these into groups for a 14 per cent (75/540 x 100) sample. I first stratified by village: 14 per cent of TVM's 200 households was 28, and 14 per cent in NPL meant 47 households should be chosen there.

Table 4.2 Classification by stratification criteria

In business	No business
Landowning:	
Merchants	Landlords
Artisans	Farmers
	Kuulies with land
	Salaried with land
No land*:	
Artisans	Kuulies
Petty traders	Salaried without land

Note: * 'No land' here means less than one acre of land, counting irrigated land as double.

Because I needed to be sure of adequate representation of the powerful classes, as well as the landless, I used two further criteria for stratifying: (1) whether a household had land of its own, and (2) whether a household was in non-farm 'business' of any kind – money-lending, grain trading, retailing, services such as barbering or running a teashop, etc. This gave a two-by-two classification with various occupations in each category (Table 4.2). The population proportions falling into each category are shown in Table 4.3 (the number of households chosen are in parentheses).

Only a few weeks later did I discover the limitations of my stratifying exercise. While it ensured correct sample proportions for the four categories and two villages shown, only half a kilometre away from the villages were hamlets with completely different proportions in each category. In particular, these more remote hamlets had few salaried workers, few landless labourers and few landlords. They had more kuulies (workers) with land and more petty-commodity producing farmers (those who worked the land themselves and sometimes hired in labour, but who would not work as kuulies). The occasional landlord in that 'hinterland' were crucial to the area's economy, yet had been excluded from my sampling exercise because their houses were outside our central villages. Even if within our central

Table 4.3 Population proportions in each category

Category (land)	In business		No business		Totals	
Nimmanapalle:						
Landowning	19%	(9)	33%	(15)		
No land	25%	(12)	23%	(11)		
					63%	(47)
Tavalam:						
Landowning	6%	(2)	55%	(15)		
No land	4%	(1)	35%	(10)		
					37%	(28)

villages' boundaries, they fell inside a much larger category of 'landed, not-in-business' households.

Secondly, I discovered that you should stratify a population to include small groups for whom adequate representation in the sample is especially important. I should have broken the population into class categories that isolated the small, economically powerful (and in Chittoor District, distinct) classes of landlords and merchants. For this, I could have used the labels that local people use to identify the major social groups (see below). My imported scheme was inappropriate and hard to apply.[9]

Further, in stratifying the population, I defined 'landless' as 'owning less than 1 acre (adjusted) of land', with irrigated land counting twice in the adjusted total. I did not take this further for three reasons: (1) initial reports of land owned are notoriously prone to misreporting; (2) land quantity is not a good index of the farmer's potential crop output, nor of the land's total market value – my quick 'adjustment' proved inadequate and I later discovered great variations in plot values even within small holdings; and (3) land has been shown (at least for a north Indian region) to be a worse indicator of social class, adoption of high-yielding varieties (HYVs), etc., than *labour use*.[10] With such doubts, I chose not to employ a more detailed breakdown of land holdings when initially stratifying NPL and TVM. I now wish I had, because instead of throwing out the baby with the bathwater I could have used land as a crude indicator for economic status. Some of the problems that emerged later would perhaps have been avoided.

Within a month of stratifying the sample, during the first monthly survey, I began to understand local concepts of class and occupation. I was then, and only then, able to go back and identify each enumerated household as fitting in particular socio-economic classes. I wish now that I had adopted the Telugu terms earlier and not stuck with my imported conceptions about landed-ness and being in business. This experience taught me that while preparation is important, over-preparation can fix labels and categorisation schemes in your mind and reduce openness to relevant, appropriate local terminology.[11]

The class categories I ended up using matched the Telugu labels for occupations quite closely, as in the following examples:

- K: labourer = '*kuulie*'. I distinguished landed (K) from landless (K+) within this class, though most people in the villages did not. Many of these workers were also tenants.
- F: farmer = '*ryotu*'. *Ryot*, traditionally, is translated as 'peasant'. In the study area, however, these households were petty commodity producers, not peasants. They used their own and others' labour but did not work as kuulies (I have tried to avoid letting a 'peasantist' terminology mask the class differentiation which exists in the study area).
- L: landlord = '*bhuuswami*', a word for landlords in pre-capitalist India,

which is still used locally today although they are now capitalists. They hire in all labour and do not work on the land themselves.

- M: merchant = '*vyaapari*' or '*shetty*'.
- O: for 'other'. This groups several types of petty-commodity producers whose main income was non-agricultural. These include barbers, clothes-washers, hotel owners, etc.
- S: salaried = salary-dependent household or '*jiitam vastundi*' (literally, 'salary comes').

Had I learned and accepted the local terms earlier in the survey, I would have had a ready-made means of accurately representing the landlord and merchant classes. These groups were easily identified by villagers of all classes. Instead, I used the inappropriate and ethnocentric occupational breakdown by 'land held' and 'business', described earlier, finding in this procedure a strangely comforting rigidity. Consequently, landlords and farmers are under-represented in the sample. This is shown in Table 4.4. A Chi-square test for class proportions showed the sample to be significantly different from its expected composition. Also by random error, neither the landlord nor merchant classes were represented at all in TVM. I now find this gap to be a horrific block to generalisations I might like to make about these classes. While I could reweight the sample, basing final class weights on the class proportions in the census, this would not solve the problem of the absence of TVM merchants, TVM landlords and all hinterland households.

Creative augmentation and replacing dropouts

However, I did have enough sense to augment the sample to boost the representation of the landlord class. The random sample, not being explicitly stratified by class, gave only one landlord out of 75 households. I chose four

Table 4.4 Population and sample class proportions

	Class							
	K	K+	F	L	M	O	S	Total
Nimmanapalle:								
Population (%)	19	18	12	7	12	19	13	100%
Sample (%)	18	11	25	5	14	18	9	100%
Tavalam:								
Population (%)	33	43	9	3	4	6	2	100%
Sample (%)	33	22	37	0	0	4	4	100%
Overall								
Population (number)	132	148	60	30	50	78	49	547
Sample (number)	17	11	21	2	6	9	5	71*
Expected (number)	18	20	8	4	7	11	7	75

Note: * There were 4 drop-outs (see below for further discussion).

additional landlords in NPL and eight more from the hinterland and along the road to town. The four from NPL have been used to create a 'composite landlord household' by averaging their data, giving each household a weight of 0.25, which was added to the random sample at the analysis stage. I felt that adding this composite household was justified, given that landlord households were 7 per cent of the NPL population and 3 per cent of TVM's. These figures suggest an appropriate sample number of four landlord households (5 per cent of 75 = 3.75). In fact, therefore, my stratifying mechanism failed (by chance) to represent this class adequately, and the composite household only partly adjusts for this random error.

The benefits of augmenting the random sample far exceeded the extra effort needed to include those households in my study. Landlords' behaviour in central and remote villages is crucial to the social system and to the development process. I learned a great deal from the respondents in the augmented households.

Finally, three merchants, two farmers and three kuulies refused to participate. I replaced one merchant and one kuulie and added one (composite) landlord.

Summary

Implementing proper sampling methodology is not a straightforward exercise. Not only is there the myth of representativeness, but in designing the survey, the researcher faces three choices: (1) depth and breadth of initial enumeration or a quicker start to the actual survey; (2) the simplicity of unstratified random sampling or the greater likelihood of representativeness by developing a stratified random sample; and (3) richness added by augmenting the sample but at the cost of time and energy needed to sustain a larger survey. There is no single solution to these dilemmas. Each must be resolved within your own research context.

4.2 Dilemmas of repeat surveys

4.2.1 *Repeat surveys in principle*

Repeat surveying can be defined as the collection of current longitudinal data through multiple interviews over a defined time period. There are two main reasons for doing repeat surveys (or multiple round interviews):

1. To collect detailed information on transactions or behaviour over a relatively long period; the period being too long and/or the transactions too numerous for accurate recall in a single interview.
2. To measure changes in variables which you expect to exhibit variability over several months or seasons.

The second reason is particularly important in rural areas characterised by seasonality and drought. These factors make the short-term fieldworker's experience unrepresentative in as fundamental a way as does the selection-bias problem. By spending a year or longer in the field, and by using repeat surveys, it is possible to capture seasonal differences in production activities, labour usage, consumption and nutrition status, crop storage, and patterns of buying and selling. The corollary of this is that if you do not do repeat surveying in a highly seasonal area, you will get a very distorted snap-shot indeed. This is especially true in my case, of research in an environment characterised not just by seasonality, but by regular droughts. (This also begs the question of what is 'usual' or 'typical' in a highly variable agricultural environment. To offset drought and bumper-crop cycles, all you can do is ask questions about specific past years and about 'usual' years, unless the research is carried out over several harvests or you move to the study area for good!)

A major practical advantage of doing repeat surveys is that it gives the fieldworker a clear timetable or fixed schedule to work to, around which your time in the field can be structured. Without this imperative to visit each household at approximately the same date every month or quarter, you can easily lose direction and motivation. On the other hand, following a rigorous schedule introduces all the dangers of inflexibility. Doing repeat surveys means you are committed to collecting the same data, from the same respondents, month after month, from the outset. In reality, there is no way that you can plan your life in a Third World village for up to a year or more ahead, and expect to carry that plan through completely. Sickness, bureaucracy and other unforeseen events are bound to intervene at some point. Furthermore, you are committed to interviewing each respondent at more or less the same time of month each round. Chasing up people who are not at home on the day can be extremely frustrating and time-consuming.

Also, the imperative to interview the same individuals throughout your time in the field means that you are vulnerable to sample decay (people who get terminally irritated with you half-way through and drop out, people who migrate or visit elsewhere for part of the research period, leaving gaps in your data). One way to offset this is to 'over-sample' at the start, say by 15 per cent, so that you are fairly sure of ending up with a large enough sample even after 10–15 per cent of your respondents drop out.

A final problem worth mentioning follows from the positivistic tendency in repeat surveying to collect vast quantities of 'hard data' (often far more than you need), and consequently to lose out on qualitative information, because of the imperative to collect numbers. Some ways to guard against this are discussed below.

4.2.2 *Repeat surveys in practice: three lessons I learned*

Pilot interviewing plays a crucial role

Pilot interviewing (testing your questionnaire by trying it out on a few people first) is always recommended in the textbooks. It is uniquely important in the case of repeat surveying because you are asking the same questions each round; so you have to get the questions right as soon as possible – you cannot go back over missed ground later, as you can with other fieldwork methodologies.

I should also say a word here about the 'pre-pilot' stage. You need to understand a lot about the community and the local economy before you can devise good questionnaires. Do not rush into Round 1 too quickly – take more time and do proper piloting, rather than letting your initial enthusiasm get the better of you. Otherwise you run the risk of wasting an entire round of interviews. Or you might consider using Round 1 as a kind of extended enumeration or baseline interview, collecting background data like demographic and historical information – 'soft' data: fairly easy to collect, not as prone to distortion or sensitivity. Also take this opportunity to introduce yourself and explain your research project, stating clearly that you will be coming back every so often. You could even 'prime' respondents to remember the transactions and activities you will be asking about, in advance of the second interview – which will be Round 1 proper.

In my case the eleven monthly surveys we carried out gave us only ten rounds of good quality data. The first round was really more like a practice run (though I did not see it as such until much later). Much of the data obtained then had to be ignored because of lies, inaccuracies, misunderstandings, and a poor method of questioning by myself and my assistants. I take the blame for these flaws, noting, however, that mistakes are inevitable. The first round is part of the learning process and it would be advisable to keep a detailed diary at this stage (to be replaced later by fieldnotes directly on the questionnaires), since you may get the urge to throw out the first month's questionnaires. (Don't do it!)

Yet Round 1 was an important temporal landmark for our respondents. From then on we aimed to arrive at each household on roughly the same day of every month, asking what wage labour, grain sales and harvesting they had done or made since we had last visited. One-month recall was thus not a mathematical calculation in their minds, but a reckoning of events since a fixed date on which we all agreed.

Monthly interviewing is tiresome for fieldworkers and respondents

I had originally intended to interview 100 families once a month for 12 months. I felt that such a programme was necessary if I (as a foreigner) was to overcome the barriers and complications of language, seasonality and respondents' recall difficulties. One-month recall is certainly the most we can expect on some specific economic transactions. In addition, since my study focused particularly on grain and groundnut storage, and as true stock figures are notoriously difficult to collect, I hoped to outwit the villagers by inquiring about all grain transactions. Calculated grain balances would then act as a check on reported stock levels.

In practice 100 interviews a month – every month – was too ambitious. Even the 75 random-sample and 15 augmented-sample households I actually selected created far too much work for one person. My assistants offered to do interviews *for* me (as opposed to *with* me), but I refused, except when absolutely necessary. I was never fully satisfied with their written notes; for all their skill and experience my friends still could not foresee my follow-up queries about stocks, debts, etc. We did between 2 and 6 interviews a day for about 20 days, and would take 10 days for rest and travel before beginning the next round.[12]

My respondents got over their suspicions about me by about Month 3; by Month 8 they (and we!) were bored by the interviews. Just then the main harvest came in, many loans were repaid, marriages were planned, and these events helped to offset the boredom. Then by Month 10 it was so bad that I sensed the accuracy of the data was falling. Each questionnaire was 5–6 pages and included 4 pages that were the same every month. We often got the response, 'Same as last month! Copy it down yourselves, we're busy!'. We proved to our respondents that there *were* monthly variations by emphasising their own travel, sickness, visitors and festivals at the start of each interview. This also made a friendly and natural introduction to the discussion. But boredom had clearly become such a problem that in Month 11 I cut the questionnaire short, leaving out labour and some grain purchases; and I ended the survey without doing a twelfth round of interviews. Even now I feel that we may have wasted respondents' time collecting voluminous details.

Unless you are prepared to shorten your questionnaires and collect fewer data, two possible solutions to the problem of respondent (and fieldworker!) fatigue are: (1) to adopt quarterly or seasonal interviewing as an alternative to monthly interviews; and (2) to use sub-surveys and multi-level surveys as a means of 'breaking up' the research and introducing more variety and interest into the interviews.

If the researcher is not set on getting exact monthly prices and wage rates, then quarterly or seasonal interviews may be a feasible alternative. Some information can be collected quarterly – data on items or activities which change slowly or infrequently, or major events which will be accurately remembered for some time. Respondents can easily add up some of the major quantities they deal with (harvests, sales, purchases, stocks, assets and debts) over longer periods than a month. They can also tell you the terms of their various contracts (rental, labour and credit) over the period since your last visit. You lose your daily contact with farming operations, but the time and energy saved are considerable. The disadvantage remains that you get only four sets of observations over a year instead of twelve. This can be a serious loss – not only of data quantity, but quality too. You miss minor transactions, and get more inaccurate recall responses, the less frequently you monitor the household. Again, it depends on what data you are collecting whether this matters or not. The trick is to identify which data must be collected more frequently than others.

One possible additional benefit for foreigners in India is that travel to other parts of India or even to Sri Lanka and Bangladesh would be conceivable in the gaps between seasonal rounds. If a long-term visa were unattainable, a series of three-month visits with gaps for extra-India travel would be a serious possibility for a well-funded researcher. I almost wish I had done this. However, the feeling of having a routine, a house and a place (however strange) in the village community made it all bearable for me, and travel abroad tended to disrupt all that. In fact, time between rounds of interviewing can be spent in a variety of constructive ways – not just to take physical breaks from the field, but also to do other types of work: talking to local officials and consulting archives, as well as preparing for the next round of interviews.

The second alternative would be to have a monthly or even bi-weekly survey on a few items (such as labour, purchases or sales) and then have seasonal interviews on a different set of items (credit, assets, family decisions, harvests, sowing, etc.). This approach sounds complicated and would tie you almost permanently to the village, but it would reduce respondent boredom. It could also provide good data, assuming you develop good enough ties with respondents for them to divulge details to the best of their ability. I adopted a modified version of this methodology, as I will now discuss.

Create your own learning opportunities

My own approach was not ideal: into a long (30–60 minutes) basic monthly survey we inserted additional questions. These special questions took up one or two pages and an extra half-hour or so for each household, but they uncovered a fascinating variety of information. At first our special questions were very innocuous, dealing wih livestock, vehicles, houses and other assets; wells and pumpsets; land quality and rental agreements. Then in Month 3 we got serious about credit. We asked about all outstanding loans (the basic survey only asked about loans taken in the current month). It was at this stage that most of the drop-outs refused point blank to participate (up to then they had avoided us or lied). However, as time went on and no harm had resulted from the remaining respondents telling us about their debts, we developed even better relations with them. This suggests another advantage of repeat surveying: that you build up respondents' confidence and trust that you do not enjoy if you interview them only once or twice.

In Month 5 we asked about the value of each plot of land owned. This inquiry, aimed initially at checking the validity of the original landholding figures, not only validated them but proved fascinating in its own right. Though there were no land sales, all the farmers knew the expected sale value of their land. Market values then proved a good index of land quality (plot-wise) and could also be used as a good proxy for overall wealth (household-wise).

In Months 4 and 7 we asked about respondents' price expectations. Most – though not all – cultivators had a clear estimate of current or future prices for each variety of paddy, groundnut and gram, ranging up to a year ahead.[13] However, I made the mistake of not distinguishing this year's price rise from the usual price rise. I am sure the villagers could have made this distinction.

Though they often laughed, the respondents found inquiries like this one interesting and thought-provoking. These detailed questions forced the villagers to admit I was serious about wanting to learn about their agriculture. Other items, such as gold and silver holdings (postponed till Month 10), experience of famine, investment plans, loan plans, last year's harvest and sales, seemed less threatening to the respondents within the context of our relationship. *They* were teaching *me*.

Here are two other suggestions for creating learning opportunities:

1. Make non-survey visits. We discovered how to irrigate by hand, who was the local witch doctor, who gets to use the cow's first milk, and all sorts of other invaluable things *only* by being in the hamlets socialising. Shared visits, meals, festivals and fun are all invaluable to the researcher. They also give respondents a better chance to ask their questions of you, making it more like an equal exchange.
2. Have special discussion sessions with groups. I learned about landlord–worker relations by listening to groups of workers and then, quite separately, listening to landlord families discuss the same issues. The villagers loved unstructured discussions and I used them to shape my basic and special survey questions. A good discussion question is open-ended and stirs up a debate. A good questionnaire question generates diverse answers from different respondents but enables the answers to be categorised and compared with others consistently.

4.2.3 *Summary*

The benefits of repeat surveying include: a more detailed and discriminating understanding of changes in the study area over the research period; longitudinal data on selected variables rather than single-point observations; having a clear structure and timetable to work to. The drawbacks include: interviewer fatigue (overwork), respondent boredom/irritation, and reduced flexibility.

The trade-off implied here requires a delicate balance to be found between the scope of the research project and its feasibility. More interviews might yield more data, or might result in increased non-cooperation and end up being counterproductive. Excessively ambitious fieldworkers might undermine their own research through trying to do too much.

There are several steps you can take to reduce interviewee fatigue. For example, keep questionnaires as short as possible. Limit repeated questions to a minimum – do not be tempted to ask about everything every month. You should have a clear idea of data requirements at the outset, and stick to that. Also prepare interview forms before each round by noting summary responses from previous questionnaires. If a household has no animals or poultry, do not irritate them by asking every month if they sold any animals. Preparing forms cuts out extraneous questions and allows you to follow up on inconsistencies or unclear points. Finally, keep respondents interested by adding a few different questions each round, especially 'chatty', less structured questions.

A broader point should also be made here, about the trade-off between frequency of visits and length of interviews. The ideal methodology might be to use sub-surveys and multi-level surveys. The idea here is to mix up repeat surveys with other forms of data collection – short, regular visits to monitor (say) asset sales and food purchases, quarterly visits to check up on seasonal events like harvests, plus a longer visit once or twice during the year to gather data which require less frequent collection (family histories, demographic and qualitative data).

The general lesson I draw from my experience is not to let the pressures of repeat surveying make you inflexible. This is a recipe for turning the excitement of fieldwork into a tedious data collection grind, a prospect which holds little charm for yourself, your assistants or the local people.

4.3 Conclusion

Like all fieldworkers, I set out with very ambitious goals, several of which I had to modify as reality got in the way. Sometimes this was very depressing; but in the end I think I did the job as well as I could. Fieldwork taught me as many things about myself as it did about crop storage in India! One lesson that I had to relearn over and over is that nobody is perfect. As Smith (1975, p. 55) once put it: 'To err is part of the human condition . . . Errors are simply that; just errors.' Somehow I find comfort in this idea, knowing that my fieldwork was full of mistakes yet had its own strengths.

Notes

1. I owe thanks to the Marshall Memorial Scholarship Fund, to the Beinecke Foundation, to the George Webb-Medley Fund of Oxford University, and to

Hertford College. These agencies put few restrictions on the use of grants given and I hope I have earned the trust they placed in me to use the money wisely.

2. Bremen (1985, pp. 7–9) develops this argument in the context of Indian village societies.
3. An overall survey of sampling methods for social scientists is Casley and Lury (1987).
4. Details about sampling procedures can be found in Yeomans (1982), Volume 2, pp. 127–42; in Spiegel (1972), Chapters 8, 11 and 12; or (for Indians who may have access to this book) in Nagar and Das (1983), Chapter 9.
5. My thanks to Judith Heyer, who first proposed this to me.
6. Standard statistical packages, such as SPSS (Statistical Package for the Social Sciences), have routines for weighting and reweighting of data.
7. See da Corta and Olsen (1990) for further description.
8. Da Corta and Olsen (1990, Table 1).
9. Certainly, the simplicity of using local categories influenced a previous generation of social scientists who used *caste* as a guide. However, in India today many people deviate from their traditional caste occupation and wealth level, and there are even inter-caste marriages. For these reasons, caste is less useful as a classifying variable.
10. Patnaik (1987, 1988) proves that labour use differentiates north Indian rural households *better* than other indicators. But net labour hiring relative to own-farm labour cannot easily be reckoned during a quick enumeration. These variables require discussion before respondents can give consistent and comparable estimates of their usual labour use. (On this, also see Chapter 7.)
11. By contrast Crow's reports on Bangladeshi economic arrangements have always used suitable Bengali terms (Crow and Murshid, 1989; Crow, 1989). See also John Harriss (1983).
12. Thanks to Liz Oughton, who has set an example for me. Recalling her hard work in Maharashtra gave me the confidence to go on even when I felt like quitting.
13. Olsen (1991) discusses these findings in their seasonal and market-wide contexts.

5

Fieldwork under time constraints

John Hoddinott

Introduction

Between January and June, 1988, I conducted fieldwork in Karateng sub-location, a rural locality in western Kenya, 270 kilometres northwest of Nairobi.[1] As part of my doctoral studies, I was interested in examining the economics of inter-generational relations.[2] I undertook fieldwork to obtain data on the migration of sons, the role of children as old-age security, and household accumulation and inter-generational mobility. A distinguishing feature of my experience was that it lasted six months, a shorter period of time than that of other contributors to this volume.

There is no 'right' length of time to undertake fieldwork. The number of weeks, months or even years spent in the field is a function of many factors, including the aims of the research, the degree of intimacy required with respondents, and logistical factors, such as ease of transport. However, for personal, professional or financial reasons, it is not always possible to spend as much time in the field as would be desirable. This constraint has a number of implications. Limits are imposed on the range of topics that can be analysed, the extent to which they can be explored and the methods of analysis. Hypotheses developed on the basis of a short period of fieldwork, particularly when there is inadequate opportunity to cross-check results and where ideas are more impressionistic, run a greater danger of being misleading. The conclusions that can be drawn from a brief fieldwork stint must necessarily be more tentative.

I decided to limit my time in the field because it was not possible for my wife to accompany me. Consequently, I had to address the problems noted above. These 'approaches to fieldwork under time constraints' are discussed in Section 5.1. Secondly, I found it necessary to make a number of compromises, both methodological and non-methodological. These are reviewed in Section 5.2.

I also discuss the extent to which the time constraint affected the collection of data, using household income as an example.

5.1 Approaches to fieldwork under time constraints

It would be incorrect to enumerate 'rules' or 'principles' for fieldwork under time constraints. However, there are several issues that are particularly important for research conducted under these conditions. Four are considered here: matching the research objectives to the time available; planning; relations with respondents; and flexibility.

5.1.1 *Matching the research to the time available*

For some research topics three weeks of fieldwork may provide all the necessary data (though this may require the use of 'rapid rural appraisal' techniques). For other topics, a year may be insufficient. Put simply, the duration of fieldwork should be a function of the aims of the research. But if there are time constraints, it is necessary to limit the research planned to that achievable in the time available. Failing to do so creates the possibility of collecting inaccurate and/or incomplete data.

Longhurst (1981) suggests one method for matching research to the time available. He argues that data can be categorised as single-point or continuous and registered or non-registered. The first distinction refers to the time-span of the activity being observed. Single-point data are events that happen once or within a defined period of time, whereas continuous events are ongoing. The latter distinction reflects how well the activity is remembered. Registered events are most easily recalled. Non-registered events are neither recorded nor easily recalled. The categories can be combined to produce a four-way classification of data. For example, the hiring of wage labour is a continuous registered datum, as it involves a monetary transaction. Family labour expended on weeding the cassava crop is a continuous non-registered datum, ongoing and less likely to be recalled accurately.

Short periods of fieldwork are better suited to the collection of single-point, registered data, rather than continuous, non-registered data. The nature of the latter makes it necessary to monitor them on a frequent and possibly ongoing basis. My research required migration histories of household members, investment in education and land transactions. As these were major events for the households concerned, and because they occurred discretely over a well-defined period of time, such a study was suited to a shorter period of fieldwork. For other topics, such as whether children acted as old-age security, it was necessary to obtain data that were continuous and a mix of registered (for example, gifts of money) and unregistered activities (getting firewood). Here, it was necessary to use a much shorter recall period.

5.1.2. Planning

Planning is obviously important to the conduct of successful fieldwork. Proper planning may not prevent wastage of time and mistakes entirely, but it can reduce the probability of their occurrence. As many aspects of planning are covered in Chapter 1, three specific to fieldwork under time constraints are considered here: preliminary reading; a preparatory trip; and thinking about methodology.

Preliminary reading

Preliminary reading is always useful: when there is insufficient time to absorb all the sociological, cultural and economic details of the locality in which fieldwork will be undertaken, it is vital. There will be cases where background material is limited or not accessible. But if a literature does exist, failing to review it means, at best, spending precious time rediscovering what is already known. At worst, it greatly increases the likelihood of making horrendous mistakes such as disregarding important cultural norms of behaviour.

A literature review can provide a guide to the relevant topics and locations for research. This applies to all fieldwork, but is especially important when time constraints circumscribe the research programme. When I began preparing to work in Kenya, I was especially interested in migration and the idea of children as old-age security. Focusing on these helped me decide which areas would be suitable for my research. It also restrained me from becoming over-ambitious. Preliminary reading is helpful, too, in determining when to undertake fieldwork, a factor particularly important if the research has a seasonal component or if extensive travel within a region or country is necessary. For example, a study of traders in several rural areas will be more difficult during the wet season when roads are poor. I gave this aspect no consideration prior to moving to Kenya – my decision to start in January was completely arbitrary! Fortunately, this did not matter greatly because the data I collected were not seasonal. (By good luck, my fieldwork coincided with the start of the growing season, and this acted as a useful temporal landmark during the interviews.)

Related to reviewing the literature is making contact with researchers already working in (or on) the same country or topic. Ideally, this exchange of information can be done on a reciprocal basis. In my case, contact with a social anthropologist and a geographer who were studying the same ethnic group gave me the chance to obtain practical information, share ideas, and confirm or modify preliminary hypotheses.

A preparatory trip

A preparatory trip can make planning much easier. Though expensive, it affords an opportunity to overcome bureaucratic problems. When time in the field is limited, it is especially frustrating spending hours waiting around government offices. A preliminary reconnaissance of the research site can also be undertaken. This reduces the possibility of picking the 'wrong village'. It can provide practical information as well as giving a sense of what living in the area will entail. A preparatory trip makes it possible to rethink the research and methodology before undertaking detailed fieldwork. Finally, it makes it easier to move into the field quickly.

Four months prior to starting fieldwork, I undertook a preparatory trip of three weeks. This enabled me to expedite research clearance, make contacts at the University of Nairobi and collect materials on Kenya not available elsewhere. I was also able to make a short trip to the area I was considering studying. While there was insufficient time to make detailed observations, I did obtain some general impressions. For example, it was suitable for my research (in that migration was common), it was relatively accessible by bus, there were no serious security problems, and there were a number of useful facilities (photocopy shops, post office, etc.) in a nearby town.

Thinking about methodology

Preliminary reading and a preparatory trip can be used to guide the selection of appropriate research methods. The ultimate choice of these is determined partly by the nature of the research and partly by conditions in the fieldwork area. Prior consideration of these factors saves valuable time.[3] I decided to concentrate on the collection of quantitative data through formal interviews, supplemented by casual observations and informal conversations with respondents. Also, given my tight schedule, it was important to try to minimise the gaps in the data collected, as there was relatively little time to return to respondents for information omitted from previous interviews.

Having decided to use formal interviews as the principal research method, I began work on questionnaires between my preparatory and main trips. At the outset, I made a list of the questions that I thought would be useful to ask. I then obtained questionnaires used by other researchers in Kenya. These suggested how questions could be asked, the order in which they were asked, possibilities for pre-coding and how physically to lay out a questionnaire. However, using other researchers' questionnaires as a guide risks replicating their mistakes. Also, there is a temptation to include irrelevant questions solely because they appeared in other people's surveys. Based on the list of questions and the questionnaires, I designed a mock questionnaire prior to commencing fieldwork. Though it was necessary to make substantial changes once in Karateng, this approach meant that I was not starting from scratch.

5.1.3 *Establishing and maintaining relations with respondents*

The most valuable lesson I learned regarding the conduct of fieldwork while in western Kenya was not to scrimp on establishing and maintaining good relations with respondents. There is a terrible temptation, when time is short, to view time-consuming social niceties as something to be avoided. Certainly, I felt this way on a number of occasions. However, there are good reasons for resisting this temptation.

First, the ethics of fieldwork rightly insist that local customs be respected. I do not believe that a time constraint is a satisfactory excuse for ignoring these. Besides, good fieldwork relies, above all else, on establishing and maintaining good relations with the community being studied. Behaving in a manner that respondents find objectionable will not facilitate this.

Secondly, these occasions can provide an invaluable setting for informal discussions. While living in Karateng, I participated in negotiations over bridewealth payment. This provided a number of opportunities to discuss with other young men in the village issues relating to marriage, bridewealth and relations with elders. This was useful in interpreting and confirming the quantitative information collected on these subjects.

My first step in establishing relations was to meet local government officials. While these were principally courtesy calls, they also served to allay possible suspicions regarding my activities. (I made a second visit half-way through my fieldwork to say how I was getting along.) I had a much longer meeting with the assistant chief of the sub-location (the local government official), with whom I was to be in the most contact. This gave him an opportunity to learn about my intentions while giving me a chance to obtain more detailed information on the area. The assistant chief then arranged for me to address a *baraza* (a meeting composed principally of village elders, though other members of the community and government officials also attend). During the *baraza*, I introduced myself (in somewhat less than fluent Dholuo) and explained what I hoped to do in Karateng. This was followed by a question period which focused on my personal background and the proposed survey.

The next step was to introduce myself to the residents of Karateng. I did this while conducting an initial reconnaissance of the sub-location and also during the creation of the sampling frame. Visiting each household allowed me to meet many people relatively quickly while satisfying local curiousity (and suspicions) regarding my activities. It also allowed me to ask households if they would be willing to take part in the survey. Only one compound refused to do so, because my research was not 'official'. However, they had recently lost a land dispute arbitrated by the sub-location elders and the assistant chief, and their refusal may have been connected to this in some way. Interestingly, one member of this compound told his neighbours to have nothing to do with me. But because he was not especially liked, the fact that he did not like me seemed to improve my status within the community!

I also arranged to move in with a local family. I did this for convenience, but it was useful, too, in developing relations with people in the community. The family I lived with was headed by the widow of a man who had been a respected government official and also the local vicar. Because of her impeccable background, I acquired additional respectability. More generally, living in the area and eating the same food as everyone else were popular moves.

Most importantly, I participated in a number of community functions, notably church services and funerals. Funerals in Luoland are an important event and attendance is considered *de rigueur*. Attending, besides being a courtesy, allowed me to converse with people on an informal basis. It was also a good way of meeting migrants, who would often return to Karateng for major funerals.

Finally, before leaving Karateng, I visited as many households as possible to pay a social call and say goodbye. Based on a very preliminary analysis of the data, I prepared a short economic profile of the area. I presented this to the assistant chief at a *baraza*, where I thanked him and the elders of Karateng. I visited all the local officials I had met on arrival, thanking them for their help and giving them a copy of the profile.

5.1.4 *Flexibility*

A typical remark found in books on fieldwork is: 'It is not unusual for research plans to change after one begins fieldwork . . . It is important that just as the fieldworker should have an open mind about what will be observed, similar flexibility should be maintained with regard to the overall research agenda' (Gregory and Altman 1989, p. 45). At a practical level, it will be necessary to adapt to the unforeseen problems that arise. However, a time constraint inevitably restricts flexibility.

At one level, flexibility can be achieved by preparing contingency plans. For example, there were often delays when I had to visit government officials. If possible, I struck up a conversation with someone. Failing that, I reviewed and coded completed questionnaires. A problem that arose early in my fieldwork was that respondents were not at home when we wanted to see them. Peter Amolo, my research assistant, suggested we make appointments to meet with people. This worked quite well. It meant that we were not interviewing people at times inconvenient to them (which hopefully improved our relationships with respondents and the quality of the data). It also meant that time was not wasted chasing people who were not at home. Also, we tried to schedule interviews with households in close proximity to each other. This reduced the travel time within the research site.

I found it helpful to follow a work plan and to be very focused in my inquiries.

Besides being a useful tool for making the most of the time available, this was a useful antidote to 'fieldwork blues'. But while schedules and contingency plans are important, so too is mental flexibility. Do not let time constraints or preconceptions stand in the way of the facts! Initially, I was interested in examining investment in cash crops funded by migrants' remittances. Half-way through my study, it became clear that there were few households growing cash crops, but that there was substantial investment in education. This led to an investigation of processes of household accumulation.

Even when operating under a time constraint, it is necessary to make allowances for being sick. As discussed in Chapter 1, the likelihood of being ill at least once is quite high. Towards the end of my fieldwork, I contracted food poisoning. Had this occurred earlier, I would have had insufficient time to recuperate and successfully complete the research. I was fortunate not to be ill more severely or frequently, as I had made no provision for this.

5.2 Do time constraints matter?

5.2.1 *Making compromises*

Inevitably, undertaking fieldwork in a short period of time required a number of compromises to be made. Rather than outline general principles, since the exact nature of these will vary, here I enumerate the more important compromises I made and assess their consequences.

One major compromise was to limit the amount of time spent learning the local language. I could have spent my entire time in Kenya becoming fluent in Dholuo. While my linguistic skills would have been enhanced, the time available to learn about other things would have been severely circumscribed. Instead, I learned essential phrases at the beginning, such as greetings, and then tried to pick up as much as possible day by day. Given the time available, this was probably the right decision. But had I allocated more time to learning rudimentary Dholuo on arriving in Karateng (for example, practising in the evenings), this would have speeded up my language acquisition.

A disadvantage of not learning the language fully was that it restricted my ability to interact with people on an informal basis. This compounded the fact that a limited amount of time was available to undertake such conversations, and this amounted to a second major compromise. As a result, I learned far less about local culture and history than I would have liked. It also meant that there were fewer opportunities to cross-check the material being collected in the interviews.

I spent very little time in libraries and none at all in land registry offices or archives. Given the nature of the research, this was probably not a major omission. As I was doing a case study, it was unlikely that there would be detailed information on Karateng in these sources. But my understanding of the wider historical processes that affected Karateng was rather limited by my not examining archival evidence.

Some of the losses entailed in these compromises were mitigated by living in the sub-location. Doing so increased the time available for informal contacts and allowed me to develop closer relationships with a number of people. Though they were not representative of the entire population, it was very useful to have discussions with them on a wide variety of topics. It also meant a considerable saving on commuting time.

The selection of the area for the survey also involved a compromise. On the basis of the preparatory trip, I had decided to use Karateng as the sampling unit. However, while undertaking an initial reconnaissance, I discovered that it was difficult to traverse the sub-location from east to west, owing to the presence of several rivers. As few of these were bridged, they posed an obstacle to movement that was likely to worsen with the onset of the rainy season. Secondly, extrapolation from census data indicated that there were approximately 1,300 households currently residing in Karateng. This was too many to enumerate if I were to visit each one and introduce myself. Thirdly, wealthier households appeared to be concentrated in the north of the sub-location, poorer in the south. Hence, using the entire sub-location as the sampling unit was going to be physically difficult, and a considerable amount of time would have been needed to construct a sampling frame. Consequently, I restricted the sample frame to three contiguous villages running from north to south and containing about 400 households.[4] This made movement easier, while maintaining representativeness.

Creating the sampling frame involved further compromises. At the outset, I decided to use the household as the basic sampling unit.[5] To create the frame, I did a small census, obtaining information on the age of the household head, as a proxy for stage of household life-cycle, and dwelling wall materials (concrete or mud) as a proxy for household wealth. An alternative indicator could have been roof construction – thatch or *mbati* (corrugated metal) – but the number of households in the latter category was so large that this would have been an inadequate means of distinguishing wealthier households from poorer ones.[6] This method was faster than collecting detailed information on household composition and asset holdings, but more time-consuming than just enumerating the survey area and choosing households by random selection.

After completing the interviews, it was possible to cross-check this classification scheme. Wall construction did serve as a good proxy for wealth. Of those households classed as wealthy on the basis of living in dwellings with concrete walls, 88 per cent were in the top two deciles of either consumer durables owned or land holdings. With respect to life-cycle position, households headed by men under 35 tended to be slightly under-represented and those headed by over 60s slightly over-represented. It is possible that the ages of some heads were under-estimated in the creation of the sampling frame. This would have the effect of over-estimating the number in the under-35 category and under-estimating the number of 60+ household heads, while leaving the 35–59 age group unchanged.

A final compromise was in the size of the sample. A large sample would have allowed greater scope for statistical analysis, whereas interviewing a smaller number of households would have allowed more detailed information to be collected. Given the aims of the research, I decided on 120 households. This was large enough to permit a reasonable amount of econometric analysis, yet small enough to be manageable in the time available. Later, an additional 40 elderly households were sampled to obtain data on the role of children as old-age security.

5.2.2 *Consequences for data quality*

The compromises necessary when conducting fieldwork under time constraints, *ceteris paribus*, increase the likelihood of obtaining inaccurate data. Therefore, it is especially important to incorporate measures to minimise these, even though this may reduce the scope of the research. This section describes the steps I took and assesses their usefulness.

The first derived from the choice of research topic. The data required fell into three categories: demographic; historical; and household income. The first two can be considered single-point, registered data and, as already noted, are suited to a shorter period of fieldwork. Data on household income are more continuous and include both registered and non-registered elements.

Considerable effort was expended on questionnaire design, both prior to commencing fieldwork and in Karateng. I tried to design the questionnaires to be easy to use and to order the questions so that they followed a logical sequence. I also found pilot testing most helpful. Having spent hours in Oxford devising the 'perfect' questionnaire, I was tempted to skip this in order to save time. This would have been a false economy. Pilot testing made a huge difference. It led to substantial amendments and improvements to all the questionnaires. Failing to pilot the surveys would have resulted in major gaps in the data collected that could not have been easily rectified.

As a substantial amount of information was required, two or three interviews were conducted with each respondent. Although this entailed a cost in terms of the time spent returning to previously visited households, it had the advantage of making each interview shorter and therefore easier on the respondents. It created an opportunity to check the information collected and to pursue unclear responses. The second round included some questions designed to cross-check answers given in the first round. In the first interview, basic data were elicited on household demographic structure, migration, cropping patterns and income. Because of its continuous nature, and the amount of time available, a one-year recall period was used. The second interview focused on household economic and demographic history. Questions were asked about investment in education, marriage and brideprice, migration histories, land transactions, crop investments and changes in holdings of consumer durables. Finally, a separate questionnaire was developed for elderly people, to obtain additional information on children as a source of old-age security. Because these data were continuous and principally non-registered, two (one-week and one-month) recall periods were used. The time constraint meant that it was not possible to undertake repeat surveys on these topics. Consequently, I have only a 'snapshot' of these at one moment in time.

Despite these measures, the questionnaires were still imperfect. The biggest mistake was to include a time budget survey in the first round of interviews. This proved to be a salutary lesson in the importance of thinking through methodology in advance. It made the interviews unnecessarily long. The information collected was incomplete as some household members were absent. Perhaps most importantly, the data were not really necessary for the research. I had included it because it seemed like a good idea, rather than for any specific reason.

I had originally intended to conduct interviews both in the daytime and in the evenings. However, for security reasons, it was not possible to meet respondents at night. Instead, this time was used to review completed questionnaires and transfer the data to coding sheets (this was possible, in part, because my living arrangements gave a reasonable degree of privacy). This had several advantages. It forced me to go through the questionnaires carefully for omissions and inconsistencies. Secondly, it meant that a duplicate copy of all the data existed, hence reducing the potentially disastrous consequences of loss or destruction of the questionnaires. It also meant that on my return to Oxford, I was able to enter the data into a computer almost immediately. Finally, a number of cross-checks were built into each questionnaire. As these are also discussed in other chapters, I will focus here on household income.[7] This is a particularly useful example because, when time is short, income data have to be collected retrospectively and this poses further challenges.

Data on incomes were necessary to determine which households were reliant on non-agricultural sources, particularly remittances from migrants. Because of the time constraint, it was necessary to rely on households' recollections of their incomes over the previous year. In obtaining this information, I asked a series of questions about income at the beginning of the long rains planting season. Since this provided a recognisable benchmark, it was possible to establish a readily identifiable one-year recall period. Secondly, the income data were cross-checked by collecting information on major household purchases. These included expenditures on blankets and sheets, baskets and pots, cooking, crockery and eating utensils, men's, women's and children's clothing, and funeral and *harambee* (community fund-raising events) contributions. Since these were all 'lumpy' purchases, they were subject to smaller recall errors or deliberate under-reporting. While in the field, this information was compared with household cash income. Households reporting no sources

Table 5.1 Comparison of income and expenditure shares

Income Deciles	Income share (%)	Expenditure share (%)
Lowest 40%	11.7	10.7
Middle 30%	21.8	23.0
Upper 30%	66.5	66.3

of cash incomes, but high cash expenditures, were asked supplementary questions during the second round of interviews to determine how these purchases were funded. A comparison of the expenditure and income data suggests that they match each other reasonably closely, as shown by Table 5.1. In addition to verifying that total income appeared consistent with other measures, I also took steps to minimise errors associated with different types of income (wages, remittances, crop sales and other sources).

A number of individuals received salaries on a regular basis (such as teachers and local civil servants). This is another example of single-point, registered data and it proved relatively straightforward to collect. There was a possibility that some individuals might conceal their earnings. For some occupations, I was able to obtain pay scales. Comparison with reported amounts suggested that deliberate under-reporting was not a problem.

Many households obtained remittances from absent children. These are an important feature of inter-generational relations in Karateng, and households could readily recall amounts received. But because of the length of the recall period involved, there was a danger of some being omitted. On the basis of the pilot survey, remittances were separated into four categories: money sent back; money brought back; value of gifts given; and money given to parents if they visited their children. This approach was particularly useful in capturing small remittances made by a number of individuals.

The crop income data were more difficult to collect. I relied on respondents' recollections of what they had harvested by crop and by plot in the previous year. Three problems were encountered. Some of the maize crop is eaten green and it is unclear whether households included this when recalling harvest sizes. As poorer households are more likely to eat maize green, it is possible that their income is underestimated. A second problem concerned crops, such as cassava and sweet potato, that are harvested on a non-registered, continual basis throughout the year. Estimates of their production were difficult to obtain on a retrospective basis. Finally, it was necessary to value crop production that did not pass through the market. I experimented with two methods. One used the average price reported by households from their sales. The second used seasonal price data obtained through informal questioning. These produced comparable results.

Some households obtained income from other sources. These included income from casual labouring, own-business activity and miscellaneous transfers. Because of the irregularity of these earnings, data quality was variable. Two important own-business activities are brewing *changaa* (a liquor) and pot-making. However, production methods for these goods did not vary greatly within the sub-location and I was able to obtain estimates of the unit costs associated with brewing and pot-making. During the interviews, in addition to asking for information on total revenues and costs, questions regarding the frequency and level of production were also included. This made it possible to calculate (with allowances for seasonal considerations) a second net profit figure that could be compared with the reported difference between revenues and costs. A similar methodology was applied to data on women engaged in large-scale trading, though with less success as they were a more heterogenous group. However, other income sources, such as earnings from casual labour and occasional transfers from other family members, were more difficult to obtain and virtually impossible to cross-check. Consequently, these data are more unreliable. I also included some open-ended questions to capture income sources not covered in other parts of the survey, but these produced a very poor response. This may have occurred because the questions were too vague and proper follow-up questions were not included.

5.3 Conclusion

Conducting fieldwork under a time constraint is a challenging exercise, but not impossible. A time constraint limits the topics that can be pursued and requires compromises in the research methods used. While planning is vital, it should not lead to inflexibility. Rather, it should be regarded as a means of getting the most out of time spent in the field. Finally, no matter how severe the time constraint, it is essential, for both ethical and practical reasons, to establish and maintain good relations with respondents.

Notes

1. This fieldwork was supported by grants from the George Webb-Medley Fund, Wadham College and the University of Oxford.
2. The results of the fieldwork are discussed in Hoddinott (1989).
3. Though, as Olsen notes in the preceding chapter, thinking about methodology before starting fieldwork should not lead to inflexibility.
4. Villages in this locality are geographical descriptions based on clan lines. They are not built-up areas of settlement.
5. As discussed by Devereux in Chapter 3, the definition of the household can be problematic. I adapted the 'common pot' definition to suit conditions in Karateng: 'A household includes all persons living under one or several roofs within a compound who share a community of life in that they are answerable to a common head and are normally reliant on a "common pot" for feeding. Sons living in the same compound as their fathers but cultivating their own land are considered a separate household. All wives of a man in a polygamous union are part of one household.' Hoddinott (1989, p. 35).

6. The actual choice of households was done through a random selection method. Households were grouped according to village, age of head and wall construction and listed sequentially by number. In order to obtain a sample of 120 households, approximately every third household was chosen from each group.
7. See da Corta and Venkateshwarlu (Chapter 7) on dating events, Christensen (Chapter 8) on livestock and credit, Harriss (Chapter 9) on traders, and Lockwood (Chapter 11) on cross-checking demographic data.

6

Qualitative research: collecting life histories

Elizabeth Francis

Introduction[1]

I carried out fieldwork on the economic and social impact of labour migration in Kisumu District, one of the home districts of the Luo people of western Kenya, between 1987 and 1989. The study was concerned with processes which have brought about agricultural decline and impoverishment in one sub-location, Koguta, over the course of this century. In the course of the research, I looked at long-term processes of household accumulation and differentiation and changing relationships within and between households. I used a variety of research methods, including a small survey for basic socio-economic data, and an individual budget study. I also had many informal discussions. But most of my information about long-term processes of social change came from sixty life histories that I collected. These are the focus of this chapter.

The content of my study and the methods I adopted were decided primarily by the issues I was exploring, but I was continually made aware of the significance of my relationships with informants for my findings. These were shaped partly by my overall situation in the field, but also by the tactics I followed in the course of different interviews. In this chapter, I suggest a framework for starting to think about roles and discuss its relevance for my own experience in collecting life histories. I also describe some of the tactics I followed when conducting interviews.

6.1 Establishing (and being given) a role

Local-level research, whether a brief, one-off survey or longer-term fieldwork, places the researcher and the researched in a social relationship. Coping with these relationships is one of the most important and difficult aspects of this type of research: important, because they profoundly affect the nature and quality of the data collected; difficult, because both sides bring expectations that are unlikely to coincide, while they may perceive the relationship in radically different ways. Uncovering the roots of such expectations and perceptions demands an acute awareness of the roles the researcher and informants are playing.

There are no general principles for role-finding, beyond an assumption that any researcher will want a role which minimises the extent to which information is distorted or withheld, while also remaining ethically acceptable. The role a researcher takes on is the outcome of a combination of factors. It is only partly a matter of choice. The researcher may find a role thrust upon her or him that she or he would not have chosen, and which may have to be adapted to, or coped with. Added to this consideration is the point that, although some factors can be surmised in advance, many may be hard to anticipate. The following list is not meant to be exhaustive:

1. Factors that affect the way in which the residents of a locality and various types of outsiders interact:
   (a) For how long and in what ways has the locality been linked to other regions and exposed to the state, to missionaries or to development agencies? For example, is there a history of conflict, or of patron–client relationships?
   (b) Will the researcher necessarily be seen initially as a representative of one of these institutions, whether or not she or he is?
   (c) How do various types of people (rich, poor, women, men, old, young) view the representatives of the state and other authority figures?
   (d) What is the class structure of the locality? (This may influence choice of living arrangements and both the nature of and opportunities for social interaction.)
   (e) In ex-colonies, what are people's memories of Europeans? For example, would a Western researcher be trying to counter an impression of arrogance?
2. The identity of the researcher:
   (a) What are typical attitudes in the community to someone of the researcher's gender, age, marital status and social class?
3. The identity of the people being studied:
   (a) How do members of different ethnic groups, social classes and age groups and people of either gender perceive and relate to the researcher?
4. The specific nature of the research project and the circumstances under which it is conducted:
   (a) What is the nature of the research project? Is it purely an academic study or is it related to the work of a government agency or other organisation?

(b) Is the researcher part of an organisation, or is she or he working independently? Is she or he alone or in a team in the field? If the researcher is part of an organisation, how much scope does the researcher have for shaping an independent role in the field?
(c) How is the researcher introduced into the community? For example, is it through an outside agency, or through a group or individual within the community? In either case, how is this 'gatekeeper' perceived within the community?
(d) Does the researcher live in the locality? If so, under what circumstances – with a local family? In lodgings? Alone?
(e) What is the researcher's standard of living while in the field? Is it greatly different from that of the rest of the community?
(f) What research methods are being used? (At one extreme are formal interviews, used exclusively; at the other is participant observation.) How do these methods condition the nature of social and professional interactions with informants?
(g) Has the researcher become involved in community activities, formal or informal? If so, in what way – observation and participation? Patronage? Advocacy?

My research was carried out alone and independently, as a purely academic study for a Ph.D., so my research activities and fieldwork location were not closely defined for me. It was important that I find a role in which I could win a substantial amount of trust, because I wanted to discuss highly sensitive topics, such as finances and relationships within the household. As I planned to live in the community for over a year, I would be dependent on informants' willingness to make time to talk to me on many occasions. Because I hoped to get beneath the surface of people's rationalised explanations of their behaviour, I also wanted to be in a position where I could observe and take part in daily life, as well as carry out formal interviews.

Before I arrived in Kenya, I expected that the most important factors affecting my role would be that I was a young, British woman carrying out research in a former British colony. Moreover, this was a region which had been a source area for migrant labour since the early decades of this century. Many of the older men could be expected to have had contact with British people only in the context of authority relationships (at work or through contact with the colonial state). Many of the women would have had contact with Europeans only through mission churches. Memories of the colonial period might be a source of hostility, but also, possibly, of a residual excessive deference. The region is also one in which representatives of the state and other authority figures are regarded as alien and perhaps hostile forces, to an extent greater than in other regions of Kenya. So I assumed that people would be suspicious of my motives in carrying out the research and afraid of what I would do with the information. All these considerations made me keen to be introduced into a community in such a way that I would not be associated with the state and that would allow me to win people's trust. It would also be important to behave in a way that would confound stereotypes people might have of arrogant or aloof Europeans.[2]

Initial suspicion of me was lessened by the fact that I was introduced into the community by a prominent and highly respected local family, with whom I first had contact in the United Kingdom and with whom I lived throughout my fieldwork. As in many other cultures, when a person is introduced to Luo people, the first questions are often about his or her clan and family affiliations, as this allows the questioner to 'place' the stranger in relation to people who are known. Cohen and Odhiambo (1989, p. 27), writing about Siaya, an adjacent District also inhabited by Luo people, make this point vividly:

> In Siaya the individual is synonymous with the stranger, an alien, possibly even an enemy . . . You do not in an important sense exist until you reveal your networks and, more importantly, until this network can be verified by your interrogators.

Living with a family meant that I could introduce myself in a way that was analogous to the cultural norm, while my hosts' accceptance of me was a sign to others that I was probably not a threat. The fact that my family introduced me to many other members of the community in their own terms – 'She is a student who is learning how we live here, so she can go and teach people in her country about us, just like students from Kenya go to her country to learn how they live' – made people readier to accept my presence and showed me how to introduce myself to others. This form of introduction was usually accepted, because a number of young people from the area have themselves studied overseas.

There are obvious potential pitfalls attached to being associated with any particular family, or clan, in a community. In becoming their 'daughter', I was identified with them, and at least one potentially valuable informant was wary of me for a long time because of longstanding poor relations with my hosts. (He did, eventually, suggest an interview, once he saw that so many other people had talked to me.) I see this wariness as an inevitable by-product of developing close relations with certain individuals, and believe that it was more than offset by the 'respectability' my association with this family brought. In general, I made an effort to spread my informants across several lineages, and my association with the lineage I lived in does not seem to have been a problem. Living with a family also gave me an opportunity to observe domestic relationships much more closely than would be revealed in even the most in-depth interview. My family was also an invaluable source of information about other people in the community, because I knew them well enough for a relationship of real trust to develop. Finally, I consider that some sacrifice of privacy was worth the gain in my feeling of belonging in a Luo home.

The pitfalls of close association with the type of family that would have overseas contacts could lead to a distancing from poorer individuals in a community where class divisions were deeper. However, patterns of sociability in this community are only beginning to be shaped by class formation and there is no clearly dominant class that I risked being identified with. Similarly, although my family's standard of living – and hence mine – was higher than average, the difference was not very marked.

For most of the time, my categorisation as a 'student' was unproblematic. My role was defined as an unmarried, European 'girl' who was studying Luo life. On the whole, this was a useful role, because it marked me out as a person who was not attached to a potentially threatening outside agency and who was not an authority figure. Being British did not present special problems. Fine distinctions about nationalities were often not meaningful and most people categorised me simply as a European – a *Mzungu*. Although some older people initially treated me with the deference that they had been taught European employers and missionaries expected, my relationships with many people were very relaxed and friendly. I found that my initial child-like incompetence in the language and in some of the simplest daily activities, such as carrying head-loads or lighting a stove, were all good counterweights. My role also allowed me legitimately to ask many naive questions.

Eventually, I became reasonably fluent in the local language, Dholuo. Being able to take part in conversations going on around me and talk to people informally made the atmosphere more comfortable when it came to interviewing them formally.

But my role was not completely unambiguous. I was living in a locality where the long-term decline of farm production has brought about serious and growing poverty. People's best chance of escaping poverty is to find well-paid urban employment for themselves or their relatives. There is an expectation that local people with the right contacts, or their urban-based relatives, should help poorer people with finding jobs or funding for education. It is also expected that they should be prepared to give money or food to poorer relatives. Sometimes these expectations are fulfilled; at other times, they are not. I neither wanted, nor could play, the role of patron, but people's very acceptance of me as a temporary member of the community created the expectation that I would give help in this way. That is what better-off relatives are supposed to do and, despite the fact that I was known to be a student, many people found it difficult to believe that a European could have limited funds and no contacts for finding people jobs.

The question of repayment and obligation became, for me, the most distressing problem in my fieldwork. This was a community in a migrant labour economy, where the link between academic qualifications and better-paid employment was clearly understood, and comments about the benefits I would gain from getting a Ph.D. filtered back to me. Even if only one person makes a remark like this, the researcher, isolated in the field, can easily start suspecting that everyone thinks the same way. It was sometimes hard to maintain a sense of proportion. Any role would have had drawbacks, as well as advantages, but this was often hard to remember.

The truth of the remarks, and my lack of a benefit for the community, prompted me to look around for some way to compensate them for all the time and information given. The role of advocate was not an option. No development agencies were operating in the study area and an attempt to play an advocacy role with the local administration would have been interpreted as an unwarranted interference in local affairs, putting at risk my government research permit.

The only realistic recompenses available were 'sop' activities. For example, I held several large parties for local people where each guest was given a small gift. Although these were a great success, the basic problem of unfulfilled expectations remained. Expectations are higher for the longer-term fieldworker, because contact with informants is so much more intense and personal than in a one-off survey, and the fieldworker's dependence on informants' willingness to give up time is so much more obvious, particularly when the novelty of the researcher's presence in the community has worn off. I found the problem manageable only when I accepted that I could never fulfil everyone's expectations.

A field researcher cannot expect to have equally good relationships with everyone she or he comes into contact with, however sensitive she or he tries to be. One reason is simply the fact that people have different personalities, but there are also likely to be some systematic differences related to the gender, age and socio-economic position of the researcher and informants. These may change over time as the researcher becomes more established in the community. They can also be at least partially offset by one's choice of research assistant. I decided before I arrived in the community to look for a young, female assistant, as I knew that research in a migrant labour reserve would involve a large proportion of female informants. I anticipated that they would feel readier to talk to me if my assistant was female. In fact, older women in the community generally had more confidence about talking to strangers than younger women and so, in the earliest days, I found it easier to get them to talk at length. Later, when younger women knew me better, this difference became much less marked. But some older men did not take me as seriously (or feel as comfortable with me) as they might have taken an older, male researcher or an older, married woman, and it was some time before I found enough older men who were ready to make plenty of time to talk to me. Accordingly, when I collected life histories from some of these older men, I was helped by a young man who was a university student at home for the vacation. His presence made the atmosphere more relaxed and we found that the most productive approach was to have a three-way conversation. Presumably, a male researcher would have a different set of problems in a migrant labour economy like this, where so many of the inhabitants are women.

I did not find that the quality of my relationships with people was systematically related to their socio-economic positions, though I could see how it easily might have been. People who could speak English, or who, because of their education, were used to thinking in a more abstract way, were easy to talk to and it was tempting to rely on them for information about the community. They were also more used to talking to outsiders and to receiving them as guests. But what they said was filtered through their personal perceptions and, although such information could be a useful way of checking my findings, it had to be used carefully. (These points are discussed below.) Conversely, with poorer, usually less educated people, I sometimes had to overcome their diffidence about offering hospitality to a European.

With hindsight, I can see that my gender, age and obvious lack of institutional links allowed me to avoid being identified with the state or other potentially threatening figures of authority. They did, however, both present other problems and confer other advantages. As difficult as the essentially methodological problem of finding an appropriate role was the ethical problem posed by being a European researcher in an impoverished rural area.

6.2 Collecting life histories

6.2.1 *The life-history approach to social process*

A central concern in my research was to explore how changes in the political economy of the region were registered and acted out at the local level during and since the colonial period. In western Kenya, a concern with processes of change implied a focus on household differentiation and changing gender relations. It was necessary to find out, for example, how people had accumulated or lost access to resources; what strategies they had followed; and how these strategies were related to changes in domestic relationships and in relations beyond the household.

In order to examine these processes, I needed to know about the changing economic activities and relationships of many different types of people, particularly with regard to access to and control over key resources such as land, labour, education and money. It was also important to try to get behind the bare outlines of reported behaviour to the underlying beliefs, strategies and constraints which had shaped that behaviour. One way into such a study of economic change as social process is through a focus on the life histories of individuals.

There were also practical considerations behind my choice of technique. I had initially hoped to collect a great deal of this sort of information informally, but I found that one consequence of people's understanding that I was a 'student' who was 'studying' their way of life was that they expected me to carry out formal interviews. Out of courtesy, people tended to stop what they were doing when I arrived at their homes and sit expectantly, waiting for me to start questioning them. There was also little public space that allowed me to observe behaviour without taking on the role of a guest in someone's home. Although I did develop a more informal relationship with many informants, as well as with my hosts, it became clear that much more of my material than I had expected would have to be collected by direct questioning. I therefore tried to develop a format for interviewing that would be both relatively informal and flexible. I eventually found that collecting life histories fitted these needs.

The usefulness of the life-history approach is critically dependent on several factors. In the first place, the researcher needs to have a thorough understanding of the macro-developments which provide the context of constraints and opportunities within which people have acted. In western Kenya, some of the most important of these factors were growing land shortage, the long-term decline of returns to farming and off-farm activities in the region and, crucially, a series of changes in the structure of demand and wages on the urban labour market. Without this kind of context, it can be difficult to interpret the reasons informants give for their actions.

It is also important to interview the widest possible cross-section of people, in order to capture the variations in social and economic processes which have occurred. For this reason, interviewing a statistically representative sample may be quite inappropriate. (I return to this point below.)

Lastly, this research technique is one in which a rapport between interviewer and informant is absolutely crucial. Because the researcher has only a general idea, in advance, which processes are likely to have been especially important in any particular life history, he or she must try to make sure that the informant does not feel overly constrained by the researcher's preconceptions. The researcher must also be flexible enough to respond to the unexpected.[3] In the discussion below, I show how I tried to apply the second and third considerations in my own research. The first point comes in more at the stage of interpretation, which is outside the scope of this chapter.

Asking other people to tell the story of their lives is a highly artificial undertaking. A 'life story' is an intellectual construct whose structure and content reflect the priorities of the researcher and the images the informant projects back into the past, as much as tangible realities. Despite this artificiality, I consider that it is possible to collect reasonably accurate material about certain topics in an interview that is structured around the chronology of an informant's life, provided that it is not done naively. I would not make any grander claim for this research method.

6.2.2 *Sampling*

My original intention was to collect around twenty life histories as a supplement to a larger number of interviews on specific topics. I finally collected sixty usable life histories, because I found this kind of interview to be a flexible research tool which also encouraged many informants to open up far more than in other types of interview. Sixty life histories gave me a good spread of informants according to the criteria of age, sex, household structure, economic activities and socio-economic position.

There is no *a priori* link between qualitative research and non-statistical sampling techniques, but my research required that I talk to individuals in a wide variety of socio-economic positions in order to explore a range of social processes and behaviour. I collected the life histories at a fairly late stage in my research, by which time some of the most important selection criteria were clear. One criterion was generation. The most important differences in experience were between the generations born before 1930, those born between 1930 and 1950, and those born after 1950. These differences largely reflected changing opportunities in the local economy and the urban labour market. Men tended to migrate, while women tended to remain behind in the rural area. Moreover, men and women had markedly different social roles and differing rights of resource access and control. So gender was another key criterion. The central historical experience in this century has been the creation and differentiation of a migrant labour force. Accordingly, a further important criterion was the employment history of the household head, his wife and their offspring.

Some types of individual whose experiences were important for my understanding of different social processes might not have been picked up in a statistically derived sample. For example, there was only one university-educated returned migrant in the village where I lived, but investigating his behaviour was important for understanding processes of social differentiation. I was also interested both to interview members of as many different lineages as possible (because there was social differentiation between lineages, as well as between households), and to talk to closely related members of the same lineage (in order to understand the transmission, or non-transmission, of economic position between and across generations). Other selection criteria became important as my understanding of social processes grew. For example, I interviewed different types of women traders in order to understand why some had managed to accumulate resources, while others were caught in a rut of low returns and under-capitalisation. Beyond basic socio-economic criteria, then, the process of selecting informants was largely additive, as further criteria became relevant, and as I met people who were interesting for my study (and also sometimes subtractive, as some people who initially seemed potentially good informants proved not to be particularly enlightening).

Also important was informants' varying ability to analyse their own situations and actions in the rather abstract way demanded by any researcher who asks questions that begin with the words 'Why' and 'When'. This factor makes certain kinds of informant superficially more attractive, particularly highly educated people who have been more exposed to formal cause – effect analysis and exact dating, but other informants' answers to 'Why' questions can be enlightening in different ways. For example, a stereotyped comment like, 'Young women don't do so much farm work nowadays because studying has made them weak' reveals much about people's perceptions of social change. (This comment, of course, also applies to highly educated people's perceptions.)

As well as theory-driven selection criteria, a major factor determining my set of informants was bound to be people's varying willingness to talk to me. In an important sense, informants partly choose themselves, because one is critically dependent on the willingness of people, many of whom are already over-stretched by their labour burdens, to give up valuable time for no tangible benefit. Winning this willingness in turn depends on the establishment of an appropriate role and an approach to interviewing that informants view positively. In my own case, as I have mentioned, I initially found it difficult to select a large enough sample of older men, but this was a problem that time, and the aid of a male assistant, helped to overcome. My association with the family I lived with helped on the occasions when I needed to introduce myself to informants, such as the women traders mentioned above, who did not know me, but who were important subjects to include in the collection of life histories. By the time I found it necessary to approach strangers and ask them to tell me their life histories, I had also learned how best to approach people in a way that in their culture was properly respectful, friendly and interested. I think that close involvement in the life of the family I lived with helped me to learn how to do this. It was not a set of skills that I picked up all at once, or completely consciously. Lastly, my clear lack of association with the state also made it relatively easy for me to talk to people who were involved in illegal activities.

6.2.3 *Interview techniques and tactics*

The life histories were collected through semi-structured interviews, in which I took rough notes that I wrote up in the form of a continuous text immediately afterwards. Most interviews lasted for around two hours, although I discussed their life histories with some individuals over the course of several interviews. The bulk of the interviews were conducted at the same point in my fieldwork, but a small number were carried out with migrant men as and when they came back for visits. Much information collected on other occasions was also relevant. For example, an important sub-set of informants for the life histories was the people who took part in my budget survey, giving me information on contemporary patterns of income receipt and use that I could fit together with the longer-term picture given in the life-history interview.

In the life-history interviews, I collected the same basic information from all informants: age (or approximate age); father's occupation and approximate size of his landholding and herd; education level; marital, migratory and occupational history of self and spouse; current landholding and land bought or sold; stockholding; crops currently grown and sold and long-term changes in these; investments; current economic activities and sources of income; children's education and occupations; and whether the children provide economic support.

Because, in many cases, I was dealing with a long time period (sometimes over seventy years), I did not expect to be able to collect accurate numerical data, particularly for the early decades. I considered that information about behaviour and social processes was less likely to be inaccurate, although it does present its own difficulties.

I have been able to use the material collected in the life histories to analyse long-term processes of economic differentiation, because the principal source of economic mobility within and between generations has been the labour market. Qualitative distinctions can often be made between households with regard to the labour-market position of their members (unskilled, artisan, clerical, managerial employment and so on), while differences in labour-market position have generated quite distinct trajectories of household development. For example, it was possible to see how some individuals were able to use resources gained through trading or better-paid wage employment to invest in their children's future labour-market position (through funding their education to secondary-school level and beyond), and how others were hampered from doing this by low wages. It would have been more difficult to collect material on very long-term changes in economic position in a community where mobility involved primarily quantitative changes (land-holding, cattle-holding and so on), which informants are perhaps more likely to misremember.[4]

Whether or not I was able to move beyond collecting a straight chronological account of someone's life to begin to understand motivations, feelings and conflicts depended crucially on the establishment of rapport. This was partly a function of my longer-term personal relations with many informants and people in their social networks and, more generally, the role which I had been given within the community. On the whole, the points made about the significance of my role for encouraging informants to accept the request for an interview also apply to their readiness to open up in the course of an interview.

But it would be a mistake to see a researcher's relationship with each informant simply as something fixed from the beginning by ethnicity, age, gender and so on. It is something to be worked at over the course of fieldwork and also during an interview. When I began my research, I expected that my role in the community, as an outsider and an alien, would make some topics much more difficult to talk about than others, perhaps even impossible. As it turned out, there were few topics that I had wanted to talk to people about but could not (though some people were more forthcoming than others).

Even if an informant thinks of one from the start as someone who is neutral and who can be trusted, building and maintaining rapport during an interview is a complex task. There are some obvious techniques, such as beginning with innocuous topics and introducing more sensitive topics in an unthreatening way (see below). It is also important to learn the conversational conventions. For example, Luo people consider it good manners in conversation to have many pauses and to say things like, 'Yes . . . indeed . . . that's the way it is' to show that one is following what is being said, and agreeing with it, but not rushing the speaker. Nor do Luos plunge into topics. They approach a subject crabwise.

The most important thing seemed to be to take the interview slowly, while at the same time assessing constantly whether a topic was worth pursuing. And there were some cases where I decided that the interview was not worth pursuing. I then just waited for an appropriate moment to finish.

I structured the interviews around likely major life events. For a woman, these included marriage and the consequent move to her husband's home, getting her own farm and cooking pot, and the final return of a migrant husband. For men, these were the first migration and subsequent jobs, marriage, and retirement. There were then several recurring themes. I asked a number of women about their relationships with senior and junior women in their compounds over the course of their lives, while I asked many men and women about the husband's involvement in agricultural decision-making while he was a migrant; I attempted to establish how prosperous male and female traders had achieved their position and why some elderly widows wielded economic power in their compounds, while others did not. Many topics emerged only during the interviews. When an informant made a remark which set off a new line of inquiry that seemed important, I followed it up. Some individuals were more informative or readier to talk about some topics than others, so it was often a question of getting a feel for how the interview was going and acting accordingly.

As an illustration, when I asked women and men about power within their households, some of them gave replies which I eventually recognised as repetition of stereotypes. Others appeared to be putting far more thought into their replies, giving reasons for the state of affairs in their households and making comparisons with other people. For example, when I asked Monica Anyango[5] about farm decision-making in her household, her replies encouraged me to ask more general questions about the reasons why some women have much more decision-making power than others. The resulting discussion gave me many insights into links between regional impoverishment, economic differentiation and gender relations.

Quite early in our conversation, I asked Martha Odiyo if she had attended school. From her reply, I learned that:[6]

> She went to Bible School. Her husband had only one brother and many sisters, so there were plenty of cattle for bridewealth. His sister lived in Martha's father's home and she arranged the marriage. Her husband brought cattle twice. She did not want to get married and leave Bible School, but her father insisted, because he had seen the cattle. She married in 1933. Her husband was still a boy. She thought that they would marry formally (in Church), but it did not happen. Her husband did not go to Bible School (i.e. he was not a practising Christian). She was pregnant

> and so she had no say in it. It is hard for a woman to get her say, because she has come from another home.

I took this reply as a sign that Martha would be prepared to talk about any subsequent marital difficulties, and this proved to be the case. This was another very informative interview, because her husband, Peter Odiyo, was one of the few relatively successful non-migrant farmers in Koguta and there had clearly been a great deal of conflict as he appropriated his wives' labour power to build up his farm enterprise.

> Odiyo is a fierce man and he liked to quarrel. The quarrels arose because he expected her to do a lot of work and she didn't like quarrelling. She did consider leaving him, but her bridewealth was high, so she could not leave. He used to threaten to bring another wife. She would say 'Just do that', because she was fed up with the quarrels . . . After the other wives came, she was left with one garden. Before they came, she worked very hard in the joint garden. The cattle Odiyo used to marry her co-wives came from her work.

This picture of marital conflict confirmed the description Odiyo had earlier given to me of his attitude towards marriage. He saw it as a relationship full of conflict, in which a husband plays off one wife against another in order to impose his authority.

When I came across particularly reflective and responsive informants like Monica and Martha, I had the chance to talk in a more abstract way about the hypotheses that I had built up from interviews with other people. I found conversations like these the most exciting and enjoyable part of my fieldwork, because a real sharing of ideas took place. The great temptations to be avoided in conversations like these, however, are over-prompting and putting words into people's mouths.

Much could also be learned from casual asides, although their significance was often apparent only much later. Wanting to find out about the extent of commercialisation of agriculture in the 1930s, I asked John Okumu whether his wife had sold crops at that time. He said no, and added, 'Who would have bought them?'. It was only a year later, when I drew together my material on the local economy, that I realised what this remark indicated about the food supply position in the 1930s – a crucial point in the periodisation of the decline of agriculture in this migrant labour economy.

Even stereotyped replies could teach me a great deal. For example, when I asked both men and women about the reasons for the difficulties women have in getting their husbands to agree to their trading, many informants stated that a woman who trades is an unreliable wife, possibly even a prostitute, and that women do not use money wisely. Such remarks are shaped by gender ideologies, that is, beliefs about appropriate behaviour and rights in specific contexts, together with more diffuse beliefs about the essential nature of women and men and appropriate relations between them. In the course of subsequent analysis, such beliefs proved to have been a powerful influence on the investment behaviour of migrant men.

I came across a number of problems when collecting life histories. A full discussion is not possible here, but the following problems were some of the most common. Many older informants were vague about dates and ages, since these were not considered important pieces of information until recently. I used various methods for establishing ages and dates. People often knew whether they were a little older or younger than other individuals who appeared to be of the same generation and who, because of greater exposure to education, knew their dates of birth, They could also tell me whether they were born, married and so on near a well-known event of which I knew the date (the coming of the first missionaries; the World Wars; a major famine in 1931–2; Kenyan Independence), or whether they were old enough to look after cattle at that time (probably over seven years old) or had given birth to their first child (probably around seventeen years old), and so on. In this way, I could usually place an event to within around five years.

Other problems were harder to avoid. Informants sometimes telescoped the past, giving a description of an undifferentiated 'long ago', in which it was hard to distinguish the 1920s from the 1940s, or they quoted apparently exact figures from one period to cover a much longer one (for example, giving their last earnings from employment as the typical wage in their career). I tried to get around this difficulty by asking informants about specific periods ('when you were first married'; 'at the time that your husband was working in Mombasa' and so on), but this was only sometimes effective. It was easier to derive a periodisation from some informants than others and for certain topics than others. Men could usually remember their dates of entering and leaving various jobs, so it was not difficult to periodise a migrant's career, but gradual changes in labour use in a rural household were harder to track. I was forced to fall back on, for example, people's memories that when they were young, most women worked on their gardens in the morning and afternoon, whereas now they farm in the morning and make baskets for sale in the afternoon. Prior knowledge of the changing political economy of the region (growing cash needs; land shortage; distance from markets for cash crops) was necessary to interpret observations like these.

Another source of difficulty was the possibility that informants' views of the past were coloured by nostalgia, or that they were projecting contemporary patterns of behaviour back into the past. These pitfalls are intrinsic to the collection of oral history, but they can be at least partly avoided. For example, I talked to a number of older women about their relationships with their mothers-in-law and daughters-in-law, in order to find out whether, and why, the access of senior women to the labour of junior women had diminished. Most older women said that they had helped their mothers-in-law more than their own daughters-in-law now helped them, but this perception could easily have been mere nostalgia. Further evidence was needed that there had, indeed, been a change, and this came from the terms in which older and younger women described their relationships with senior women. Older women described the relationship in the following terms:

> I would work in my mother-in-law's garden roughly every three days. I just went, without being called.

> I would help my mother-in-law in her garden until the work was finished.

> I would spend equal amounts of time in her garden and my own.

Younger women described their current labour input into their mothers'-in-law gardens quite differently:

> I work in her garden if she is sick.

> She may call me and, if I have finished, I help her.

Asking the informant a more specific and less emotionally charged question than a direct comparison between generations produced answers that I could then myself use to make comparisons.

Perhaps the most difficult problem to deal with, however, was the possibility that an informant was withholding information, or not telling the truth. Outright lying was difficult to prevent, but could sometimes be spotted because the information was inconsistent, or implausible. Because this was such a small community, I was often able to cross-check information through discreet enquiries.

There are some obvious tactics for lessening the possibility that an informant gives misleading information. I always began interviews with innocuous topics and slowly worked my way towards more sensitive subjects (this is also how Luo people behave when they want to discuss a delicate topic), and I tried to introduce potentially embarrassing questions indirectly. For example, many people are reluctant to admit to having little or no education, so I often prefaced a question about educational attainment with the question, 'Were there many schools in your community when you were a child?'. The informant could then explain that there were very few schools and the admission that he or she had received little or no education was easier to make. Introducing a sensitive subject too quickly could destroy the process of gaining an informant's trust and ruin the interview, so I tried to pick up conversational cues. If an informant was ready to volunteer information, I then pressed a little harder, but brief answers were often a sign that the informant did not want to pursue a subject and I moved on to another topic. I initially found the need to make such adjustments to my interview schedule frustrating, because I would prepare a list of topics before the interview and wanted to cover them all, but, as in so much of my fieldwork, I eventually realised that a researcher has to go with the grain, and not against it.

6.3 Conclusion

In this chapter, I have argued that a researcher is necessarily involved in a series of social relationships in the course of fieldwork. These relationships are partly conditioned by factors outside the researcher's control. The latter include, for example, the researcher's ethnicity, gender, age and socio-economic position, or historical conditions affecting attitudes in the community to outsiders. These simply have to be adapted to. Other factors affecting a researcher's role in the community can be anticipated and acted upon. These include choice of research techniques, living arrangements and manner of involvement in community affairs.

The discussion of my collection of life histories has attempted to show, however, that the social relationships in which the research was embedded were not fixed by immutable social roles taken on by my informants and myself. They changed over time and were also profoundly influenced by the tactics I followed in the course of interviews. Fieldwork turned out to be as much about learning to handle the dynamics of individual interviews as about learning what opportunities and constraints were set up by my social role in the field.

Notes

1. This fieldwork was supported by grants from the Economic and Social Research Council, the Wenner-Gren Foundation for Anthropological Research, Somerville College, Oxford, and the Royal Anthropological Institute.
2. A valuable source of advice on many of the issues mentioned in this section is Ellen (1984).
3. Bozzoli (1985) provides a useful discussion of these issues.
4. Da Corta and Venkateshwarlu discuss this in Chapter 7.
5. To protect informants' anonymity, I have changed their names.
6. This is a condensed version of a longer conversation with the informant.

7

Field methods for economic mobility

Lucia da Corta and
Davuluri Venkateshwarlu

Introduction[1]

> Studies based on research in two villages must inevitably be subject to criticisms on the grounds of their limited usefulness for the purposes of generalisation. But it is not the purpose of village studies to provide a foundation for generalisation. Rather such cases are intended to *make possible the determination of processes*.
>
> (Harriss 1983, p. 71: our emphasis)

Our field study addressed the nature and causes of economic mobility and social change in drought-prone villages of south India, in the context of developing capitalism since 1950. Rather than relying on written sources, we followed a structured approach to 'oral history' by asking villagers themselves about their economic histories and about changes in class, community and gender relations.[2] This was an immensely satisfying experience, because villagers offered hitherto unknown and fascinating explanations for different aspects of agrarian change, and because collecting such data ourselves assured us of their reliability.

One of our chief aims was to collect sufficient data to test, or at least comment on, the applicability to our survey areas of variations on the classic (Leninist and Chayanovian) theories of agrarian change. This involved following methods of analysis found in Neo-Populist studies of 'peasant household mobility' – which are concerned with changes in individual household wealth – and methods found in Marxist studies of 'class differentiation', which analyse transformations in social relations and class formation. Taken together, these demand a great deal from field researchers, who must reconstruct enough data to cover the social, economic, demographic and cultural life of the family as far back as memories permit, including both quantitative data to capture magnitudes of change and qualitative data to explain the circumstances surrounding such changes.

At an early stage, we discovered that we could not rely on written sources for data on economic mobility (see Section 7.1.1). Consequently, our study depended heavily on the development of a comprehensive and systematic method of assisting villagers to recollect information about their family, community and village histories. Of course, we anticipated some problems in developing such a method, but during our trial interviews we began to despair at the difficulties which emerged. Drawing on our fieldwork in the villages (Nimmanapalle and Tavalam, and four outlying hamlets) in Western Chittoor District, Andhra Pradesh, from July 1988 to March 1989,[3] this chapter describes the methods we eventually adopted to overcome the following problems:

- For a representative sample from the earliest period of our study we required an accurate census of the population in 1950, which was not available (Section 7.1.2).
- Our original, and somewhat ambitious, questionnaire took 16 hours (and about 8 visits) to complete! Such lengthy interviews led to respondent boredom and unrest (Section 7.1.3).
- Many villagers did not know their ages and had difficulty dating events in their life histories (Sections 7.2.1 and 7.2.2).
- It was impossible to record precise quantitative evidence for routine activities before 1986 (Sections 7.2.3 and 7.2.4).
- Our analysis of social relations rested on the respondents' ability to recall amounts of time allocated to different occupations and income derived from such occupations, for which they could only give rough approximations (Sections 7.3.1, 7.3.2 and 7.3.3).
- Individuals within each household differed from the head in terms of patterns of labour use, asset ownership and status (Section 7.3.4).

7.1 Preliminary problems

7.1.1 *Limitations of written records*

There are very few studies of economic mobility, because most existing data sources do not trace changes in the asset ownership of individual households over time.[4] The *Census of India*, for example, presents static impressions of economic class structure every 10 years which mask individual household movement underlying net changes. An empirical analysis of processes gleaned from such data would be, as Shanin (1980, p. 96) wrote, 'very much akin to guessing from a snapshot how a ballerina dances'. Moreover, the *Census of India* could not be used to investigate class differentiation because such categories disguise certain important segments of the population and in any event endure transformations with every new census.

We did not find land records from local offices useful for verifying changes in land ownership.[5] Unfortunately there has been no land survey for the village of Nimmanapalle since the *Re-Survey and Re-Settlement Register* of 1917 (India, Government of, 1917). If land transactions were registered at all after 1917, they were pencilled into the 1917 report. Moreover, it was difficult to relate present-day households to the names of the owners (for example, their grandfathers or the people who sold them the land) in 1917. The critical problem, however, was that many families did not register land transfers, either because the transaction involved illegally owned land or because of the large registration fee (equivalent to 10 per cent of the land value). Indeed, one official in a nearby district admitted that in his office nearly 80 per cent of the land was not registered with proper names. Only large landowners tended to register land transfers, but their multiple plot sub-divisions and transactions meant that it could take days to substantiate just one of their histories of land transfers through written records.

While we could not use written sources to trace household mobility, they often contained some valuable information. For example, the 1917 report stated that Nimmanapalle had about 5000 acres of government waste land, a great deal more than is available now. This alerted us to the need to obtain accurate details on the extent of land seizures. The use of official sources for supporting information, however, was generally limited, as they were frequently incomplete, unreliable or both. They tended to aggregate across districts or *taluks* and seldom referred to specific villages and hamlets in our survey area (see Section 7.2.1 below). Moreover, authors of written documents were usually male and either British or from dominant castes. Their remoteness from the lives of the poor and of women was often reflected in their writing. The problems encountered with written sources for the study of household mobility forced us to be heavily dependent on oral accounts.

7.1.2 *Obtaining a representative sample*

Obtaining a representative sample for the study of economic mobility is far more complex than for static studies. Our original aim was to take a random sample from the 1950 population of our survey area, and then trace the progress of each household to the present day.[6] But we possessed no reliable records of the 1950 population. The only technique for reconstructing the 1950 population would have involved first asking each of the 1092 households in our area for the name of their household head in 1950 (that is, father, grandfather or uncle), then arranging all the census papers of the households with the same name for the 1950 head into groups (that is, of extended families). While this may be feasible for a smaller survey area, implementing this sampling method in our survey area would have taken several months at least.

We eventually abandoned this option (after much agonising) in favour of taking a random sample of today's households and tracing the mobility of each back to the father and grandfather. Our sample of 75 households was drawn from the census executed by Wendy Olsen in 1986. Tracing one collateral branch was the method used by Attwood (1979), who notes that while this restricts the analysis to a 'single line of descent', the 'sloughing off' of collateral branches 'is necessary to avoid analytical confusion' (p. 499).

There are several drawbacks to this approach. While the 1988 sample households can be said to be more or less representative of the survey area,[7] their fathers' households do not typify the population in earlier periods. Secondly, it neglects those households that have migrated out. We compensated for this somewhat by reconstructing a detailed list of all emigrants from the survey region since 1950 in order to estimate the nature and extent of such emigration.

7.1.3 *Developing an appropriate interview approach*

The success of a village-level study intent on identifying such complex processes as economic mobility and social change rests heavily on the thoroughness of the questionnaire and on the imagination deployed in its design. The preparation of our questionnaire began with the construction of a series of critical hypotheses from variants of the theories of Lenin and Chayanov as applied to south India. Questioning with reference to these hypotheses helped us to avoid collecting a confusing mass of detail. We then broadened our inquiry as important information lying outside these theories came to light.

Conducting as many trial interviews as possible with a cross-section of the population before implementing the survey was tremendously useful in determining the order and structure of the questionnaire so that one set of questions could flow naturally into the next. The most sensitive questions were asked at the end of the interview, or whenever the greatest level of intimacy had been established.

Studying economic mobility, perhaps more than single-focus studies, impels one to collect a complete portrait of household histories, including changes in wealth ownership and in class relations, and also supporting information such as details of tenancy contracts, patron–client relations, farming operations and gender relations. Trial interviews helped us to distinguish between essential supporting data required on a random sample basis, and supporting information which could be obtained more casually. We found that we could break our 16-hour trial questionnaire into three parts, as follows:

1. Our original, time-consuming *extended family history questionnaire* was kept intact and used with 14 households (2 from each class). They remain valuable for our analysis of detailed case histories.
2. A *main family history questionnaire* was conducted with the 75 random sample households. It included quantitative questions relevant to testing

theories of agrarian change (such as assets, consumer/worker ratios, social relations and loans) and essential supporting qualitative information ('Why did you take that type of loan?').

3. A series of *special topic questionnaires* enabled us to choose those respondents best suited to answering questions on select subjects of agrarian relations. These questionnaires divided into two types:
   (a) The first covered aspects of agrarian change (such as gender relations, patron–client relations and tenancy relations). Because we sought to understand historical changes among different strata, we chose three or four older respondents from elite, subordinate and intermediate, castes or classes. Different classes were chosen to avoid bias. This was vividly illustrated in the collection of data on patron–client relations where landlord accounts of generosity in times of famine contrasted sharply with those of labourers. Each respondent for these questionnaires was interviewed independently.
   (b) The second covered those questions best answered by *groups* of elderly people in each locally defined 'community' within each hamlet or village (such as the Muslim, Mala and Reddy sections). Here respondents would 'knock heads' together to reconstruct their local history and specific histories (such as a list of migrants from their community since 1950).[8]

Despite our efforts to reduce lengthy interviewing, long-term recall interviews will always be drawn out and run the risk of respondent boredom. Yet the quality of the data depended on how far we could succeed in maintaining respondent concentration and enthusiasm. We found that if they understood *why* we were asking such questions they would try more earnestly to remember events. We therefore described the purpose of our study in detail at the outset, as clearly and simply as possible.

We also repeated our purpose throughout the interview by explaining each set of questions (for example, how questions on illness are related to the study of social mobility). This also encouraged respondents to criticise our line of questioning or to raise issues we had not thought of. Examples occurred when we prefaced some inquiries with: 'We are asking this question because the books [or my teachers] in England say that Indian farmers do this or that. What do you think?'. Here we would summarise the essential theories of major studies to get their view about their applicability to the survey area. This process also established a sense of frankness and intimacy with the respondent (that is, that we were doubting our teachers and relying on them to correct us). Having decided on our interview strategy, we were prepared to confront our first methodological problem – dating major events.

7.2 Dating major events

7.2.1 *Verifying reference points*

Most villagers did not know their ages or the actual dates of changes in their family history. They could, however, describe the timing of an event by relating it to an event in their own family history (such as a marriage or the birth of a child)[9] or local history. We therefore found it very worthwhile to compile a chronology of local events which most villagers could remember well. For instance, we used the famine of 1952, the construction of a new school in 1968 and the construction of a dam in 1978 as reference points. Other useful dates included the electrification of each hamlet, the introduction of bus services to each area and the construction of temples.

We had to be careful to verify the exact dates of such events before using them. In the first instance, oral accounts often differed from written accounts, partly because the latter often referred to the district or *taluk* level and could not be generalised to all the villages and hamlets within it. This is well illustrated in post-independence drought reports, which identified Chittoor District as suffering drought in 1973, yet local oral sources claim there was no drought in our survey area. Even when written accounts occasionally related to the central village, they could not be generalised to the whole survey area. We learned at an early stage that signs of economic development, such as electrification, came to the central village much earlier than to the hamlets.

Moreover, among oral accounts, local history was inevitably seen differently by people from different areas, castes, classes, households, gender and ages. This is epitomised in the case of identifying years of drought. Throughout our interviews, respondents recalled curious 'drought' years: 'You know the drought of 1969?'; 'There was surely a drought in 1972!'. There were several reasons for this. One explanation is that experiences differed among different areas. For example, for the past four years one entire *taluk* in Guntur District (coastal Andhra Pradesh) had been declared drought-prone by the government of India, but only the unirrigated, cotton-growing part of the *taluk* was actually affected by drought. The irrigated, paddy region was not affected at all.

Furthermore, the identification of drought years varied among different classes. Everyone agreed that there had been a severe famine in 1952 in Western Chittoor District except the merchants. One rich merchant did not even agree that there had been a famine at all! In a similar vein in Guntur District, accounts of 'good and bad times' differed between farm-dependent and wage-dependent households. During a drought in Guntur District, wage labourers suffered from falling wages, but farmers did not suffer. Though their yields of cotton fell, their returns were normal because the price of cotton rose. In 1978, a year of good rains, the reverse occurred. Labourers found much employment, and better wages, while farmers suffered as the price of cotton plummeted. Severe drought years were more easily identified as they tended to affect both labourers and farmers.

Finally, accounts differed among different households within the same class. In our survey area, dry years are followed by a few wet, then by a few dry, and so on. For some households the dry years were so difficult that they suffered as much as during severe drought years, perhaps because of a combination of a poor harvest and heavy consumption demands (having a young family, or an illness). For example, one downwardly mobile big landowner in Western Chittoor argued forcefully that the 1986 drought began in 1981. The reason is that his well went dry earlier than others, and he felt the full impact of this calamity because he was already getting poorer and had heavy debts. In the end the only drought years which we could rely on were those of the 1986 drought and the 1952 famine.

7.2.2. *Charting demographic histories and land transfers*

After verifying reference points, we began each random sample interview by identifying the ages of all household members in 1988 and in 1950, by relating them to the dates of local events. We then set out to reconstruct the dates of deaths, marriages and household partitions. A crude family tree was drawn for each household, outlining their composition in 1950 and in 1988. This greatly facilitated our questioning about each family member throughout the interview.[10] (Appendix 1a quotes part of an original interview we had with one villager, which illustrates this process.)

Although collecting dates of demographic changes was sometimes a gruelling process, it made further questioning on the dates of asset transfers much easier. First, demographic data, combined with our list of dates of local events, enabled us to draw on a store of reference points. Secondly, the exercise of dating demographic events mentally prepared respondents to recall other facets of their family histories in a similar fashion. Finally, beginning our interviews with demographic questions was a polite way of showing an interest in the respondents' family, helped to develop a fluid rapport, and anticipated a later stage of intimacy when more sensitive questioning could commence.

The interview in Appendix 1b demonstrates how easily dates of land transactions can be determined once this vital armoury of reference points has been established. We found it useful to ask about current land ownership before proceeding to trace land transfers from the grandfather. At the end, all land transfers should add up to the current land owned. It was methodologically imperative to ask for information surrounding land transactions, such as the class of partners in transactions, the source of finance for purchase or conversion, why that transaction took place, and so on, in order to analyse land transfers correctly later (see Section 7.3.4 below).

In a similar manner we identified the dates of other asset transfers (such as house purchases or construction), dates of adoption of new technology, changes in occupations, major loans taken, major illnesses and other crises, good and bad agricultural years, and migrations.

7.2.3 *Ease of recall for different types of data*

The ability to recall different types of data depended on: (1) the period in question, (2) the amount of detail sought, (3) the class of the respondent, and (4) whether the information involved a regular or major event. The period from about 1970 to the present could be better covered than earlier periods. When young respondents had difficulty with earlier periods, we would question their father or grandfather.[11] Although young people had trouble generally with earlier periods, they could always provide details of their parents' and grandparents' land transactions with great clarity! Patterns of labour time and of incomes for 1988 and 1986 were difficult to reconstruct. While the recall period was much shorter, it demanded that the respondent remember a great deal over that period (see Section 7.3).

For most villagers, demographic information was easier to recall than data on assets. Among assets, house and well exchanges were easier to recollect than land transfers. However, it is difficult to generalise about the order of difficulty of recall beyond this point. For the majority of our respondents, land transactions were followed by major loans, regular loans for farm and consumption needs, livestock exchanges, and time and income proportions (see Figure 7.1). But ease of recollection on these issues did vary. For example, labourers with a small piece of land could more easily remember the details of past land transfers (they had so few and each was significant) than each loan taken in their histories, as many small loans were taken each year. By contrast, large landowners could as easily recollect loans (since they tend to take a few major loans rather than many small ones) as each land transaction, because there were so many.

Finally, it was far easier for respondents to recollect *major* events – particularly those that affected the family of the respondent – than regular events (such as yearly loans or asset transactions). For example, cultivators found it less difficult to recall land transactions than cattle transactions, because the latter were exchanged regularly. Similarly, major loans – such as those for investment or marriage and big loans for illness – were much easier to recollect than regular, seasonal loans for farming or consumption needs.

7.2.4 *Quantitative precision versus qualitative description*

The quality of quantitative evidence inevitably erodes the further back in time one explores. Figure 7.2 illustrates that for data on consumer/worker ratios,

SENSITIVITY

Information about the past and about others						Information about the present day and about own family
Least sensitive						Most sensitive
1 Demographic	2 Time and income proportions	3 Cattle, land, well or house transfers	4 Major and regular loans	5 Encroached land	6 Gold and bank savings	7 *Vaisha* information and moneylending

PRECISION

Information regarding major incidents and about the present day						Information regarding regular or minor incidents or about the distant past
Most precise						Least precise
1 Demographic	2 House and well transfers	3 Land transfers including encroachments	4 Major loans	5 Regular loans	6 Cattle transfers	7 Time and income proportions

Figure 7.1 Ease of collecting select types of data

Variables	*Before 1950* Information on whatever is available	*Long-term, 1950–86* More systematic information	Comparison between a drought and non-drought year *Short-term, 1986–8* Detailed qualitative information and more precise and disaggregated quantitative data
Consumer/ worker ratios	No ratio	*Discrete categories:* In 1950, workers described crudely as 'those old enough to do kuulie work' and consumers as those 'too young to work'	*Continuous values:* Actual ages of all household members
Land ownership	*Discrete categories (2):* In terms of wet and dry land – sometimes only rough approximations	*Further disaggregated categories (14):* In terms of 14 different types of land	*Continuous values:* Land values (for each of the 14 types)
Occupational patterns	*Listing:* List of chief occupations of ancestors	*Banking:* Occupations *ranked* (1′,2′,3′ . . .) by: (1) amount of time devoted to each activity, and (2) contribution to total income	*Proportions:* More precise proportions of time allocated to each activity, and of income per activity per year
Farm loans	*Anecdotal:* Stories of usufructuary mortgage arrangements and of notorious merchant land-grabbers	*Descriptive:* Description of yearly farm loans and relations with moneylenders	*Quantitative:* Precise quantitative details of all loans taken since 1986 (interest rate, amount taken, terms of loan, etc.)
Famines/ droughts	*Anecdotal:* Stories of 1936 famine	*Descriptive:* Account of how the family survived the 1952 famine; but land transfers were the only precise quantitative details recorded Note: This information was much more detailed for 1970–86 than for 1950–60	*Quantitative:* Details of how households coped with the drought, supported by precise details of loans taken, cattle transfers, changes in labour use, etc.

– Increasing amount of total information
– Increasingly disaggregated and accurate quantitative information

Figure 7.2 Examples of data available during different time periods

land ownership and occupational patterns, moving from the present period to the past leads to increasingly aggregated and less precise quantitative data. For classifying occupations, for example, the quality of information deteriorates through time, from proportions which can form a *ratio* level of classification, to ranking which can construct an *ordinal* arrangement, to listing which can produce a non-hierarchical *categorical* taxonomy (see Section 7.3).

Indeed, quantitative data to express changes in mobility are simply not available in some cases. For example, most villagers could only recall accurately the specific details of all ordinary loans for farming needs since 1986 (amount taken, interest rate, terms of repayment and so on). While they could not recall exact quantitative details for 1950–86, they could draw a verbal portrait of the nature of regular yearly loans for farming and consumption needs, as well as describe interesting changes in their relations with moneylenders. For instance, they could state the approximate minimum and maximum amount of such loans, classify whether their labour or harvest was tied to such credit, mark when the types of loans changed, for example, from moneylender to bank credit and – most crucially – outline the reasons for such changes. For earlier periods, villagers could not describe ordinary behaviour, but they could recall interesting or amusing incidents, such as stories of notorious merchant land-grabbers or anecdotes about earlier famines.

The value of qualitative evidence is not restricted to cases where quantitative data are not available. Often quantitative economic data cannot sufficiently capture qualitative changes in class relations. Many class relationships in our survey area remained the same in *form*, but have changed in important ways with the development of capitalism. For example, 'small peasants' have always borrowed from 'merchants'. The nature of moneylending arrangements between merchants and small peasants, however, has been transformed from a usurious credit relationship (which might have interfered with production for home consumption) to one which is far less so (and can be said to encourage petty commodity production). Seizing on qualitative changes is particularly important in the case of the assetless, where major alterations in the status of households are reflected in variations in their relationships with their employers; for example, from bonded to semi-bonded to free wage labour. Similarly, changes in the bargaining power of women *vis-à-vis* men cannot be measured exclusively by changes in the ownership of assets.

Finally, even precise quantitative data can be misleading if there are no explanatory data to accompany them. Quantitative economic or demographic data analysed in isolation may lead to baseless theorising about change when it is not supported by qualitative data detailing why the household chose (or was forced) to make a change, how the change was made and who was involved. Interesting cases of this occurred when many wealthy households in our sample sold land. If we had collected only amounts of land transferred it would have appeared that they were getting poorer and that there was an overall trend towards equalisation of asset ownership in the villages. By collecting supporting qualitative information, however, we found that rich households sold land to invest in mechanised pumps or non-land assets. Hence many wealthy households actually experienced decisive upward mobility, and our evidence suggests that there was not an overall trend towards levelling in asset holdings.

As satisfying as it was to ask villagers why a change occurred, it must be pointed out that villagers offered only the *proximate* causes for change and not *overall* contributory causes such as changes in social, economic and political structures. For example, a farmer might have said he sold his dry land to buy a mechanised pump. But this investment only became profitable because of prior technological changes associated with the Green Revolution, and in government policies which subsidised well improvement.

7.3 Estimating quantities: determining occupational ranks

Another set of interview difficulties relates to shorter-term recall of very detailed data on routine activity. Here we focus on problems involved in recollecting and estimating occupational patterns; that is, the amount of time spent on different occupations and on income earned from different activities within one year, for 1986 and 1988. Clearly, exact figures were not available, but obtaining at least a rough estimate of such occupational activity was essential to classify households both in the field and for later analysis.

7.3.1 *Importance of occupational data for mobility*

During our trial interviews we found it extremely frustrating not to know exactly how respondents spent their time and which activities contributed most to their overall income. Often household members would participate in six or seven different types of activity, but only one would be mentioned when we first inquired. Moreover, it would surface later in the interview that the occupation initially mentioned was not the most important, in terms of either labour time or the proportion of income which it contributed. For example, some villagers identified themselves as 'cultivators' when in fact they spent three-quarters of their time doing assorted labouring activities. Some employers also classed themselves as 'cultivators' when most of their income was from business or salaried activity. Obtaining the relative importance of different occupations was crucial to informing later questioning. For instance, if a respondent did a good deal of labouring work, questions concerning labour relations with landlords should have been asked.

Reconstructing the relative importance of different occupations is also important theoretically. Leninist studies of class differentiation underscore the need to classify households by a criterion which reflects the degree to which a household appropriates surplus value (and is hence able to invest in assets) and alienates surplus value (and is therefore far less likely to accumulate wealth). Such a criterion can reflect the future mobility of different households and differentiation of classes, and thus predict overall social change. But stocks of assets are not always good proxies for relations of surplus appropriation. Quantifying yearly labour use for each activity for each household, on the other hand, is a more direct measure of the overall class position. Patnaik's (1976) Labour Exploitation Criterion (E), for instance, identifies classes by comparing the use of outside labour relative to the use of family labour:

$$E = \frac{\text{Labour-days hired in} - \text{Family labour-days hired out}}{\text{Family labour-days in self-employment}}$$

Collecting occupational information to reflect the variety and importance of activities outside agriculture was also crucial for our survey area, and we suspect that it should be relevant to other increasingly non-agrarian rural economies of south India. Furthermore, considerations of household vulnerability to asset mortgage or disposal in times of crises, based on Sen's (1981) entitlement paradigm, imply that occupational groups are useful in assessing the degree of market dependence, and are therefore helpful in determining a measure of vulnerability to crises.

7.3.2 *Ranking occupations*

Useful measures of the relative importance of different occupations include: (1) labour time spent on different occupations, and (2) income accruing from each occupation. Occupations refer to activities within agriculture (that is, class divisions such as hiring out labour, own labour, tenancy and landlordism) as well as to occupations outside crop production (artisan work, merchant activity, firewood collection).

When collecting occupational data it is important to cover one complete year, because activities vary greatly from one crop season to another. In our survey area, most small peasants who own only dry land mostly cultivate their own land in the first crop season (July–November). In the second and third crop seasons (December–June) they do labouring work or lease in wet land. In the first crop season they have enough work on their own land and even hire in labourers during the harvest season. The same peasants in the second and third crop seasons, however, work for others as labourers or as tenants for big farmers who own wet land. If one were to focus only on the first season, dry-land cultivators might be misclassified as 'exploiting' cultivators, whereas in the second and third seasons they might be classified as 'exploited' wage labourers or tenants. We found similar changes in the activities of wage labourers as the seasons changed. Landless labourers were well employed during the first crop season when both wet and dry lands are cultivated, but found only occasional non-agricultural work in the second and third crop seasons, such as collecting firewood or tamarind to sell.

The optimum methodology for collecting time allocation and income data is to monitor each individual daily, but this is time-consuming and intrusive. A more widely used method is to make an inquiry once or twice a month, asking villagers to record or recall their labour use and income for the preceding period. In studies where repeat surveys over the course of the entire year are not possible, however, the long-term recall method described below may prove to be a worthwhile option.

To construct proportions of (1) time allocated to different activities and (2) income earned from different activities, we followed several steps:

- *Listing* all activities and discussing comparisons among them.
- *Ranking* activities according to their relative importance.[12]
- *Constructing proportions*.

We found that villagers could *list* activities before 1950 and *rank* activities from 1950 onwards in terms of their first, second and third greatest contribution to overall time spent or to overall income (see Figure 7.2).

To trace occupational change we chose particular years from each decade since 1950 which the villagers were most likely to remember: 1950 itself (two years before the 1952 famine), 1967 and 1973 (the last year of exceptionally good rains). We asked our respondents to rank their occupations in terms of contribution to total income or the proportion of time allocated to them. We also asked respondents to date major changes in occupation or occupational pattern and to explain the circumstances surrounding these (for example, if they were attributable to a land purchase, to getting a salaried position, to investing in a tea stall, etc.). For 1986 and 1988, we could obtain more precise estimates of the relative importance of time allocated to different activities and income derived from each activity: 1988 was easily recalled because it was the year preceding the survey, while 1986 was well remembered because it was a drought year and the year that Wendy Olsen travelled to the villages to conduct her survey.

We began reconstructing labour-use patterns by listing agricultural occupations, discussing comparisons among them and then ranking them in terms of labour use. Respondents would suggest dividing their labour use into sections based on how they estimated difficult quantities in their daily life.[13] For example, a respondent might estimate proportions of his labour use as follows: 'Out of five days, three were spent on my own land and two on my leased-in land.' Alternatively, he might have gone directly to precise amounts: 'Last year we went for wage labour for three months in all – in stretches of ten days each.'

We would next ask respondents to translate these estimates into approximate months or fractions of months out of twelve. We refined these estimates by inquiring about months completely unemployed, employed for half days, doing exchange labour[14] and performing non-agricultural work. The proportions were then adjusted accordingly until we arrived at more refined figures. We continued until the respondent concurred with the final proportions. As Western Chittoor is marked by striking seasonal variations, we occasionally found it worthwhile to guide respondents mentally through each season; that is, through the groundnut season, noting days spent preparing the land, sowing, weeding and harvesting, then through the next season and so on.

This method could not be used to determine the extent to which a household hired in labour. For this, we obtained a rough figure by asking villagers one of the following questions:

1. How many days did you hire in labour and how many labourers were hired each time?
2. What was your total wage payment this year and what was the average wage paid each time?

We obtained income derived from each activity in a similar way. We began, as with the labour-use proportions, by listing activities, discussing comparisons among them and ranking them.[15] Then respondents would suggest breaking their income down into parts, again based on how they ordinarily estimate difficult quantities. For example, a respondent might do one of the following:

- Use fractions, as follows: 'Half of my total income comes from cultivation of my land, a quarter from wage labour and the remaining quarter is divided into half on selling milk and half from selling sheep' (that is, an eighth from each of the last two activities).
- Suggest a convenient unit, such as 5 rupees, and construct proportions as follows: 'Say my total income is 5 rupees, 2½ comes from cultivation, 1½ from wage labour, 1 from tenant work.'

After respondents had constructed simple fractions or proportions, we found it very useful to ask them to imagine that their total income was Rs 100. They would immediately come up with revised estimates, and whenever they were not clear would give a single estimate for two or more activities (such as wage labour). Using Rs 100 gave them the flexibility to make further refinements on their proportions and to disaggregate groups (for example, wage labour into agricultural and non-agricultural wage labour). A simple example of the steps taken is shown in Table 7.1.[16]

Table 7.1 Constructing proportions for income from labour

1 Discuss agricultural activities	2 Rank them	3 Respondents' fractions out of 5 units	4 Suggest Rs 100 and refine		5 Disaggregate wage labour	
Own farm	1	2.5	50%	45%		45%
Wage labour	2	1.5	30%	30%	Agricultural	20%
					Non-agricultural	10%
Tenant	3	1.0	20%	25%		25%

In the field we would often make on-the-spot calculations and refer to previous answers to test the accuracy of the respondents' answers. Finding a gap, we could offer them a chance to re-examine answers and thus to report details they might have been trying to hide or had simply forgotten to mention, and ask them to adjust the proportions accordingly.

7.3.3 *Testing the validity of reconstructing proportions*

Collecting data by this 'proportions method' is not precise and we are conscious that data gathered in this way must be analysed with great care. Yet requesting villagers to construct proportions compels them to adjust and refine original rankings, and as a result, at the very least, we obtained more disaggregated and superior rankings. Perhaps even more importantly, the process of asking villagers to estimate quantities in this way led to a far more in-depth knowledge of the nature of different activities than would have been obtainable otherwise.

We were uncertain of the reliability of this method until Venkateshwarlu tested its validity in his own village in Guntur District in early 1990. He compared the results of our method with those acquired by a more sophisticated approach involving the collection of each and every detail of income and expenditure. In the first method respondents were asked to construct proportions directly; in the second method Venkateshwarlu calculated proportions himself using details procured from the interviews.[17] Thus he collected two separate sets of statistics from nine cooperative respondents from different classes. Whereas the original method took 30–40 minutes, this more detailed study took 3–4 hours. The results of the longer study were collected together with the rough observations and a pair-wise statistical test was conducted to compare them. We found no statistically significant difference in the results. We found this encouraging and hope it lends some credibility to our method of collecting proportions.

7.3.4. *Intra-household differences*

An important reservation about this 'proportions' method of data collection, and about our method of data collection on household mobility in general, is that much of it was collected on a *household-wide* basis, thereby casting a veil over intra-household differences in labour use, titles to wealth, status and autonomy, which vary with the class and caste of the household. We were able to collect most of this whole household information for about 25 per cent of our sample. Analysis of this sample revealed, for example, that even if housework were excluded, other household members could have patterns of labour use very different from that of the household head (see Table 7.2, which shows that women in this household did more wage labouring than men).[18] Nevertheless,

Table 7.2 Time allocations for each household member

Labour use	Head of family (56 years)	Son 1 (35 years)	Son 2 (28 years)	Grandson 1 (12 years)	Grandson 2 (8 years)	Wife (50 years)	Daughter-in-law 1 (28 years)	Daughter-in-law 2 (24 years)
Farming own land	3 months	8 months	2 months	4 months	–	7 months	8 months	8 months
Grazing cattle	7 months	–	–	3 months	–	–	–	–
Wage labour	–	15 days	–	–	–	2 months	1 month	1 month
Driving bullock cart	–	1 month	7 months	–	–	–	–	–
Studying full-time	–	–	–	–	12 months	–	–	–
Not employed	2 months	2½ months	3 months	5 months	–	3 months	3 months	3 months

the time needed for collecting our detailed family histories prevented us from gathering data from each individual for all 75 households.[19] A rigorous study of intra-household mobility for a random sample of 75 households or more requires a separate field investigation in itself. Such a study must first overcome: (1) the temporal demands of such an ambitious field research endeavour, and (2) the analytical problems associated with classifying each individual's status and tracing her or his mobility through time.[20]

7.4 Conclusion

This chapter has outlined a field methodology designed to help determine processes of economic mobility and social change in rural India. We have highlighted the importance of developing a workable interview strategy when collecting very detailed family histories under time constraints. To encourage respondents to recall quantitative information, we employed a series of methods to simplify recall *based on an understanding of how villagers themselves recollect the timing of events and estimate quantities*. Reconstructing the dates and extent of demographic and economic changes drew us nearer to understanding the direction and magnitude of such processes of change. This quantitative evidence was, however, crucially deficient without supporting qualitative information which could interpret such change.

Clearly, precision cannot be guaranteed through recall, but sufficiently convincing data can be realised by encouraging respondents to quantify whenever possible, and to describe events when not. Indeed, the arduous process of trying to collect figures that were difficult to recall was fruitful in exposing the nature of such data, which otherwise might not have been understood at all.

We found it necessary to deploy imagination and persistence in trying out different ways to obtain difficult information from villagers. Often a villager's response to our first question was, 'I don't know', 'How can I tell my father's age then? I do not have any idea!' 'How can one remember such details?'. If we had stopped there, we would have no data. We were frequently amazed at how the use of improvised techniques, care and diligence enabled us to tap quite fertile memories.

Appendix 1 Excerpts from an interview with a landed labourer

Appendix 1a Eliciting dates of demographic change

Interviewer (I): Sir, how old are you?

Respondent (R): My age . . . around 50 years, or one or two years more or less than 50. What do you think?

I: *(It is very difficult to guess his age.)* Um, you look like around 50 years old. Sir, it seems that a long time ago people in this area suffered from major famine called the 'Gruel Famine'. Do you remember that famine?

R: Oh yes! How can I not remember the Gruel Famine? I remember very well. [. . .]

I: How old were you during the Gruel Famine?

R: I was this much. *(Tries to show his height with his hand)*

I: 'This much' means that you were six or seven years old?

R: Yes! – six or seven years old. In the famine year I was admitted to the first class in the school. [. . .]

I: If you were in the first class, it means you were six or seven years old then; not more. The Gruel Famine came in 1952. That means you are now 43 or 44 years old?

R: Yes, you should be correct sir. I look like over 50 years old but I am young. Only one year back my youngest son was born.

(After establishing the date of birth of the respondent, we set out to reconstruct the dates of births, deaths, marriages and household partitions:)

I: Can you tell me the approximate age of your father during the famine and whether he was in a joint family with your grandfather and uncles or separated from the family?

R: Sir, how I can tell my father's age? I was small then. But one thing I remember very well, by that time only my father separated from my grandfather. It seems that two years after my father's marriage, the year I was born, quarrels between my mother and grandmother started. My grandfather decided it would be better for my father to have a separate establishment.

I: How many brothers and sisters did you have at the time of the Gruel Famine?

R: I was the only child. I am the first born. Later after the famine my sister was born.

I: Sir, tell me at least this. In those days generally at what age did men get married?

R: At a very young age. My father also got married at a young age. My father used to tell me a story. It seems he started moving around with girls after he started getting a moustache. He fell in love with my mother and had a premarital sexual relationship. My grandfathers came to know about this and decided to get them married. It seems my father was only 17 years old then. My mother was a little younger than my father.

One could work out the approximate years of birth for the respondent and his parents, and the year of the respondent's parents' marriage and partition, as follows: his father got married at the age of 17 and partitioned two years after his marriage, and the respondent was born in that same year. The respondent is about 43 or 44 years old (that is, his year of birth was 1944 or 1945). Thus, we can assume that his parents got married in 1942 or 1943. His father was about 17 years old at the time of marriage and his mother was a little younger than him (by one or two years). So:

Respondent's year of birth:	1944 or 1945
Father's year of birth:	1925 or 1926
Parent's marriage year:	1942 or 1943
Mother's year of birth:	1926 or 1927
Father partitioned in:	1944 or 1945
During the Gruel Famine:	
Father's age:	26 or 27
Mother's age:	24 or 25

We went on in this manner to reconstruct the approximate ages of members of the 1950 household.

Appendix 1b Eliciting land transfers

I: Sir, when did you partition?
R: I partitioned . . . twenty years ago.
I: Do you have any other clues?
R: Sir, it happened exactly three years atter my father's death, the same year my brother got married and my first daughter was born.
I: How old is your daughter now?
R: She is about 20. Two years ago she got married.
I: Sir, do you have any other clue regarding the partition date? Twenty years ago the new school building was being constructed. Do you remember that incident?
R: Yes! – the same year my daughter was born.
I: *(The school building was constructed 19 years ago, in 1969. It seems he partitioned in 1969, 3 years after his father's death. Thus his father died in*

1966.) Sir, can you tell me about your father's land sales, purchases, development of dry land into wet land and encroachments [seizures of government land], if any? When did he first buy or sell the land?

R: In the Gruel Famine [that is, 1952–3] my father purchased an acre of dry land from my uncle – who went to Tungabhadra Dam for work. He also purchased 0.75 acre of wet land and 1 acre of dry land in the same year when my sister was born. My father used to tell us that my sister brought 'Lakshmi' [the goddess of money] to our family. That year we had very good rains and got profits from cultivation.

I: Can you tell me the approximate age gap between you and your sister?

R: Ten to twelve years.

I: *(That is, in 1952–3, during the famine, his father purchased 1 acre of dry land from his uncle and in 1956 or 1957 his father purchased another 1 acre of dry land and 0.75 acre of wet land.)* Sir, next . . .

R: Next . . . I purchased 2 acres of dry land a year after my father's death. I managed to finance it by selling all the goats and sheep because after my father's death there was no-one left in my family to look after them.

I: *(One year after his father's death means 1967.)* Any more purchases or sales?

R: I sold one acre of dry land to meet my brother's marriage expenses [that is, in 1969].

Notes

1. We wish to thank the Leverhulme Trust, the George Webb-Medley Fund, Oxford University, who funded the initial pilot study in January 1987, and the American Association of University Women, who funded the fieldwork in July 1988. We are also grateful for the patient and generous help of all our friends in India. Da Corta was assisted by Venkateshwarlu in the field, and by Aloor Vidya Sankar for research in government offices. P. Rangaswami, B. Prasad Babu, Jaleel Kahn and many others also provided invaluable assistance. We also thank our supervisors, Barbara Harriss and Santa Sinha, for their encouragement, Wendy Olsen for introducing us to her villages, and Mark Tomlinson for his comments.
2. This approach to history is discussed in Thompson (1978) and employed in such studies as Vaughan (1987).
3. We also draw to some extent on Venkateshwarlu's fieldwork in Guntur District in early 1990.
4. There are a few exceptions to this; for example, ICRISAT (the International Crop Research Institute for the Semi-Arid Tropics) have been building up a data set amenable to the analysis of household mobility since the early 1970s by questioning the same households over a period of time.
5. However, van Schendel (1981) found the land surveys in Bengal somewhat more useful.
6. This was the approach taken by Rahman (1986) for his study of class differentiation in Bangladesh.

7. The 1988 sample is 'more or less representative' as there had been some minor migration in or out of the survey area since 1986.
8. Because respondents often chose to elaborate on the unanticipated, we found it useful to come prepared to all interviews with all these questionnaires so that we could interview respondents on the spot.
9. We found we had to guard against relying on rounded figure responses, such as 'about twenty years back'. While this would put us in the right area, we could rarely rely on it.
10. We were able to reconstruct a crude consumer/worker ratio for the 1950 household, even if we did not have precise ages, by asking the villagers which household members were 'old enough to work on the farm or for a wage' and which were too young.
11. Inter-generational interviews were often useful, as older family members would recall details of earlier periods while younger members were good at providing the details of recent loans and investments and future planned investments.
12. The method of ranking by relative importance was useful in other parts of our field research. For example, we also asked respondents to rank coping strategies employed during severe crises.
13. Venkateshwarlu's background as the son of a small farmer and his extensive experience conducting fieldwork helped us to be sensitive to this.
14. Exchange labour is a form of labour barter occurring between households of similar socio-economic status during peak agricultural seasons.
15. Some respondents could calculate exact figures for income earned from different activities (especially salaried households).
16. We used a similar method to determine the proportion of income spent on different items, that is, expenditure patterns.
17. For example, expenditure on food was estimated by collecting the physical quantities of average family consumption (grain per day, spices per month, vegetables per month, and so on), and scaling these to a common time frame (one year) before calculating values on the basis of market prices.
18. Da Corta and Olsen (1990) found a similar trend in their analysis of 1986 data on labour use in Western Chittoor.
19. In the field it took 30–40 minutes to reconstruct proportions for the household head; to reconstruct them for each member with the same care would have taken hours and several visits. Because of these time constraints, we collected lists of occupations for other household members and collected full-time allocations for other adult household members only when they differed exceptionally from that of the household head (for example, when the household head was very old), when women were the acting head of a household (for instance, widows and divorced women) and when an agricultural respondent had children with non-agricultural occupations.
20. We made some efforts to trace the 'status mobility' of a very small sample of women within households, by criteria such as 'degree of influence over budget decisions', 'actual ownership of assets' and 'ability to make independent journeys' with our special topic questionnaires. Da Corta hopes to return to the survey area to study the 'status mobility' of women since 1950 within the context of her present study of economic mobility and social change.
21. This interview was written out in longhand by Venkateshwarlu in Western Chittoor. Here we deleted parts where the respondent went into long explanations and the conversation between da Corta and Venkateshwarlu which took place during the interview. It is important to note that we interviewed the respondent in a distinctly inquisitive tone, not an interrogative tone. Moreover, this interview

came along after the original fact-finding, trial interviews. The knowledge gained during these interviews is employed frequently to jog the respondents' memory. We caution that without such knowledge, the interviewer runs the risk of interviewer suggestion.

8

Sensitive information: collecting data on livestock and informal credit

Garry Christensen

Introduction

Information which is sensitive for personal, cultural or legal reasons poses a special set of problems for fieldworkers – irrespective of the conditions under which it is collected. If these problems are not resolved there is a high risk that informants will either transmit the information in a biased manner or withhold it entirely. Either response precludes completion of the research for which the information is intended. Potential informants must thus be convinced not only that the information has a wider value, but also that it will not be used against their wishes or interests. The difficulties inherent in this process are compounded when the work is conducted in a Third World community, as foreign to the researcher as he or she is to them.

As with all fieldwork, there are no standard procedures or formulae for addressing these problems. Approaches tried elsewhere often provide a useful starting point, however, and this chapter is presented in that spirit. It begins with some thoughts on the nature of sensitive information drawn from a range of experiences in the field. A general strategy for the collection of sensitive data is then outlined, followed by a discussion of the way in which this strategy was applied to the collection of livestock and credit information in Burkina Faso.

8.1 Sensitive information

Information is sensitive when it can be used in a manner contrary to the interests or wishes of the informant. Informants therefore tend to be most wary when the information sought has some association with illegal activities, closely guarded cultural or religious practices, or personal characteristics associated with shame or dishonour, wealth or income. The level of sensitivity and its manifestations vary enormously from one research setting to another (even from one interview to the next), so it would be specious to use these categories as the basis for a hierarchy or typology of sensitive information. Sensitivity is a function of the kind of information sought, the uses to which it might be put, the informant's perception of and interaction with the interviewer, and the setting of the interview itself. Furthermore, even the best fieldworkers find that their initial notions of sensitivity are often awry – in terms of their notions of what is sensitive as well as what is not.

Information on illegal activities is likely to be sensitive where the controls on these activities are pervasive and the penalties against them severe. Smuggling commodities and trading food in a manner which contravenes official regulations are good examples of this, as are tax avoidance through the disguise of assets or income, and the 'sale' of customary land. In these situations it is essential that the fieldworker establishes full independence from the authorities that control these activities, and guarantees confidentiality of the data after they have been collected. Where these preconditions are met most interviewees will usually volunteer information quite readily (see Morris and Newman 1989). But there will always be some people, particularly those who operate illegally on a large scale, who will avoid contact with anyone even remotely associated with officialdom or authority.

The sensitivity of information on personal characteristics and events is also readily understood. Many people are reluctant to discuss highly personal subjects such as sexual practices, difficulties in personal relationships, serious ill-health and antisocial behaviour. The interviewer's own perception of the sensitivity of this personal information may not always be accurate, however. In his Kenyan fieldwork, for example, Hoddinott (personal communication) deliberately omitted questions on deceased children from a questionnaire on family demography, believing that respondents would find this topic difficult to discuss. To his surprise the informants not only volunteered this information, but also queried its omission. Nevertheless, where personal information is clearly sensitive it is essential to preserve both the privacy of the exchange and the anonymity of the information.

Information on cultural practices such as initiation rites, religious ceremonies and witchcraft is often closely held to protect their integrity and sanctity. In the absence of social taboos against discussing these activities, the establishment of a trusting working relationship may eventually afford access to this information. But where explicit taboos against discussing these practices exist, and the sanctions against those who break them are severe, obtaining access to this information will be very difficult. A further constraint arises when this type of information is held by a relatively small group of people within the community. This might apply to the secrets of a particular skill or craft, such as the making or rendering of iron and precious metals, which is held by a particular lineage or family group. Any desire to retain control of this information may be an important element of its sensitivity, in addition to innate cultural or religious factors.

Long-term fieldwork has much to recommend it, in these contexts. There are many instances where a researcher living in a community has ultimately come to be regarded as an 'insider' and has been privileged to learn details of cultural practices and beliefs that would never normally be divulged to an 'outsider'.

Cultural factors may also limit discussion or acknowledgement of certain kinds of event. Twins, for example, are regarded as evil in some cultures and so may be described simply as brothers and/or sisters. Muslim cultures regard charging interest on loans as sinful and so may disavow the use or extension of interest-bearing credit, even though these kinds or transactions do occur. Morris and Newman (1989) overcame this latter problem by asking informants to discuss credit transactions in hypothetical terms, so allowing them to distance themselves from an otherwise 'sinful' practice.

Many situations or activities are sensitive because they bring shame on the individual or household. Among the most demeaning are survival strategies such as begging and the pawning of wives or daughters, which are sometimes forced on households during periods of severe food shortage. Informants are likely to describe such activities, if at all, as occurring in a more innocuous form. Informal credit transactions are another frequently reported 'shameful' activity, although the cause of this shame varies significantly. In the Asian context, *lending* is considered shameful, reflecting the often usurious practices of moneylenders; in Africa, by contrast, *borrowing* is sometimes considered shameful, reflecting the disgrace of being unable to provide adequately for the family. In fact, African respondents often mention that, if anything, shame is associated with not being able to meet a request for a loan, where it is needed to support friends or family.

Measures of wealth, income and expenditure are widely sought by field-workers, often with limited regard for the extent to which informants consider this to be sensitive information. Subjecting the poorest households in the village to a detailed questionnaire on wealth and income may, unintentionally, expose the extent of their poverty in a humiliating manner, especially where the interviews are conducted in a 'public' setting. This sensitivity stems partly from a natural reticence about disclosing precise measures of economic status – particularly among the very rich and the very poor. If this detailed information were widely known in the community it could lead to increased demands on wealth for those who are rich, and/or prejudice access to resources for those who are poor. In some cultures there is also a strong belief that the precise enumeration of certain things brings bad fortune.

Once again, it is stressed that these attitudes are not universal. Respondents in Devereux's (1989) preliminary census in northern Ghana did not consider questions on assets and incomes to be particularly sensitive, but questions on the number of children in the family were. This was probably not unrelated to the fact that the last time a white man had gone around the village listing household members was when the British imposed a head tax in 1936 – bad fortune indeed!

To compound this diversity and disparity in the nature of sensitive information, levels of sensitivity are also highly variable. For instance, there is a gradation in sensitivity from information which is widely held in the community to that which is held solely by the individual. Thus a household head may readily acknowledge that he is wealthy by local standards – a fact which is likely to be widely known in the village – but be reluctant to disclose precise details of this wealth. Similarly, the number of marriages by the household head may be readily elicited, but not the reasons for separation or divorce. For an alert fieldworker these gradations will become apparent through a combination of careful observation and casual conversation.

Perceptions of the sensitivity of information will also vary according to the respondent's desire for privacy, and his or her level of aversion to the risk that the information will be used indiscriminately. Hence the same questions will frequently elicit different reactions from different respondents. Where interviewers are in a position to benefit from the information which is being sought, at the expense of the informant, this problem will be particularly apparent. This does not mean that potentially sensitive issues should be addressed circuitously or with undue deference, however. In many circumstances, a frank, direct approach may be the best way to dispel respondent suspicions and to develop greater respect between respondent and interviewer.

These observations indicate that the interviewer must negotiate his or her role *vis à vis* the informant to a considerable extent. This process of negotiation occurs through a combination of respect for community customs and behaviour, increasing awareness of the nature and level of sensitivity of the information which is sought, and constant explanation and clarification of the way the information will be used. Thus sensitive information may be accessible by some people and not others depending on how effectively the process of negotiation proceeds.

Attributes of the interviewer such as sex, ethnicity and age may also be important. In one village in Burkina Faso, the respondents refused, politely but firmly, to divulge information on either livestock or credit to a female enumerator – whereas they discussed these same issues quite freely with a male enumerator. This certainly did not reflect the woman's ability, as her other work was of an extremely high standard and she was well liked and respected in the village. Rather, there appeared to be a view among the household heads (all of whom were male) that these issues should not be discussed with women. The ethnicity of the interviewer can have either a positive or negative influence on the level of access to sensitive information. For instance, a 'local' person who has the advantage of knowing the language and customs, and being more readily accepted, may also be perceived as being in a better position to use the information for his or her own ends.

These same attributes in the informant may also have a bearing on access to information. In Burkina Faso, junior household members who were acting as household head while the true household head was absent often refused to discuss livestock and credit. Each one politely deferred these questions to the true household head, who on his eventual return responded quite readily. It appeared that as junior household members they were unsure of their authority to discuss these issues. On the other hand, women invariably prove to be the most effective respondents for discussion of sensitive issues such as birth control. Various relationships or conflicts within the household add a further dimension to this, in that different views of the same situation will emerge from interviews with different household members. For instance, wives or junior siblings will be reluctant to divulge information on activities done without the knowledge or consent of the household head, especially if the interview is conducted in his presence.

Finally, when, where and how information is sought will affect respondent perceptions of the confidentiality which will be accorded the information. Waylaying the respondent on the way to the fields or the local market, and/or when she or he is in the company of others, is unlikely to inspire much confidence.[1] Wherever possible, interviews of this nature should be conducted in a private environment where the respondent feels at ease.

All the fundamental requirements of good fieldwork must thus be invoked if sensitive information is to be collected effectively. In particular, the interviewer must first gain the respondent's trust and respect. Fieldworkers implementing 'one-shot' surveys are at a considerable disadvantage in this regard, as it is difficult to hurry the process of negotiation. As there is often a pronounced asymmetry between the respondent's view of what is sensitive information and that of the interviewer, he or she must also guard against inappropriate perceptions of the data being collected. Finally, throughout the fieldwork there must be a continuous evaluation and monitoring of respondent perceptions of the survey, and attitudes towards the fieldworker and/or enumerator. Even where all these conditions are satisfied, however, some kinds of information will always be inaccessible – irrespective of the skill of the fieldworker.

Faced with this last situation, the fieldworker may still be able to obtain useful information by indirect means, although it is unlikely to be as accurate and comprehensive as that obtained first-hand. Asking informants to discuss the subject of interest in hypothetical terms, as noted above, thus avoiding any direct personal implications, may elicit useful normative information. Often, it is also possible to piece together the nature of otherwise sensitive issues from information volunteered by secondary sources. This takes time, however, and the fieldworker must be careful to cross-check the veracity and consistency of the various sources of information used. The magnitude of illegal activities can sometimes be gauged by comparisons of official secondary data with the fieldworker's own primary data, but this must also be done carefully, as official data usually have their own inherent biases and inaccuracies.

Having now discussed the issue of sensitivity in rather abstract terms, I next relate this to my own fieldwork in West Africa.

8.2 The research setting

The methodology described below was developed during a World Bank research project on capital accumulation and formal and informal credit markets in rural West Africa, conducted in Burkina Faso during 1984–6. Fieldwork was carried out in collaboration with researchers from ICRISAT and IFPRI, in the villages of ICRISAT's Village Study Programme.[2] My initial work was thus made easier in that informants were already familiar with the interview process.

ICRISAT had begun this work in 1981–2 with a sample of 150 households in 6 villages located in the three agro-climatic regions characteristic of the West African semi-arid tropics – the Sahel, the Sudan and the northern Guinean Savannah. The wide geographic spread of the villages along a northeast–southwest axis of 400 km precluded permanent residence in any one village, requiring instead a great deal of travelling in order to supervise data collection by enumerators effectively. It also meant that there were five different ethnic groups in the sample (Mossi, Fulani, Rimaibe, Bwaba and Dagari-Djoula), each with its own language and culture. For these reasons my knowledge of the respective languages extended only to the traditional greetings.

Permanent enumerators were allocated to each village and housed there with their families. Interviews were conducted with household heads at intervals of one week to one month throughout the project.

8.2.1 *Eliciting sensitive information*

Three elements characterised my approach to collecting sensitive information. These were applicable to both livestock and informal credit data, and are probably sufficiently general to transfer to most field situations:

- Establishing and maintaining respondent trust.
- A phased series of questionnaires which moved from general, non-threatening information to precise data on individual transactions.
- Consistency checks.

Each element addresses one or more of the facets of sensitivity discussed above. The first two were used to effect a gradual build-up of the rapport and trust between interviewers and respondents, which served to assure respondents that the interviewer would not use the information in a manner prejudicial to their wishes or interests. Concomitantly these measures facilitated a better understanding of the extent to which the information sought was in fact sensitive, and so amenable to systematic and unbiased collection. A series of checks was then implemented to assess the quality and completeness of the data collected.

Respondent trust

The foundation for good fieldworker–respondent relationships is always the goodwill of the community towards the project and the fieldworker. Measures to establish and maintain this goodwill are discussed in other chapters, so I will not dwell on them here. Instead I will elaborate on the measures used to develop respondent trust as the essential precursor to collecting sensitive information. I would stress nevertheless that the establishment and maintenance of community goodwill is critical. It may often be a time-consuming and tedious process, but it should never be hurried or neglected if the fieldwork is to proceed effectively.

My use of enumerators meant that initially I had to establish respondent trust at two levels – their trust in me and their trust in my enumerators. To establish my own credibility, I met initially with the sample members and elders of each village to describe the nature of the research and the way the data would be used, and to stress the confidentiality of all information provided to us. To demonstrate this commitment further, all questionnaires involving potentially sensitive information were 'tested' with the village chief to elicit his comments and approval, before being implemented. I also spent as much time in each of the six villages as possible – carefully following village protocols – and over the two years of the project I conducted interviews (translated by the enumerators) with as many sample members as possible.

Ultimately, however, the critical consideration was the level of trust between the respondents and my enumerators. My approach to this was based on two factors: the need for enumerators who would be readily accepted by the respondents; and strategies to minimise the possibility that information acquired by the enumerators would be used to further their own social or political objectives in the village, or simply transmitted indiscriminately. The immediate decision was thus whether to hire someone from the village who would satisfy the first criterion but perhaps not the second; or someone from outside the village to satisfy the second criterion at the possible expense of the first.

Burkina Faso was undergoing a major social revolution at the time, with widespread repercussions for politics from the national to the local level. Attempts to replace traditional village authorities (chiefs and elders) with committees formed from disciples of the revolution had created significant political divisions and tensions within villages. For this reason, I chose to employ enumerators from outside each village. I also found that older, married enumerators (of either sex) were most readily accepted by the villagers, and that maturity and the ability to get along with people were more important enumerator attributes than IQ or level of education.

The character and conduct of enumerators are also critical in developing the trust of respondents, particularly in reassuring them that sensitive information will not be passed on indiscriminately. To this end I developed a code of enumerator conduct in collaboration with village elders, which forbade among other things: behaviour which was objectionable to the village (such as drunkenness), borrowing money from village residents, and disclosure of information obtained during interviews. Any breach of this code meant dismissal – which occurred in the case of one enumerator – a harsh but necessary step in the interests of retaining respondent trust and village goodwill towards the project.

The importance of respecting the confidentiality of information was stressed to the enumerators at all times. My emphasis on this was further demonstrated by insisting that interviews be conducted in a suitably private location (preferably in the respondent's own compound), with no-one else present but the household head. The interview was stopped whenever the inevitable visitors dropped by, and restarted once they had left – although with the benefit of hindsight I should have had my enumerators adopt a far more diplomatic approach to the intrusion of these visitors. This practice caused some hilarity among the respondents initially but came to be respected quite quickly. It is difficult to know if this reflected the respondent's own wish to maintain the privacy of the interview, or acceptance of this practice as a tangible demonstration of my commitment to confidentiality.

Phased questionnaires

A deliberate decision was made early in my fieldwork to introduce questionnaires on 'sensitive issues' later in the project, after a good working relationship had been established with respondents. Actual data gathering then proceeded in two stages: an initial questionnaire on the general perception of attitudes and practices, followed by a more detailed instrument on individual transactions.

The first questionnaire introduced the respondent to the idea of sharing information on the subject, without seeking data on his or her own transactions. It also alerted me to aspects not previously considered, guided the design of the subsequent instrument, and provided valuable indications of potential biases in the final data. In fact, this questionnaire confirmed for me the inappropriateness of assuming that south Asian attitudes towards informal credit applied in West Africa. These insights could have been obtained just as easily by interviewing key respondents, but not all the informants would have been exposed to the subject. The value of this questionnaire as part of the process of negotiation would have then been lost.

The second questionnaire followed individual transactions on a detailed, case-by-case basis. It was simple and direct and the respondents accepted it quite readily. The only sample members who objected to the nature and detail of the questions were those one or two who were reluctant to participate in any aspect of the fieldwork – and they were dropped from the sample for that reason.

Consistency checks

Finally, a series of consistency checks was used to pick up bias or error in the data. Some of these checks were built into the questionnaires, and others relied on the use of village norms and the perceptiveness of the enumerators. In general, the errors detected by these checks tended to indicate recall problems rather than a deliberate withholding of information. Examples of consistency checks are provided for the case studies of livestock and credit data which follow.

Livestock data

Livestock are a highly visible form of property in West Africa. The general extent and composition of an individual's livestock holding therefore tends to be widely known within each village. Informal discussions invariably elicited comments such as, 'Mahmadou and Saidou own the most livestock in the village, but Mahmadou has many goats whereas Saidou has the most cattle.' This community-wide information also extends to livestock owners who graze their animals away from the village (for herd management or strategic reasons), although of course these observations are less reliable.

Problems began to emerge when detailed livestock counts were sought from individual owners – especially those with large herds. This reaction often occurs where farmers are taxed on the number of livestock they own (usually cattle), a policy which is common in sub-Saharan Africa. (As tax avoidance is a universal phenomenon, their reason for withholding information in this situation is easily understood.) Even though Burkina Faso's cattle tax had been discontinued a few years previously, many farmers were still suspicious that the data would be used to assess taxes in some other form. My immediate concern was thus to assure all respondents that government in general and tax departments in particular, would in no way be privy to the information.

The extent to which detailed information on livestock holdings is sensitive because it is an indicator of wealth was more difficult to ascertain. My impression is that this source of potential sensitivity is perhaps over-rated in the literature on fieldwork, though of course this impression derives only from my own experience. Community perceptions of the relative wealth of individual households, even without precise information, tended to be fairly accurate. Fortunately there were few indications that disclosure of detailed information on wealth would bring bad fortune, although this belief should always be given consideration.

Not being quite sure of the sensitivity of enumerating livestock holdings, my approach was to frame this aspect of data collection within a broader set of questionnaires on livestock management. Hence the elicitation of livestock inventories was preceded and followed by more general questions on various aspects of management – with equal emphasis on each issue. Interestingly, this approach resulted in an unexpected and different kind of 'sensitivity' – the embarrassment of some farmers that they did not know how many livestock they had (particularly small ruminants and pigs) or what their levels of reproduction, off-take or losses were.

As described above, the questionnaires were implemented in a two-stage approach which involved a general (non-sensitive) questionnaire, followed by more detailed data collection which directly sought the sensitive information. The general questionnaire began by asking which kinds of livestock were owned (a Yes/No response), and then focused on their management and production. Issues of interest included: how and where the livestock were fed/pastured at different times of the year; who, if anyone, was responsible for herding; expected levels of production (reproductive intervals, fecundity and productive life); diseases and their treatment; breeds; and uses (sales, gifts, consumption and draft). Valuable information was thus obtained on the importance of livestock to family welfare (which varied widely by locality and ethnic group); expected levels of production; consumption; and so on.

Key respondents from each ethnic group were then interviewed to determine 'taxonomies' of age, sex and class for each type of livestock. A wide variation in these taxonomies was observed, which became more detailed as livestock ownership and management assumed greater importance to household welfare. In those ethnic groups where livestock were of limited importance, the taxonomy was a simple three-way classification of: 'young' stock of both sexes, adult (reproducing) females and adult (breeding) males. At the other extreme, the taxonomies went beyond detailed age and sex groupings to include separate categories for colour, breed and region of origin. These taxonomies (in the respective languages) were then used to develop the livestock inventory instruments.

This approach improved data quality, in that total numbers for each livestock category could be checked against the numbers in each age–sex grouping, as a simple, initial internal consistency check. To provide a further, more comprehensive consistency check, the inventory was designed to include a full reconciliation between beginning and ending livestock numbers, and the additions and subtractions which had occurred in the interval between. It thus took the following form:

Beginning inventory + Births + purchases + gifts received
– Sales – deaths – losses – consumption = Ending inventory

Once the nature of this reconciliation had been explained, the respondents became quite interested in it, although as noted above they often admitted that they had no accurate knowledge of births, deaths and losses. This problem was overcome by increasing the frequency of the interviews and conducting them at times when livestock were managed more intensively, such as during the breeding season and in the period from planting to harvest. It also required considerable tact by the enumerators.

While I did not expect this reconciliation to balance exactly, especially with larger herds, I often found that it resulted in substantially revised reporting of livestock numbers. Fortunately there was no consistent pattern to the revisions prompted by this reconciliation – in terms of either under- or over-reporting. This suggested that the initial inaccuracies resulted from hastily given answers and inadequate recall, rather than a deliberate attempt to misreport information. There is always a danger in such situations that even cooperative informants, in their desire to provide answers to all the interviewer's questions, will make up numbers rather than admit that they simply do not know.

In fact, some respondents discovered that it was to their advantage to give accurate answers; for example, when the livestock data being collected were used to verify ownership and so settle disputes. It is a common practice among the sedentary agriculturalists of Burkina Faso to 'entrust' their cattle to Fulani herdsmen in return for an agreed fee – usually any milk produced plus a proportion of the offspring. In principle, this benefits each party: the farmer is spared the difficult and time-consuming task of having to take his cattle long distances from the villages in search of grazing, and the herdsman earns additional income at little extra cost by grazing the farmer's cattle along with his own herd. In fact, the relationship is an uneasy one, as the cattle must often be grazed away from the village for weeks at a time, by an ethnic group whom the farmers regard as thieves and tricksters. Disputes about the fate of animals which fail to return from these grazing trips occur frequently. One such conflict occurred during my period of fieldwork between a farmer from one of my study villages and a herder. (Incidentally, this case also provides a good example of how the process of data collection can be of direct and immediate benefit to respondents.)

I arrived at the village one morning to learn that my enumerator was away giving evidence to the village chief on a dispute between one of the farmers in the sample and his herdsman. The latter had returned from an extended grazing trip minus two of the ten cattle which the farmer had allegedly entrusted to him. When confronted by the farmer, the herdsman denied all knowledge of the other two cattle – claiming that the farmer had only entrusted eight animals to him in the first place. The farmer had taken the case to the village chief, citing the livestock inventory which had been prepared by my enumerator some months previously as evidence to support his claim. As it happened, my enumerator had compiled most of the original inventory with the farmer, but had completed and verified the age and sex breakdown with the herdsman. So the inventory constituted an independent, *written* record of the number of cattle involved. When confronted with this corroboration of the farmer's case, the herdsman eventually admitted that he had sold the other two cattle, and he was banned from the village. My enumerator, on the other hand, had his status in the village considerably enhanced.

8.2.3 *Informal credit*

The term 'informal credit' refers to lending and borrowing activities which occur outside the sphere of formal financial institutions such as commercial banks, government development agencies and cooperatives. These informal transactions usually occur between individuals, and include interest- and non-interest bearing loans of both money and goods. They can be distinguished from gift exchanges in that there is usually an explicit undertaking to repay the transaction at some future date, agreed on by both parties.

Accurate data on informal credit transactions are considered difficult to obtain due to the connotations of exploitation, usurious interest rates and shame. Thus the data are prone to severe bias and their use may lead to incorrect research conclusions. In fact, the few careful studies published show that claims of usury and exploitation are probably wildly exaggerated, being based on anecdotal evidence or practices which depart drastically from the norm.[3] This in itself indicates the danger of strong preconceived ideas about informants' sensibilities. Nevertheless, I approached the collection of these data with some trepidation.

I used the initial general questionnaire to obtain an idea of the uses of informal credit, the amounts of money likely to be transacted, and the kinds of actors in the market; and to explore the extent to which transactions were in fact 'sensitive information'. The responses suggested that all households used informal credit frequently as both borrowers and lenders, but that the amounts involved were very small. Most transactions occurred between friends and neighbours, and the credit was used to finance household expenditure on food and other personal consumption. Lending was considered an honourable activity and borrowing a normal part of life – except where it was used for shameful purposes: to finance food shortages, brideprice or 'gambling and womanising'.

Reassured by these findings, I designed a straightforward questionnaire which monitored each credit transaction on a monthly basis. Data recorded included: the date of the transaction; amount transacted in cash or in kind; security required (if any); conditions specified for the date, form and amount of repayment; and the timing and amount of subsequent repayments. The questionnaire was readily accepted and easy to implement, and the results confirmed the trends suggested by the preceding, general questionnaire. Gratifyingly, the data did include a large number of the supposedly shameful credit transactions associated with financing food shortages and brideprice. However (not surprisingly), none of the respondents reported borrowing or lending for 'gambling and womanising'.

One limitation which I was unable to overcome was the bias which results from restricting interviews to household heads. In the general questionnaire, I tentatively explored the extent to which the household head was cognisant of all economic activities in the household. While most male respondents stoutly proclaimed absolute authority over all transactions and transfers, some acknowledged that smaller transactions were conducted independently – particularly by senior wives and adult siblings. This was confirmed in general conversation and by other questionnaires, and it gradually became apparent that transactions undertaken without the knowledge of the household head were much more widespread than was being admitted. By then it was too late, so I am not sure how large this bias was.

The consistency checks on these data were less structured than for the livestock inventory and were done after the interview. They relied first on the enumerator's ability to note when credit transactions between two sample members were not described by both parties – fortunately, a fairly rare occurrence with no systematic pattern. Secondly, since most of the informal credit was very short-term and was transacted between borrowers and lenders in the village, I also calculated the ratio of borrowing to lending within each village. Apart from two villages where there were a severe crop failure, this ratio was close to 1:1, as would be expected if there were no bias in the data. The ratio in the remaining two villages was closer to 2:1, presumably because many of these households had borrowed heavily from outside the village to buy grain when their crops failed. This view was supported by an analysis of the changes in net indebtedness in these villages, which showed that it had increased substantially. On this basis, I was satisfied that the data were reasonably free from systematic bias.

Subsequent comparisons with other similar studies showed an additional advantage of the approach used, resulting from the relatively high (monthly) frequency of interviews. While this approach is very resource-intensive, it picked up the innumerable small, short-term transactions which turned out to account for over half of all the informal credit transacted. Contemporary studies which relied on retrospective data collection for a 12-month period captured few of these transactions, reporting only the larger transactions for consumer durables and bulk purchases of cereal.[4] This probably leads to a major bias in any analysis of these retrospective data in terms of the uses of informal credit, and the average and total amounts transacted.

8.3 With the benefit of hindsight

Looking back, my initial views of the sensitivity of information on livestock and informal credit were exaggerated and not always appropriate. Livestock data proved readily accessible once the general nature of the inquiry had been established, and its association with taxation had been dispelled. Access to informal credit data also proved less sensitive than indicated by previous researchers, once the confidentiality of the information was assured. Nevertheless, these topics still retained significant elements of sensitivity – as indicated by the inability of the female enumerator to elicit information, or the reluctance of junior household members to discuss them without the authority of the household head.

A more informed view of the nature and level of sensitivity would not have led me to change the overall strategy used to collect this information, except perhaps by interviewing women as well as men. The successes achieved were based more on the initial development of goodwill and trust than on the technical tricks of questionnaire design, implementation or data verification. Ultimately it is this goodwill and the attendant patience and courtesy of the villagers which allow fieldwork to proceed, despite all the mistakes which are made along the way.

Notes

1. But see Rudra (1989) and Heyer (Chapter 13 in this volume).
2. ICRISAT is the International Crop Research Institute for the Semi-Arid Tropics. Although based in Hyderabad, India, it has projects in Africa as well as Asia. IFPRI is the International Food Policy Research Institute, based in Washington, DC.
3. See, for example, the chapters by Harriss, Bottomley, Singh and Wilmington, in Von Pischke, Adams and Donald (1983).
4. See Tapsoba (1981) and Graham *et al.* (1988).

9

Talking to traders about trade

Barbara Harriss

Introduction

Empirical measurement is at the heart of all positivist economic, social and geographical analysis, and of all Marxist attempts to grapple with forces and relations of production and circulation, and with political and ideological 'superstructures'. But economic data are not as easy to elicit as many of those who plunder them to operationalise models and to test or verify theories seem to suppose. The case of collecting data on trade and traders exemplifies these problems.

9.1 Why traders are understudied

Many social scientists who have carried out fieldwork have spoken with farmers and labourers about farming. Merchants or traders, on the other hand, are studied comparatively rarely. The reasons for this range from theoretical neglect to (presumed) methodological difficulties.

Merchants have been thought to present an extreme challenge for fieldwork, for a variety of reasons. They refuse to talk: 'A more tight lipped group of interviewees would be hard to find anywhere' (Neale *et al.* 1965, p. 33). They lie: 'When it comes to statements about wealth, business, capital, turnover and so forth, which they never correctly told to anyone, it was impossible to get figures with any assurance of accuracy' (Fox 1969, p. 148). They evade: 'Merchants are extremely reticent regarding money matters in business' (Mines 1972, p. 47). 'The investigator would have to make frequent visits, often listening to most unconvincing excuses about why the stock books could not be made available' (Lele 1971, pp. 248–9).

These authors hazard some explanations for this behaviour. For Fox, crime and fraud (what others know as primitive accumulation) form the basis of profit: adulteration, hoarding and chicanery characterise what he called 'subsistence' trade in a semi-subsistence economy where profit is to be grabbed as a windfall. For Mines, fear of reprisals both from government officers and from other traders accounts for such unforthcoming encounters. The need to evade grounds for jealousy and for retaliation from the evil eye is another potent sealer of lips. Mercantile castes may be subject to social ostracism and/or may hold themselves apart socially. Such was the case with Fox's *baniyas* in Tezibazaar and Mines' Muslims in Pallavaram (Fox 1969; Mines 1972). Trade records are considered highly secret – *mutatis mutandis*, on a par with landholding data and fertility histories. Questions about these matters are a serious intrusion into privacy.

These considerations naturally make interviewing traders a highly sensitive business. But this is not to say that traders cannot be interviewed at all, nor that the data collected from them should automatically be discounted as erratic and unreliable. Below, I discuss problems in creating a sample of traders and methods I have used to obtain data from them. The experience drawn on consists of long talks with about a thousand traders over the period 1973–90 in India, Sri Lanka and Bangladesh.

9.2 Finding the traders to talk to

Much social science, especially economics, relies on secondary data. But in south Asia, data relevant to the study of trade are so deficient as to render them almost unusable. First, they have been collected to serve certain regulatory needs of the state, and hence are blind to many aspects of social reality. (In India, the lack of data on caste or gender is particularly striking. With respect to trade, assets and commodity flows are invisible or highly distorted.[1]) Secondly, they are collected from primary sources. These give rise to the following three further sources of awkwardness:

1. *Problems of quality*. Price data, for instance, are so abundant as to have recreated the study of markets as that of price behaviour. Prices are collected by departments of statistics using investigators who batten on to trustworthy trading contacts. This practice can be seen (by anyone who dissects the mouldering heaps of local language carbons) to introduce both variations in the quality of information and a certain tendency to underestimation, presumably in order to evade fees and taxes.
2. *Defective and incomplete information*. Measurement errors in secondary data are so serious as often to invalidate the uses to which they are put. In 1980, for instance, records of private storage available to the Tamil Nadu state represented under 1 per cent of that of trade supply records. Data on processing costs and commodity flows are acknowledged as guesswork.
3. *Variable coverage*. What might be thought to be quintessential information

on intermediaries – their identities, for example – shows enormous variation in different parts of government. Agricultural trading and processing enterprises recorded in Factories Acts lists contain only the largest firms. The commodity associations lists feature the most powerful and active firms. Commercial taxes and excise lists are most comprehensive for those commodities which happen to be taxed, but even then exclude petty trade under defined thresholds. Regulated markets lists are not the most accurate, but cover the largest range of crops traded.

Given the problems of secondary data, primary research is indispensable. It is also problematic. If the number of firms exceeds the resources available to study them, it is necessary to obtain a representative sample. The sample size should be based on the noble consideration of variances. If it were known that populations or strata were homogeneous then very small samples (characteristic of studies of trade) would be entirely justified. But populations of traders are not homogeneous and variances are usually unknown. Trading firms are differentiated on a massive scale in terms of size (as exemplified by turnover or assets), commodity traded, location, type of activity mix and internal organisation. It is hard to accept that firms have the same objectives or can be compared and aggregated.[2]

Attempts to sample and to stratify trading firms are also dictated by base considerations such as resources of time and money. Furthermore, in fieldwork on a subject that moves, there will be a trade-off between geographical coverage and depth. If a minimum representation of a stratum is decided upon, sampling fractions may vary. With large numbers of variables, the representativeness of the sample will vary. One is left with case studies and larger groups of case studies, rather than with proper samples.

Further, lists from which samples might be drawn have certain unattractive features, as follows:

- Multiple firms trading on one licence from one address.
- Firms trading in multiple commodities (and where the commodities sampled are an insignificant part of total gross output).
- The existence of unlicensed firms within the region.
- Untraceable firms with fictitious names and addresses (11 per cent of my original sample in Coimbatore District, Tamil Nadu).
- Cessation or intermission of trade (66 per cent of the millet trade in Coimbatore).
- Unindicative labelling ('wholesaler' is actually a 'processor' or a commission agent).
- Control of trade by firms located outside the area.

In the complete absence of population lists, towns can be visually inspected and mapped, but this is time-consuming and rarely exhaustive. Rapid appraisal techniques for the selection of respondents run to surveys of a settlement transect (such as firms located along one routeway) and surveys via a network of recommendations. Mostly the data gathered will describe the firms studied and are not statistically amenable as a basis for generalisation.

All these factors make sample creation and selection a hazardous business. In practice, most students of trade have used samples, but they have 'found' samples rather than selected them (Alexander 1987). On the assumption that reasonably reliable and rich information about complex phenomena is more useful than defective data in large quantity, what has been found practical is the purposive sub-sampling of very small numbers of reliable, knowledgeable and friendly informants. Dewey (1962) in Java, for example, used five informants. Fox in Uttar Pradesh, Lele generally and Mines in Madras relied on a 'few trustworthy informants'.

My three most exhaustive field studies of trade in south India and Sri Lanka used the most detailed official lists (which in the case of fertiliser traders had to be compiled aggregatively from each manufacturer and distributing company). I knew nothing more about the subjects of my research than their names, their addresses and the commodity in which they dealt. These lists were then stratified geographically, first by administrative subdivision within the territory studied (to ensure fair spatial coverage) and secondly by rural or urban location. Total sample size was dictated by time in the field (7–9 months). Sub-sample sizes for different commodities were usually made proportional to population lists, with ten as a minimum. Having arranged my strata, and calculated sample sizes, I then screened the lists for obvious systematic biases (such as caste, which often appears as a 'surname' on lists) and, assured of their absence, selected samples systematically. False trails were substituted for randomly within the relevant strata. Certain avid informants gave qualitatively and quantitatively superior interviews. These were often used as profiles or case studies in the subsequent analysis (see Harriss 1981, 1984b, for examples).

My ongoing study of the economic base of a south Indian market town (Harriss 1990) has proceeded differently. All businesses within the organic (rather than administrative) boundary of the town are mapped each decade (a laborious activity!) and a 6 per cent sample is drawn randomly, stratified by quartier. The sample fraction was dictated by the time available in 1973 – three person-months – when the first such field survey was carried out.

Finally, both of my two field studies in West Bengal and two in Bangladesh have been carried out under far more severe time constraints (the former both two months and the latter both two weeks). I have resorted to rapid appraisal methods, using a combination of social networks and transects in the settlements studied.

9.3 The field experience

In the field study of trade, the researcher is necessarily always an outsider. The 'participant observation' of trade is never undertaken (and it is rarely undertaken for any kind of rural research). My personal experience derives from accounts of the experience of traders. Of course, all this does is narrow the gap between the two experiences. My encounters with traders remain essentially vicarious.

The concepts, language and topics of any participative, first-hand field experience are the results of a process of *a priori* reasoning and the preoccupations of existing literature. Fieldworkers face responses and reactions such as dishonesty, piety, uncertainty, ignorance, dramatisation, curiosity and politeness, as well as more or less fickle memories of trading filtered through varying capacities and motivations in a meeting. Here I set down some of the methods I have used to obtain reasonably meaningful economic data from traders, under five broad categories: establishing independence from government; minimising observer error; minimising environmental error; managing the meeting with traders; and dealing with error due to the observed.

9.3.1 *Establishing independence from government*

Markets are set against states. Traders are assumed to be and described as mistrustful of contact with predatory governments. It is therefore important for researchers working with traders to distance themselves from the state – but it is very difficult to do so successfully. At a deep level, it is obvious to all respondents that no powerful person in government disapproves of the researcher sufficiently to prevent her or him from conducting field research. At a less deep level, there are visas, research clearance and official affiliations to be negotiated, which may compromise the independence of the researcher. The most it is possible to do during fieldwork is to avoid all contact with government in the field locality (over and above a necessary introductory meeting with the administrative and political heads of the local district) until after the fieldwork is completed. I also have tried to avoid the taint of living in government rest-houses – though in Sri Lanka, when my choice was between a rest house and a brothel, I capitulated!

That much of the fieldwork on markets and trade in south and southeast Asia has been carried out by foreigners is not coincidental, despite the much-vaunted mistrust of strangers by traders. There may be a point beyond which it is a positive advantage to be strange, since the likelihood of collusion between foreigners and the threatening state or other prying traders is minimised. 'Traders said they would not mind showing records to an outsider so much as to another trader' (Lele 1971, p. 82). There is clearly a trade-off between, on the one hand, foreignness *qua* independence from the state (or from other merchants) and, on the other hand, foreignness *qua* ignorance and stupidity. This ambiguity about foreignness is continually checked by merchants via tricks and challenges in interviews.

It is possible that the evidence of a massive nexus of material interests between merchants and local bureaucracy is such as to challenge the assumed dichotomy between state and market. On several occasions, I have wondered whether the careful avoidance of government was necessary. Because of the risk of getting that answer wrong, I have never altered the tactic of trying to avoid identification with government.

9.3.2 *Minimising observer error*

A businesslike procedure helps to minimise observer error. Such error results from the inevitable projection of the observer into the situation being measured, and generates a systematic rather than random bias. Personal collection of the data and the use of an interview procedure which sets out consciously to minimise observer interaction can reduce these errors.

I have found it useful to enlist the support of commercial organisations in establishing networks of contacts. Overtures are made to the relevant trade associations, to lobbies representing agro-industry and to chambers of commerce. Through such overtures, networks of 'useful contacts' inevitably create themselves, a process strengthened when names in the network bubble up in random samples. Other *dramatis personae* may be visited expressly for a case study. Having selected but not yet found the sample, letters in English and in the local language are delivered in advance of any personal contact. These letters contain a fairly full explanation of the reasons for my interest, the purposes of the research, the procedure of selection (as in a lottery), the subject of the matter to be covered in our meetings and an assurance of confidentiality (see Appendix 1a). I always try to explain my research interests as openly as possible and in such a manner as to appear unthreatening. The development of mercantile portfolios, for instance, is best justified in terms of their contribution to the national economy and not in terms of modes of appropriation of surplus.

I then make personal contact and agree the date and time for our meeting. This is easier in towns than in villages, where I am often forced to turn up somewhat speculatively, but can always renegotiate the encounter. Appointments must be sensitive to the time of the day when the trader and the market are not busy, so that the opportunity cost of conversation (and the size of the possibly pressurising crowd) are minimised. Not only are there antisocial hours, there are also antisocial seasons. Fieldwork around harvest time in India may have to be conducted, if at all, well into the night (though at such seasons markets may hum with life continuously, night and day, and never be quiet).

9.3.3 *Minimising environmental error*

Tactics to minimise environmental error aim to make the fieldworker familiar *with*, not just *in*, a research locality. Fieldwork over a long period and interactive visits over one's professional lifetime help to establish rapport, to crush rumours and generally to flatter people by one's enjoyment of and commitment to the community. Iteration generates unique historical databases, such as those for the town of Arni in 1973 and 1983, which trace the evolution of the economic base, financial and labour relations, investment and savings and the commodity flows of a market town. With regard to the duration of fieldwork, I took 9 months to interview 220 traders in North Arcot in 1973–4, 7 months to interview 90 distributors in Sri Lanka in 1974 and the same time to interview 150 merchants in Coimbatore District in 1980. Total time in the country tended to be double that spent actually doing fieldwork. Obtaining local administrative and political permissions, gathering secondary data and population listings, running in a local research partner, sorting out living, eating and transport arrangements, and waiting out various kinds of biological adjustment and/or illness occupy as much time as interviewing, and are just as legitimate a part of the field experience.

I always carry a fact sheet about my project in the local language, which I dish out to anyone who comes up full of curiosity (Appendix 1b), in order to minimise the potential damage of rumour (though it is hard to explain to a sceptic that a biro on a leather thong is not a microphone). For the same reason, I try to give the same account of the project to all questioners. Consistency is important, and the temptation to modify the description of the research depending on the audience should be resisted. (For example, a mill owner first encountered under pressure from Communists for party funds was next met as a member of a farmers' lobby when I interviewed their leader!)

It is probably no coincidence that the study of trade is rather a female preserve. Not only do male traders prefer talking to female interviewers, it is also less likely that a female researcher is colluding with the (male) state. With regard to age, the older the better (and auburn or fair hair may connote age). With regard to cultural moorings, to have children around is auspicious socially, though it may not always be auspicious for the children concerned. Mine, notwithstanding the love for them of many people in India, have had to put up with cultural isolation, with disease, with being treated like toys and with one incident of physical ill-treatment. These experiences are set by them beside the immensely rich socialisation they had in early childhood in south Asia.

The presentation of self through lifestyle is a delicate thing to manage. In my own fieldwork, there has never been any question of identifying with my respondents. (This does not mean that I dislike the traders I interview. I feel distinctly ambivalent towards some of them as exploiters, and as intelligent and interesting entrepreneurs.) Nearly two decades ago, I started by living in the kind of dosshouse or 'hotel' that was used by traders' clerks. As a result my visiting cards were distributed to all and sundry by marauding wild monkeys; I was privy to screeched telephone calls about prices and quantities at 3 a.m.; I knew the habits of bedbugs and cockroaches as well as I knew the soundtracks of the most popular Tamil movies; and I grew very thin on the kind of food eaten by clerks. Later on, when doing fieldwork with very young children, I managed to live in modest houses located close to market-places, suffered the same water shortages as everyone else and was helped by an elderly nanny of legendary resourcefulness who also acted, often unknown to me, as my ambassador at large.

I have always adopted local clothes, though the sari is a garment as full of hidden meaning as are earrings, bangles and hairstyles. Mindful of possible hazards such as the dirtiness of market-places and the need to jack up the car should a tyre be punctured, I often wear cheap, serviceable clothes which send out disconcerting and contradictory messages about my status. Similar contradictory status messages are emitted if I walk or am taken by rickshaw to my interview. On the other hand, using a car can intimidate (small) traders.

I decided early on to eat local food and to drink local water and beverages, assuming that people were not out to poison me. Since an essential act of welcome is to offer a drink, my digestive tract has often had to cope with tender coconut, tea, coffee, soda, coloured soda, cold water, hot unboiled water and hot milk in a single day. Taking risks with food and drink means paying certain penalties with health.

Investment in the local language pays high dividends for both the presentation of self and comprehension of the environment – but at high costs.[3] The acquisition of language is doubly time-consuming when the form of tuition is classical and literary, while the form needed for work is technically specialised and colloquial – literally, from the gutters. Conventional language teachers, tapes and textbooks are not set up for the 1000–2000 words of business useful to my interviews. (Moreover, having mastered this vocabulary, I am then disabled in conversation with women because a gendered world is reflected in mutually exclusive vocabularies.) Nor can businessmen take time during interviews to be language teachers. Many, while sensitive to regional accents, are unused to hearing their language mangled by a foreigner and cannot make head or tail of my approximation to one of five types of 'n' or 'l'. The importance of intention and goodwill in the learning of language, however, is not to be underemphasised, even if one is forced also to have linguistic intermediation.

9.3.4 *Managing the meeting with traders*

The fourth aspect of the field experience concerns the management of the meeting with traders itself. These are best conducted in private, though a public encounter cannot always be avoided. I have always used an assistant to work not independently but closely with me, not (only) for translating but because of the pleasing nature of a triangular encounter.

The assistant has responsibility for public relations and the order of the interview and I act as the scribe, check the questions and answers and ask the extra questions provoked by the interview itself. My research assistants have always been highly qualified (the first more so than me) and often have had previous experience of working with foreigners. I have been extremely fortunate in them, though the relationship is rarely free of frustration. The only disastrous assistant was chosen for me, not by me. Common difficulties with assistants – and faults from which I am myself not exempt – include putting answers into respondents' mouths, and asking questions in the form of assertions which require mere agreement by the respondent. Talking to traders requires street wisdom and technical knowledge, neither of which is necessarily possessed by the holders of good degrees and fluent English.

The questionnaire is invisible. The basic, skeleton one was piloted in 1972. It is memorised and rehearsed in advance. An ordinary notebook is used, in which the interview is anonymous. There is a separate mechanism to relate numbered interviews to the random sample checklist, but I have never used it. The interview notes need early scrutiny for legibility, coverage, error and inconsistency. The interview is flexible and allows for giving as well as getting: common topics are the British royal family, love marriages, local imperial history, Indians in Britain and the British connection. Attempts to test my knowledge of trade and to trick me are also quite common and need rapid reaction. Offers of hospitality, to meet families, eat meals, look around factories and farms, even to attend weddings are taken up whenever possible. I have also been used for purposes of intermediation with the cooperative and revenue departments and the hospital.

These techniques and styles have enabled me to ask a number of questions of traders. In formulating the initial set, it was useful to start with a scheme of final tables (showing the data I planned to collect) from which I derived the questions. Equally, it has been essential to allow latitude for new questions which result from the inductive aspects of fieldwork. My questions cover family and personal business histories; the organisation of the firm; investment histories; turnover; data on price information and price negotiation; the organisation of contacts; the geography of commodity flows; details of storage, transport and travel; costs of trading and processing products and byproducts; moneylending; family size, composition and occupations; the occupation profile of the kin group; land owned, its size and organisation; other income and other investment; employment of family, of casual and non-casual wage workers and of agents; political activity of the workforce; contact with government; and, lastly, the political activity of the respondent.

Some of these data, notably those concerning information flows, inventories and costs, might be improved by iterative interviews, but much of this information refers to long time periods and would not be improved by revisits. This set of questions is memorised and asked in any order that seems natural to respondents. I follow their initiative in this respect. At the conclusion of such interviews, an open question along the lines of: 'Is there anything else important to your firm that I have not asked you about?' occasionally yields a rich lode of information.

9.3.5 *Dealing with error due to the observed*

The fifth and final aspect of the field experience considered here is a set of techniques to deal with error due to the observed, meaning the continuous changes of opinion and behaviour in a reactive situation epitomised by a long interview. A utopian tactic is to minimise the number of onlookers. The majority of questions (including some which may be perceived by the outsider as sensitive) cause no greater problem than is engendered by number heaping. While different categories of trader may have different sensibilities, certain kinds of question are very commonly sensitive. These concern income, gross output, profit, savings, assets and investments, moneylending, crime and corruption. I try to have questions on these subjects asked in a matter-of-fact style, with a ready explanation of reasons for wanting to ask them. I readily exploit insights from comparative experience elsewhere in south Asia, and also use historical information to draw out responses. I assume the existence of sensitive behaviour: 'All traders lend and borrow money. How does it work in your firm?'; not 'Do you borrow money?', but 'From how many Cold Store owners do you borrow money?'.

I try to build in cross-checks. For example, with respect to gross output, estimates can be elicited by direct questioning, by the description of seasonal profiles of trading activity using the traders' own seasonal categories, by seasonal profiles of stocks, by a historical account, and by estimates from other associated costs such as those of gunny sacks, labour, electricity and sales taxes. Expenditure on labour may be obtained per day or per job, multiplied by the numbers of workers at various seasons. Data on profits can be determined by a direct question, as a residual on accounts, or through an estimate of a minimum profit per unit of output deemed acceptable. The mercantile portfolio is best elicited in terms of types of investment rather than in quantities. Use of indirect methods generally yields a range of estimates and I render them consistent in an upwards direction. If a merchant resists, it is my policy to explain carefully the aims of the research and to persist, but not to push further if this approach irritates him.

These techniques for talking to traders have never been problem free, as the last remark implies. My biggest problems, however, have not come from my informants. They result from being a time-bound foreigner. I have not programmed time for illness (or childbirth!), though such matters have absorbed months of time in the field over the years. Markets are dirty environments, and this form of fieldwork is physically taxing. My original field technique, which involved transferring interviews that day on to schedules, was masochistic, and would not have been compatible with family life. Later I had to slow down and take days out for this practice; finally to jettison it altogether. Before starting the study of traders, I thought that mountaineering was the ultimate test of my endurance. I found that fieldwork was a more complex psychological experience; not only something to be endured but also a marvellously enriching, conscientising, difficult and enjoyable way of life.

9.4 Inevitable paradoxes

Using techniques such as those described here, one can end fieldwork with a solid core of quantitative information, a penumbra of numerical data varying in its validity because of the problems of retrospective questioning, and some qualitative data which may be quantifiable (for example, histories of skill acquisition) if codable patterns can be perceived. Much data is unquantifiable. It is incomplete because of its sensitivity or because it has resulted from an interactive practice wherein counter-intuitive results generate secondary or alternative hypotheses, which can only be investigated in the residue of interviewees in fieldwork which is non-iterative.

Two paradoxes rule. One is that the hypotheses are refined and the story is established at the end but not at the beginning, so that the data to test them with are often incomplete. The second is that the random sample may be useful as an organising concept but that it hardly ever exists in reality, for reasons already discussed.[4]

Talking with traders involves the challenge of sensitive data, the near impossibility of the divulging of secrets. Any response to this challenge needs planning of the type described here. Even so, much routine data will be given in terms of rough orders of magnitude. The value, under these circumstances, of very detailed case material (both for parametric purposes and for the explanation of process, relation and history) cannot be overstated.

At the end of this period, the subject of the next piece of field research will be obvious. Yet even iterative fieldwork contains many surprises and can be confounding. We are left with impressionistic cartoons, not high-resolution photographs: Toulouse-Lautrec, not Cartier-Bresson. But without these cartoons, traders and trade would remain invisible.

Appendix 1a Letter of introduction to selected traders (in English and the local language)

United Nations University,
Project on Rural Change and Public Policy,
housed in Viswa Bharathi,
Santinketan 731235

Project Directors
Prof A. K. Sen
Sunil Sengupta

August 1990

Dear Sir

I am a teacher from Oxford University in England. I am presently working on the above project. Just as many people come to England from India in order to study, so I have come to India. For the past 20 years I have been learning and teaching about agricultural marketing. I have studied the wheat trade in Punjab, and the rice trade in Tamil Nadu, Sri Lanka, Bangladesh and also in Birbhum District of West Bengal. In the course of these studies I have talked to hundreds of traders about trade. I have written three books as a result.

I am now studying the marketing of agricultural products in West Bengal. I am interested in the history and growth of such trade (especially over the last 10 years) and how it contributes to economic growth both in agriculture and in other parts of the economy. I am also interested in how markets are regulated here; and in new crops and the problems of marketing them.

The name of your firm has been chosen entirely by chance. I would like to talk with you about the subjects I have mentioned. We can talk in English or in Bengali or Hindi at your convenience. The Government of India and West Bengal have given their permission for this project to take place but it has nothing to do with government. Naturally anything we discuss will not be divulged to others and will only be used for research purposes.

Traders are busy people, but I hope that you can spare some time to discuss these things with me. I shall be visiting you in a few days' time and I look forward to meeting you.

Thanking you,

Yours sincerely

Dr (Mrs) Barbara Harriss
M.A., Dip.Ag.Sc., Ph.D.
Governing Body Fellow of Wolfson College, Oxford, UK

Appendix 1b Letter of introduction to anyone curious (in Bengali)

United Nations University,
Project on Rural Change and Public Policy,
housed in Viswa Bharathi,
Santiniketan 731235

Project Directors
Prof A. K. Sen
Sunil Sengupta

August 1990

Project on Agricultural Marketing in Burdwan District

This is the fifth piece of field research which I have undertaken in south Asia on the subject of agricultural markets. I have worked in Tamil Nadu (1973–4 and 1979–80), Sri Lanka (1974), Bangladesh (1978 and 1989) and in Birbhum District of West Bengal in 1982. I have been interested in the way in which agricultural marketing contributes to economic development, the history of the development of trade, the use made by traders of their resources, the employment created by trade, changes in the flows of commodities traded, and the way traders help form government policy.

Burdwan District has been selected by the United Nations University, an international organisation devoted to research, as the site of a project examining agricultural change.

My role on this project is to find out about the development of agricultural marketing over the last decade and about problems faced by traders in the expansion of their businesses.

To this end I hope to be able to interview a number of traders in various agricultural commodities and talk about the history of their firms. I shall also be interested in price data if that is available and in information about government policy towards traders.

The project has the permission of both the Indian Government and that of West Bengal. The research is completely independent of government however. Details of interviews will be kept confidential as they have been in all of my research, and they will only be used for the purposes of research. I shall be accompanied by Bengali language assistants.

Dr (Mrs) Barbara Harriss
M.A., Dip.Ag.Sc., Ph.D.
Governing Body Fellow of Wolfson College, Oxford University, UK.

Notes

1. An appendix in Harriss (1984b) lists all known sources of Indian secondary data on agricultural trade.
2. As Rudra (1989) has observed in relation to agrarian research, there really is no solution to the problem of ideal sample design.
3. See Devereux (Chapter 3).
4. Also see Olsen (Chapter 4).

10

Fieldwork in a familiar setting: the role of politics at the national, community and household levels

Shahrashoub Razavi

Introduction

My fieldwork explored the relationship between women's labour participation in agriculture and their relative decision-making power and welfare within the household. The research was carried out in two contrasting regions of the Iranian province of Kerman – Rafsanjan and Bardsir – between September 1988 and August 1989. A number of different research methods were employed, including a general census questionnaire (covering 600 households), in-depth interviews with a stratified sample of 90 women, a large number of casual, unstructured interviews with villagers and landlords (living in the adjoining towns), and an anthropometric survey of a small sample of infants and children.[1] Since I was working in my home country, I spoke the language fluently. This enabled me to carry out the research without an assistant.

This chapter relates some of the problems I encountered in the field to political issues at various levels. I begin by discussing problems arising at the institutional level, with respect to bureaucracies and the legal system. In the second section, I address some of the contextual factors shaping my role in the village (class and power asymmetries) and, in the third section, the influence of gender on my interpersonal relationships. My status as an 'indigenous' researcher was significant at all three levels. The impact of the fieldworker's status (insider/outsider) on this type of research remains a contentious point among anthropologists. In the final section of this chapter, I assess some of the arguments raised in this debate, in the light of my own experiences in the field.

10.1 Political factors at the institutional level

Anthropologists generally agree that the 'fieldwork concept' is, to some extent, a product of history (Ellen 1984). The conditions facilitating contact between Western observers and 'exotic' societies were closely related to European colonialism. Similarly, new political forces, whether in the shape of nationalism or Islamic fundamentalism, are bound to affect the viability of this method of research in many parts of the developing world.

Third World governments are frequently suspicious of Western researchers. In post-revolutionary Iran, it is virtually impossible for non-nationals to carry out village-level fieldwork. But Iranian researchers, too, are subject to suspicion, especially if attached to Western academic institutions. I faced two problems in securing clearance for my research. First, the concept of village-level fieldwork is almost unknown in Iran. The number of in-depth village studies carried out over the past three decades can be counted on one hand. Consequently, there are no regular procedures for dealing with research applications, as there are for more popular fieldwork destinations in Africa and south Asia. More significant, however, was the impact of the Islamic Revolution and the highly charged political atmosphere which followed. This has added an extra layer of paranoia to the process of obtaining research clearance. The fact that the new regime has suffered from an adverse 'academic press' (mostly by Iranian academics in exile) is also partly to blame.

It is hardly surprising, therefore, that my case was regarded with some suspicion in official circles. In the Ministry of Science, after much vexation, I was finally interviewed by a high-ranking 'brother'. As became clear in the interview, his initial distrust was based on several fears: of left-wing agitation, foreign espionage and my presumed antipathy to the Islamic Republic. It was a pleasant surprise when my permit was issued shortly after the interview. The main factor working to my advantage was the fact that my family had remained in Iran, and my father had maintained his academic post at Tehran University – 'proof' of his impartiality. Furthermore, the nature of the work I was proposing to undertake (which involved interviewing women and doing anthropometric surveys) was 'apolitical' and thus unthreatening. Finally, as a young woman I was probably not taken very seriously. This too must have helped.

But being a woman was not always an asset, as I subsequently discovered in attempting to set up my research. In Tehran I approached a number of research institutes and academics about the possibility of working with them, or using their facilities in rural areas. Their answer was negative, for two reasons. First, they themselves never stayed in one place for more than a week or two; the mere concept of doing long-term fieldwork was almost ridiculed. More restricting, however, was the fact that they were unable to obtain permission for me because I was a woman.

The post-1979 change in state ideology in Iran, from secular to Islamic, brought with it severe restrictions on women's activities in a number of spheres, including travel and accommodation. All hostels and hotels are strictly forbidden to accommodate single women (especially if young) unless they are accompanied by a male chaperon (husband, brother, father, son). Consequently, these research institutes had confined their own female staff to desk jobs in Tehran and only the men were allowed to do 'fieldwork'. Even if they could get a permit for me, they said (by pulling some strings in Tehran), the local Revolutionary Guards would not tolerate it for long. How could a female researcher possibly live in the same house as male researchers? Or on her own? Without a male chaperon to accompany me, it soon became clear that my options for doing fieldwork in Iran were restricted to my home province of Kerman. There I could rely on my informal network of friends and relatives for accommodation and protection.

Iran admittedly provides an exceptional case of a society where the independent functioning of female researchers has been made practically impossible by law. In other strictly sex-segregated societies, however, the same types of pressure might arise from the society itself, without being sanctioned by law and force. For example, El-Solh, a female anthropologist working in Iraq, was unable to live in the settlement where she was working without her husband – she had to commute from her hotel to the settlement every day (El-Solh 1988). Similar social constraints in Saudi Arabia led Altorki (a Saudi anthropologist) to study the urban elite of Jiddah rather than any other group: 'I knew that, as an unmarried woman, I could neither travel alone in the country nor wander around with nomads. Living alone, anywhere in the country, was out of the question' (Altorki 1988, p. 51). Given my status as an indigenous unmarried woman, social pressures comparable to these would probably have restricted me to my home province of Kerman, even in the absence of official or legal constraints.

10.2 Contextual factors at the village level: class and power asymmetry

A central theme in all fieldwork, one which has been raised by many contributors to this volume, is the fieldworker–respondent relationship. This is a pivotal issue not just because of its intrinsic value, but also because it is generally believed that these relationships determine the reliability of the data that are gathered. In this section, I examine some of the factors that were crucial in shaping my role in the village communities where I worked, and thus my rapport with the respondents.

Relationships are not created in a vacuum. Upon entering any community as an outsider, various suspicions have to be dispelled, depending on the particular circumstances of the community and the individual researcher. Fears of espionage (on behalf of the state) and of taxation are two of the most common.[2] In politically tense situations, such fears may be heightened, and the researcher's task of showing herself or himself to be trustworthy becomes even more demanding.

In many Third World countries, villagers have had some experience with research work (as distinct from their contacts with officials). This is the case in many regions of India, for example. But in societies where village-level research is a novelty, the first generation of researchers face the difficult task of having to construct an 'independent' role for themselves.

Working in Iran meant that I was subject to both sets of problems – the novelty of research, as well as political tensions. Going through the official channels, though safe, would have associated me, in the eyes of the villagers, with the government. I would have been suspected of being an official in disguise, collecting data for future taxation. Alternatively, I could have risked the consequences and gone directly to the village. In this case the 'revolutionary' elements in the village would probably have accused me of espionage or left-wing agitation. Given the various political tensions in the country, a report to the local Revolutionary Guards could easily have escalated into a major event, destroying whatever level of trust I had managed to establish.

Having relatives and friends in Kerman meant that I could be introduced to villagers through these safe channels. Other researchers working in different circumstances have also found that being identified with a highly respected local family allays initial distrust.[3] During periods of crisis and rupture, local families who are impartial provide an exceptionally appropriate medium for an outsider to be introduced into a community. The importance of this factor became clear to me when I started work. As soon as I told the villagers who my relatives were and why I had chosen to work in their village, their suspicions subsided. I was not just 'a researcher', but 'the daughter of landlord Razavi, who is studying our village'. It was in fact due to my status as Razavi's daughter that I was trusted and accepted, and not because of the dubious connotations associated with being a 'researcher'.

I believe that in the Iranian context, where villagers are extremely suspicious of officials (for historical reasons) and are not familiar with independent research work, and where political tensions are significant, it would have been impossible to get the same level of cooperation had I not gone through these long-standing families. This comment, by one of my older informants, was particularly telling: 'The Shah and his *Sepah-e Danesh* came and went, the Revolutionary Guards and the *Jihad* we have recently got to know . . . but your grandfather we knew and your father we know . . . we can tell who is going and who is here to stay.'[4] My initial aversion to this role, and in fact my preference for working in another province, were due to misleading notions I had about what constitutes proper 'fieldwork' (studying what is different rather than familiar, and being a classless researcher rather than *x*'s daughter or *y*'s relative). This tradition has been shaped by generations of Western field-workers working in 'alien' societies, as well as by the empiricist demands placed upon social scientists for 'objectivity'. I was also uneasy about working in Kerman because of the discomfort I thought I would instil in my respondents by being a *landlord's* daughter. Due to the circumstances described above, I ended up working not just in my home province, but also in those villages where I could establish contact through some family network. In retrospect, I believe my initial fears were misplaced.

Next I look at the issue of power asymmetry, leaving the question of researcher 'objectivity' to the final section of this chapter.

Power asymmetry

Even if one is able to dispel initial fears and suspicions, the nature of one's relationship with the host community remains problematic. Most fieldworkers working in Third World villages are aware of asymmetrical power relations with their respondents. Various factors enter this equation, including the researcher's nationality, class, gender, age, institutional and other links.

Working in one's own society does not resolve the issue of power asymmetry. Although nationality or colour may not present a problem, the fact that the researcher (by definition) has had educational opportunities not available to many others means that she or he is relatively privileged in terms of background as well (unless one chooses to work among the elite). I come from a land-owning family in the Kerman region. This would have been a significant disadvantage prior to the 1979 Revolution, when urban-based landlords were respected and feared, since it would have created a barrier between myself and the villagers. But today the political balance in the Iranian countryside has been substantially altered. Although the new regime has not carried out a radical land redistribution programme, the anti-rich and anti-Westernisation rhetoric of the Islamic Republic, together with the threat of land expropriation, has weakened the position of the old class of absentee landlords. The revolutionary leaders have also been successful in giving some standing to the traditional (as opposed to modern and Westernised) strata of both rural and urban Iran. Many revolutionary organs (the Revolutionary Guards, the Revolutionary Courts and *Jihad*) are staffed by members of these less privileged classes, and have remained hostile to the urban and rural (Westernised) elites.

Ironically, these developments had positive implications for my rapport with the villagers, as the traditional asymmetry between us had been significantly reduced. Villagers openly criticised some of the landlords, which they would not have done in the pre-1979 years. In addition, some of them had close ties with the local revolutionary organs, upon whose goodwill (that is, non-interference) my work depended.

Another significant factor in the power equation is gender. Being a woman turned out to be an asset in this respect, especially since I was young, single and physically small. The superior position that I had due to my class was somewhat redressed by my inferior gender position. A good indicator of this was the greater degree of respect and deference shown to the middle-aged man who accompanied me as my driver/chaperon.

There are also more subtle and perhaps personal factors which affect the researcher's power *vis à vis* the host community. The fact that I spoke Persian with a Kermani accent made me seem more 'rural' and less intimidating. Most of my respondents commented on this factor, which I think made it significantly easier to establish rapport. Like most researchers, I did not share the disdain and the prejudices that many educated and urban Iranians hold against villagers. This must have come through in my behaviour.

Although the above factors contributed to a more balanced relationship between myself and the respondents, the underlying class and income asymmetries were not negotiable. This had practical implications as well. There were demands for cash, introductions to doctors, lifts in my car and so on. My strategy was to meet these demands as much as possible, for a number of reasons.

Western researchers working in Third World countries experience feelings of guilt when in the field, due to their various material and non-material privileges. What I found most disturbing was the predatory nature of my work, since it was patently obvious to myself and to the villagers that I stood to benefit substantially, while there was 'nothing in it for them'. Given the lack of communication between policy-making bodies and independent researchers in Iran, I found it very difficult to convince myself (let alone the villagers) of the value of my work to them. In fact I did not even suggest this, as it would have seemed almost ridiculous. At a practical level, I tried to come to terms with these feelings by adopting ways of reciprocating the respondents' time, effort and hospitality. My car was used frequently for taking people to nearby towns (to see a doctor or for shopping) and to other villages to visit friends and relatives. Two seriously ill patients were taken to Tehran for medical treatment. In some cases (those of widows, for example, who constituted the village poor), a day's wage was offered for the respondents' time. In Bardsir, since women participate in farm work intensively, respondents were also remunerated with a day's wage. This was arranged several days before the interview, so that they could hire someone to do their work for them on the day of the interview.

This system worked very well in Kerman, due to the general level of prosperity in the region. Offering a wage did not encourage others to ask for money, something that would probably have happened in a poorer society. By meeting these demands, the class asymmetry between us was of course confirmed and reproduced. It should be said, however, that as my class origin and even family income were already known, the villagers would always be conscious of the asymmetry, even if I had not reciprocated.

10.3 The politics of gender at the household level

In recent years, female fieldworkers have highlighted the relevance of the researcher's gender to the process of fieldwork and the information that is gathered. The gender of the researcher becomes particularly significant in the context of strictly sex-segregated societies. Some analysts have argued that gender may be a 'potentially limiting factor in the female researcher's efforts to work in societies characterized by a high degree of sex segregation . . . restricting exploration mainly to the world of women' (Altorki and El-Solh 1988, p. 5). By contrast, others have argued that 'the lone female fieldworker is usually (but not of course always) better placed than the single male worker' (Ellen 1984, p. 124). My experience confirms the second view.

My decision to concentrate on women's issues was influenced by two principal factors. At the personal level, I wanted to explore the gender aspects of my cultural identity as an Iranian woman. Academically, since gender relations and female welfare in the rural areas of Iran remain largely under-researched, their investigation seemed worthwhile. I chose to work with women rather than men, but this was not because I anticipated difficulties in establishing rapport with respondents of the opposite sex. In fact, I encountered no such problems during my fieldwork. This may seem puzzling at first, for it could be argued that, as a *female* researcher, it must be very difficult to enter the male realm of a strictly sex-segregated society. But this view ignores a subtle relationship between gender and other variables. Factors such as class and outsider status can interact positively with gender, thus reducing its constraining influence on the researcher's accessibility and freedom. As described below, I had not only a relatively privileged access to the female domain, but also an altogether unproblematic relationship with the village men.

Being a female researcher made it easy to develop a close rapport with the women. In rural Kerman (especially Rafsanjan) a male researcher would not have been able to speak to women in a relaxed manner, let alone discuss any subject which was even slightly personal. This was confirmed during my pilot study, when I had a young man from the village as my assistant. His presence made the women more reserved and less talkative. We were not even asked to enter their homes if a male member of the household was not present, and the atmosphere became serious and official. After I decided to dispense with an assistant and work alone, the women's reservations disappeared immediately.

In fact, I was pleasantly surprised at how well I was received by the women and how outspoken they were. The shy and austere appearance wrapped up in *chadors* (the veil) would be transformed dramatically once we were on our own. On several occasions Rafsanjani women mentioned that they stole pistachio from their husbands and sold it to local vendors in return for fabrics, household goods and shoes. Bardsiri women talked very openly about sex, divorce and maltreatment. A number of women complained about their husband's opium addiction. This was particularly significant because it coincided with a government campaign against drug addiction. There were of course other subjects which aroused more sensitivity: such as marrying a daughter to a man who already had a wife; or prematurely withdrawing a daughter from school to ease the work burden. (Incidentally, these were issues of which the village women assumed an urban and educated person would disapprove.)

I had a particularly good rapport with older women and widows. This was partly because I wanted to hear their accounts of 'the old days', which did not interest other young people. The fact that the widows were household heads also meant that they had more freedom in deciding how they spent their time. In other households (especially if the women were younger), their time and attention would be taken up not just by their many children but also by their husbands, who expected tea and food when they came in from work. With older married women this was less of a problem, as their husbands seemed to place fewer demands on them.

When women in a household did not know the details of its agricultural activities, I interviewed their husbands or sons. Being a female researcher was not a drawback. As I have already argued, in the female researcher–male respondent relationship, the class asymmetry is somehow redressed by the sex asymmetry. Moreover, a female researcher does not threaten respondents in the same way that a male researcher might do. But there was a fine balance to be maintained here. I found that it was essential to show a good understanding of the agricultural system (prices, agricultural operations and local terminology) in order to get accurate answers. In fact, my familiarity with these matters was very much appreciated by the men I interviewed, rather than making me appear threatening or intimidating.

I had a number of male key informants (mostly relatively old men) with whom I spent a considerable amount of time, discussing both economic and social issues. Since I was trying to construct the processes of socio-economic change over time, older informants were more appropriate. It was also easier for me to talk to older rather than younger unmarried men, because I did not want to violate social norms. I would usually speak to the younger men if their female relatives (mother or wife) were around; if not, I would ask my driver/chaperon to accompany me.

It is worth reiterating that it was my class, education and researcher status that allowed me to talk to *gharib* (non-kin) men at all; no other unmarried woman in the village could do so with such ease. These factors put me in a separate category. My female respondents (in Rafsanjan especially) often told me that my contact with the village men was acceptable because I had a reason for doing so; it was for my *work* and not for fun.

10.4 The outsider versus the insider

Among anthropologists, as Ellen (1984, p. 23) notes, fieldwork has become a '*rite of passage* by which the novice is transformed into the rounded anthropologist and initiated into the ranks of the profession', a ritual by which the 'student of anthropology dies and a professional anthropologist is born'. In this mysterious initiation ceremony, the researcher experiences 'cultural shock', a revolutionary experience in personal life, with adjustment back into her or his own society being equally stressful.

For me, writing and thinking about 'fieldwork' after the event turned out to be a difficult and frustrating experience. Initially, it was not clear to me why this was so. I did not share many of the experiences, feelings and problems which researchers doing fieldwork usually have. Had I done something wrong? Gradually I realised that my discomfort arose from the fact that my experience did not correspond to the conventional view of 'fieldwork', as I had worked in my own society. I was used to this cultural schizophrenia: being in Iran did not therefore constitute a 'cultural shock', and settling back in England was not psychologically 'stressful'. My sense of isolation arose from what Morsy (1988, p. 70) calls 'a form of scientific colonialism that maintains the "distinctive other" tradition'. As more anthropologists study their own societies this hegemonic tradition will no doubt change, making the indigenous researcher feel more at home and less isolated among her or his fellow fieldworkers.

Working within your own culture has many advantages besides the obvious and crucial one of language. My relationship with the men and women I studied was surprisingly close. This had a lot to do with our cultural affinity. There was a store of knowledge that I had acquired over the years which came in very handy in the field, especially since I was a novice. It was easy to understand people not only by the words they used, but by their tone of voice, the way they reacted to certain subjects, their gestures and so on. Having this better understanding enabled me to behave and react more appropriately and, I hope, with greater sensitivity.

This familiarity worked both ways. My respondents too, knew more about me and my world (the Iranian side of it), making me less of a novelty, so that the relationship we built up was more relaxed. When we discussed different topics (female labour participation, marriage, etc.) we compared the way things were done in the village and in my town (Tehran). They knew my world almost as well as I knew theirs, if not better. I was asked all the usual questions fieldworkers are asked about their family and friends. In addition, I was also able to provide interesting news about the local landlords whom we both knew – their marriages, quarrels, financial situation and harvests.

It is often argued that being an insider erodes your objectivity and ability to analyse. But it should be said that, even when anthropologists work in their own societies, they are rarely complete insiders. Most Third World fieldworkers are urban and middle class, rather than residents of the village or slum communities that they study. In my case, I was at best a partial insider. I was brought up in Tehran. Because of my family background, however, my world was always partly that of rural Kerman (the world of absentee landlords rather than that of sharecroppers and agricultural labourers). There was some minimal contact with villagers during our frequent visits to Kerman. I was thus more familiar with the rural scene of Kerman than many urban Iranians would be. But in any case I was certainly not a complete insider.

Even if you study your own sub-culture, the criticism that insiders are not objective is open to question. Being an insider is a problem for those who hold the positivist view that there should be a distance between the subject and the object, to allow 'objective' analysis. Today, few anthropologists would maintain this view, as the virtues of *verstehen*,[5] empathy and 'subjective soaking' are advocated, and the pertinence of 'objectivity' to the social sciences is questioned. If, within a phenomenological or interpretive frame of reference, the purpose is somehow 'to think and feel oneself into the minds and emotions of one's subjects' (the definition of empathy), then being an insider should enhance one's understanding of the host community (Giddens 1974, pp. 1–22; see also Giddens 1976).

In my experience, the more of an insider you are the better your understanding becomes. I certainly feel that I have more empathy with the absentee landlords of Kerman than with the villagers I was studying. This does not mean that I have more respect or affection for the absentee landlords as people; but I certainly understand them better, in terms of how they feel and think. The fact that I am 'one of them' does not mean, however, that I am incapable of analysing them. I can be as analytical about the landlords as I am about the villagers. This I think arises from being a researcher, which makes total immersion very difficult; it distances the researcher even from her or his own supposed class and sub-culture. Thus by virtue of being a researcher, one is rarely a complete insider anywhere (except perhaps in the sub-culture of the university/research institute).

It is often said that the ethnographer must have both empathy and detachment (Ellen 1984, p. 129). This is usually seen as a tension, where the insider obviously lacks the latter. I believe that due to our training as social scientists (especially those of us who come from mixed cultural backgrounds), we already have sufficient detachment to allow analysis. Empathy, however, is relatively easier to achieve in a familiar setting.

On the negative side, being 'one of them' (even in the limited sense that I was) meant that I did not have some of the freedoms that a complete outsider would have had. It was interesting that nearly all my friends and acquaintances in the village commented on the fact that an old and respected *Haj Aqa* (a term which refers to men who have been to Mecca) drove me around and protected me. They often said that it was very wise of my father to leave me in the safe hands of such a man when he himself had work to do in Tehran. It was in fact true that my parents (and not just my father) had insisted on an elderly man accompanying me, despite my initial protests. This probably reflected their fuller immersion in the Iranian culture. When I was well into my work I realised that if the villagers were going to accept me, I could not appear like an abandoned female. The fact that I had a male chaperon showed that my family cared about me. But given the various advantages that come from studying one's own society, I found this restriction on my freedom a small price to pay. An Egyptian female anthropologist working with the Bedouin community in Egypt was, for the same reasons, introduced into the host community by her father:

> By accompanying me, my father had shown those with whom I would be living and those on whose good opinion and generosity my life and work would depend, that I was a daughter of a good family whose male kin were concerned about her and wanted to protect her, even when pursuit of education forced her into potentially compromising positions. (Abu-Lughod 1988, pp. 149–50)

Similarly, as I became more integrated into the village culture I realised the advantages of *not* working with a young male assistant. This would have created serious problems in terms of people's perceptions and hence their acceptance of me. Incidentally, this was something that my parents had not regarded as a problem, which probably indicates their distance from the views dominant in the village (and even among the majority of absentee landlords, who would have frowned upon my association with a young unmarried man).

I have argued here in favour of the indigenous fieldworker, partly to redress the balance which has been tilted against the insider for both historical/political and methodological reasons. Furthermore, when time is short, the insider has many advantages. The outsider has to acquire various tools with which the insider is already equipped (language being perhaps the most important). Having both perspectives (as insider and outsider) is ultimately far more enriching, since they provide different representations of society, neither having a monopoly over 'the truth'. First, however, it has to be accepted that there is no such thing as the 'objectivity' of the outsider, only the different subjectivities of the outsider and the insider.

10.5 Concluding remarks

Every fieldwork experience is unique, and in my own case there may be few lessons that can be drawn for the benefit of others. Working in a country ridden with political tensions, and distrustful of independent researchers (especially those connected to the West), I found local families the most appropriate channel for being introduced into the host communities. This practice may become increasingly useful, at least in the Middle East, as political tensions and distrust of the West permeate the region once again. More generally, with the conventional requirement of 'researcher objectivity' becoming increasingly redundant, the task of providing insiders' insights has become all the more urgent – though this does not endorse the idea of a monolithic indigenous anthropological orientation, which is rejected on epistemological grounds.

Notes

1. I will not examine research methods here, as other chapters discuss this subject at some length. See especially Francis (Chapter 6), since she too was looking at gender issues and conducting interviews with female respondents.
2. Christensen (Chapter 8) adds other examples.
3. See Francis' experience in Kenya, for example (Chapter 6).
4. The *Sepah-e Danesh* was the literacy corps established in 1962, which sent young recruits to villages as teachers. *Jihad* is the organ established in the post-revolution years which deals with rural development.
5. The concept of 'understanding' (*verstehen*) was developed by Max Weber. In his essay, 'The Meaning of Ethical Neutrality in Sociology and Economics', he observes: 'The means employed by the method of understanding explanation are . . . on the one hand the conventional habits of the investigator and teacher in thinking in a particular way and, on the other, as the situation requires, his capacity to "feel himself" empathically into a mode of thought which deviates from his own and which is normatively "false" according to his own habits of thought' (Eldridge 1970, p. 28).

11

Facts or fictions? Fieldwork relationships and the nature of data

Matthew Lockwood

Give me Facts, Sir.
(Mr Gradgrind, in Charles Dickens' *Hard Times*)
No-one carries the truth in his pocket.
(Primo Levi)

Introduction

Economists and other quantitatively trained social scientists are turning to fieldwork in greater and greater numbers. They often carry out surveys on a scale until recently associated more with anthropologists. However, their methods remain distinct. They are trained in disciplines which view the data collection process as impersonal and neutral, and the formulation of questions from theory as entirely separate from fieldwork. They are encouraged to write up their research as if data collection were not a personal, social and political activity. There is a 'transparency of representation' (Clifford 1986, p. 6) in the reporting of 'facts', whereby the respondent, the fieldworker and the relationship between them are rendered invisible. In contrast to this Gradgrindian approach, my view is that fieldworker–respondent relationships matter. They have consequences for the nature of data and for the interpretation of data. In particular, close examination of the processes of choosing questions and collecting data suggests that the boundaries drawn between theory and observation, and between quantitative and qualitative data, are both false and limiting. In this sense, no theory is independent of observation, and all quantitative data is qualitative. The fieldworker should seek to use these relationships, not deny them.

In this chapter I illustrate these points with examples from my own fieldwork. During 1985–6, I carried out research in three villages in Rufiji District in coastal Tanzania. Most of the time was spent in Mng'aru, a small settlement of just under 600 people, about 5 miles away from a larger town. I lived in one household, but carried out a number of surveys of both the whole village and smaller samples. These covered birth and marriage histories, household structure, asset ownership, time use and migration. The time-use surveys were multiple round. A female assistant – a young woman from the village – carried out the birth and marriage histories. She worked unsupervised on these interviews, a point I shall return to below. Most of the other interviews I did myself, or with help from a young male assistant. In addition to these structured interviews, I tried through participant observation to collect qualitative information on a range of issues, including rights and responsibilities in agricultural and domestic labour, perception of the control of fertility, the organisation of land use, and rites of passage through the life-cycle.

As I was working within the confines of a tiny village, one of the most important aspects of the fieldwork experience was my relationship with the villagers – my 'respondents'. This chapter is concerned with the issues that arise essentially from those relationships. However, it seems to me that cautionary fieldwork tales on their own are of limited value. They are usually specific to the research site, to the individual characteristics of the researcher – that is, whether male or female, old or young, studying his or her own society or being an outsider – and to the researcher's personality. They can make fascinating, amusing and sometimes moving reading, but in the end they may not be of much use to the new fieldworker. Therefore, I have tried in this chapter to use my particular experiences to investigate the general question of why fieldworker–respondent relationships matter.

In the following section I look at some different views of the fieldwork process, from deciding which questions to ask, to identifying units and categories of analysis, to obtaining answers and interpreting them. In Sections 11.2 and 11.3, I discuss how these issues arose in my own fieldwork, and examine different responses to problems of theory and data. In the final section, the implications of taking the fieldwork situation seriously are looked at briefly for the ethics and politics of fieldwork, and the presentation of research.

11.1 Ask me no questions . . .

There are many books by anthropologists about fieldwork. One collection of readings (Freilich 1977) was entitled *Marginal Natives: Anthropologists at work.* If one were to seek an epithet for economists at work, I suggest that 'marginalising natives' would fit the bill. Neo-classical economists can be labelled 'marginalising' in three senses. First, in their intellectual imperialism, in the sense in which, believing economic explanation to be basically correct and universally applicable, they marginalise other disciplines. In the study of many countries in Africa and Asia, they especially marginalise anthropology,

Marxist economics and sociology, both in universities and in resource-rich research institutions such as the World Bank. Secondly, in their confident application to all problems of a single method, based on the concept of marginal changes in behaviour, with its roots in Marshall and Jevons. Thirdly, in the manner in which, through the formulation of hypotheses from models, they marginalise the use and discussion of certain kinds of information, both in the construction of problems and in the collection of data.

The first marginalisation is a suitable topic for a study in the sociology of knowledge, and perhaps a target for intellectual and political agitation. The second was the topic of the debate between two groups of economic anthropologists – the formalists and substantivists – in the 1960s and 1970s.[1] Here, however, I wish to concentrate on the third marginalisation.

All field research starts with theory, whether the theoretical postulates are conscious or unconscious (Hill 1982, p. 2). Our theoretical approach determines which questions we think are important, and which units and categories are to be used, both in fieldwork and in data analysis. How fieldwork relates to theory is probably the most important methodological issue raised by the process, and is therefore a good place to start.

Conventional economics is the *a priori* social science *par excellence*. Models based on rational choice are central to deciding which questions to ask in surveys, and to interpreting the data afterwards. Fieldwork is irrelevant to theory. This view continues to sustain many economic field studies. One of the few dissenting voices is that of Hill (1982, 1986). Her plea for the revision of ethnocentric theoretical postulates through fieldwork itself is based on anthropological method. One of the main points of participant observation is to contribute to the choice of questions, and to be able to give meaning to data (Bernard 1988, p. 151). Thus, as the subject matter and scale of anthropological and economic studies converge, it becomes clearer that what distinguishes the two is method.[2] This has consequences for the way fieldwork can inform theory. In the debate between the formalists and substantivists, the issue for the substantivists often appeared to be truth – for example, is it true that people actually maximise objective functions, such as utility or profit or income? But economists (although perhaps not always the formalists) use the maximisation idea only as a heuristic, an 'as if' postulate, because it generates predictions about behaviour which, claims Friedman (1979), work well. It is therefore a waste of time to find out what people actually do, in order to counter the maximisation postulates. What is required is a better heuristic. 'Better' here means two things: first that more powerful and accurate predictions are made, and secondly that a wider and more relevant range of questions can be addressed. It is this second point that shows up a weakness in economics, since the range of behavioural questions addressed by economic rationality is narrow (Sen 1979). Equally, it is the area where fieldwork plays an indispensable role, as the example given below from my own research shows.

Another way of looking at the issue is to note, following Leach (1967, p. 78), that economists (like quantitative sociologists), seek to establish the truth or falsity of statistical relationships between units of population, income, property, etc., while anthropologists 'endeavour to investigate the total network of interpersonal relationships'. In other words, anthropologists look at economies as cultural systems. It is the information about these systems, gained from fieldwork, which can help us think of better questions to ask. However, choice of questions also necessarily involves choice of categories and units. If economists marginalise the information available from looking at economies as cultural systems at the level of theory, problems will also arise at the level of measurement, because inappropriate categories and units of analysis have been used. There are many examples of this. A hardy perennial in Africa is the household. The wide variety of domestic groups, with multi-level and multi-functional definitions, involves notorious conceptual complexity.[3] Yet singular household units are still used almost automatically in many surveys, mainly because they derive from standard economic models with the familiar economic 'actors' of firms and households.

Does this matter? Again, while it may matter to the substantivist simply because the theoretical categories are wrong, the issue for the economist is whether the categories 'work'. Importantly, the use of inappropriate categories will frequently give rise to mis-specification errors. A good example from a survey of villages in Sri Lanka is given by Leach. He criticises a finding that three-quarters of households were categorised as landless, on the grounds that while 'households' were defined in the survey on the basis of cooking pots, land is actually jointly owned by compounds which consist of a father together with married sons. He therefore concludes that the degree of effective landlessness in the survey area is overestimated.

The final aspect of fieldwork I wish to focus on here is the nature of data itself. Even if the economist allows fieldwork experience to inform the choice of questions, units and categories, there remains the question of how 'good' the data eventually collected are. Again, the epistemological approaches of economics and anthropology are distinct. Here, I want to emphasise the significance of the context of collecting information – who the respondent is, who the fieldworker is, how they get on, how each thinks the other thinks, what the question means to both people, who else was there. These are, of course, an old set of issues in anthropology, but they are still new and relatively neglected in disciplines such as economics and demography.

The topic may best be approached through a route opened up by recent developments in anthropology. While 'traditional' ethnographers recognised that their respondents were often presenting their own versions of phenomena, or that the ethnographers' own presence might have an effect upon a practice under observation, reflexive anthropology expands the cultural field one step further to include the ethnographer *in the ethnography itself*. The person of the ethnographer, past experience and present personal reactions to fieldwork, are acknowledged to be an integral part of the 'data' of an anthropological study.

This is especially true of the written text of an ethnography (Clifford and Marcus 1986). In its radical form, the post-modernist critique in anthropology sees the text not as the respondent's interpretation of some 'cultural facts', faithfully translated to the reader by an invisible anthropologist, but rather as the outcome of a set of dialogues between the anthropologist and respondents. On this view, there is no single truth to be discovered by an absolute scientific method. Rather, 'method *includes* the experience of the observer and defines the experimental field as one of interactions and intersubjectivity' (Jackson 1989, p. 4). As Taussig (1987, p. 13) states: 'my subject is not the truth of being but the social being of truth, not whether facts are real but what the politics of their interpretation and representation are'.

I have invoked this rather crude representation of reflexive anthropology because I think it contains two useful messages for economists. One, an epistemological point, is that what economists treat as discrete, immutable 'data' to be collected are in fact the outcome of social interaction – 'the banal claim that all truths are constructed' (Clifford 1986, p. 6). The other, a more political point, is that much economics is based on an 'ideology claiming transparency of representation' (Clifford 1986, p. 2). These messages are important because, of these two points, economists acknowledge one in only a very partial way, and the other not at all. Economists, in designing and administering survey questionnaires, are aware that there are problems of reporting. It is for this reason that good surveys include pilot studies, as well as training and written instructions for interviewers. However, these interactions between interviewer and respondent, labelled 'problems', are treated in an *ad hoc*, instrumentalist manner, as 'getting in the way' of measuring the truth. These interactions are not included in the methodological field of economics as phenomena to be analysed. Rather, they are to be overcome by the use of techniques for removing bias.

The position regarding the alleged transparency of representation by the economist herself or himself is still worse. In a particular sense, when it comes to writing economics, economists, especially those not working in the field, *are* invisible, vehicles for the application of an institutionally powerful set of rules about analysis and writing. However, in the reporting of fieldwork, this apparent invisibility is less comprehensible. At one extreme, all literary or personal elements in the description of data collection are purged. As in the mode of scientific writing found in the reporting of laboratory techniques, to which this style clearly aspires, it is as if the processes were not actually done by people.[4] I return to this point at the end of the chapter.

The implication of this view of the economist's treatment of fieldwork is that there is a danger of not recognising that economic data are never 'true'. We can all think of examples of bad fieldwork by economists, but even the most diligent and sensitive fieldworker will not, according to the post-modernist critiques, produce 'facts', but rather only 'fictions'. As Clifford (1986, p. 6) points out for ethnography, this:

> may raise empiricist hackles. But the word as commonly used in recent textual theory has lost its connotation of falsehood, of something merely opposed to truth. It suggests the partiality of cultural and historical [and economic?] truths, the ways they are systematic and exclusive.[5]

Economic data can thus 'properly be called fictions in the sense of something made or fashioned . . . but it is important to preserve the meaning not merely of making, but also of making up, of inventing things not actually real' (Clifford 1986, p. 6). On this view, then, the economist, in designing and carrying out a survey, is not simply applying a method, as is commonly thought, but is creating a text, which not only selects some accounts and excludes others, but also helps to shape the representation of what those accounts are about.

Before going on to discuss various practical examples, I would like to examine one potential rebuff to the argument. This is that whatever the problems anthropologists face in tying themselves in knots, they are irrelevant to economics. For while anthropologists attempt to describe and analyse culture as representations of behaviour and thought, economists try to measure, describe and analyse behaviour itself. Thus while it may matter a lot to ethnographers how the cultural significance of cattle in Nuer society differs from that of camels in Rendille society, it matters not one jot to the economist, who is interested in how many livestock are owned by whom, how many are bought and sold, what the costs of feeding and herding are, and so on. The kinds of information that constitute the field of economics, and hence of economists' data gathering, are simply much less open to contest in their construction than are cultural representations.

This is of course related to the argument about economies – are they cultural systems, open to contention and arbitration, or are they closed systems, describable with a certain set of behavioural postulates? The answer to this question matters a great deal to the interpretation of data collection. For if economies are indeed cultural systems, then economic data can be contested in their construction. In the next section, I give an example of this from my own fieldwork, namely the measurement of age. It is instructive that such a basic datum may be cultural in nature. However, in principle, many other kinds of datum may involve an element of construction: in fact, any datum that cannot be directly measured and that therefore involves asking questions.

In this section I have raised several doubts about the way economists have traditionally approached theory and data. I have argued that the choice of questions, categories and units and the derivation of data are thoroughly social processes. The fact that the answers people give to questions in surveys are not true is known in abstract by all social scientists. But being in the situation of asking the questions often gives further information about how those answers are negotiated. In the next two sections, I explore some examples from my own fieldwork.

11.2 Finding the right questions

A recurrent feeling which I experienced during fieldwork was the irrelevance of the tools of research. Oxford University, the requirements of doctoral research, theoretical debates – all seemed distant and incomprehensible. If anything, this feeling grew stronger over time.

There were three sources for this feeling. First, events occurred in Mng'aru that were more visible than the subject I had come to study. Work would be abandoned for long periods, such as when a team of specialists arrived to drive out witchcraft from the village (the specialists were then expelled by the local Party officials, leading to a near riot). Closely associated with the lack of immediacy in what I was researching was a set of challenges from some villagers themselves. As is often the case, they wanted to know what was in all this for them: What good would it do? What difference would it make to their difficult lives? What was the point of the study? Apart from the political issues these questions raised, they, together with the frequent need to explain what I was doing, led me constantly to reflect on the premises of the research.

I had started by developing economic models of fertility behaviour, in which the constrained maximisation of a utility function would lead to an implied demand schedule for children. Fertility in such models is thus a choice variable, for which numeric targets may be related to relevant conditions, such as the costs and benefits of children.[6] This work was done before having gone to the field, and before having a single exchange of views with anyone in rural Tanzania. Once I arrived and started fieldwork, I was presented with an entirely new possibility. In conversations with villagers about children, they would reply to my question about how many they wanted by saying, 'It's a matter for God.' Such responses, common in African countries, are problematic for economists using models generating numeric targets for fertility. Consequently, I spent much time in the early part of the fieldwork feeling quite upset about the status of these economic models. I could not see how they might be adjusted to be consistent with what oi heard, and yet cast more light on the subject. Eventually, I decided that fertility was simply not a choice variable. Rather, people in Mng'aru were experiencing what demographers call a 'natural' fertility regime, defined by an absence of fertility control that depends on the number of children a woman has had.[7]

Approaching the question from a different angle, it is easy to see that the question 'How is fertility chosen so as to maximise utility?' only makes sense where couples or individuals exercise a great degree of control over their reproduction. This requires two conditions (Coale 1973). First, contraception must be available and efficient. Secondly, fertility control must be within the 'calculus of conscious choice'. These two conditions were not met in Mng'aru. The 'Up to God' response acts as a signal about the conditions prevailing in the population studied.[8]

The more I thought about these matters, the more I became convinced of two corollaries. The first was that economists, including myself, instead of trying to recast or ignore the meaning of such responses, should take them seriously by abandoning decision-making models of fertility. The second was that, while it was clear that individual fertility control was largely absent in the area where I was working, fertility was nevertheless controlled, or at least well below that of other non-contracepting populations in Tanzania. It therefore seemed inevitable that such controls were communal in nature. Once this was recognised, a whole set of new and more relevant questions was raised. Once the focus is shifted away from a model where fertility is determined as if it were the means to individual utility or income maximisation, to fertility as the outcome of a set of communally mediated processes – marriage, divorce, remarriage, breast-feeding practices, a taboo on sexual intercourse after birth, polygyny – then a large number of explanations of fertility behaviour become potentially relevant. Some of these might be economic. For instance, it emerged that gender relations within marriages, and hence divorce, were intimately linked to the division of labour and rights to crops between men and women. Changes in relative prices, production conditions and migrant labour opportunities led at points to increased conflict and increased divorce rates.[9] These considerations therefore became dominant in guiding the rest of the study and in the interpretation of data in writing up the thesis.

11.3 Facts or fictions? Fieldwork relationships and the nature of data

One of the things I wish I had been made to understand more clearly before I did fieldwork was that I was bound to get on better with some people than others, but that this was a help, not a hindrance. Indeed, it is of major importance in the collection of qualitative information. This misapprehension that one could and should get on equally well with everyone may seem laughable on reflection, but it was largely bound up with the concept of representativeness imposed by survey work. Alienating people by siding with particular factions, or simply by disliking them, seemed to jeopardise being able to get good response rates from a sample survey.

In retrospect, the extreme forms of invalid response or non-response I got in my survey were not associated with the question of whom I got on well or badly with. A handful of people would not answer my survey questions, but were otherwise friendly. They refused out of indifference and obstinacy, rather than hostility. One old woman was initially recorded as having had ten husbands. But I knew her well enough to recognise this mischievous answer as an expression of how pointless she thought the survey was. Later on, in informal conversation, she told me that she had been married four times. This was much more reasonable, and the circumstances of the telling made it much more acceptable. However, should I have treated it as true? I will return to this question below. By contrast to non-respondents, particular people whom I did not like, and who did not like me, generally agreed to take part in the surveys. (Sometimes they did this only once they knew I had the permission of the village secretary. Invoking the authority of structures in this way involves political questions which are pursued elsewhere in this volume.)

Affinity with certain people did, on the other hand, turn out to be important for learning qualitative information about aspects of life in Rufiji. My relationships with some half a dozen people became the major routes for this kind of fieldwork. However, the dominance of the quantitative survey in my own particular study tended to be disruptive in the development of such relationships. It was difficult to reconcile the need to keep to a timetable, especially that of a multiple round survey, with the flexibility necessary to develop interesting and informative dialogues.

In the early part of the fieldwork, this was indeed paradoxical. Doing the preliminary household questionnaire brought me into contact with most of the people in the village, and reduced a feeling of aimlessness, when my language skills were still rudimentary. But there is no point in creating conditions for the opening up of discussions, if another part of the process precludes being able to take advantage of these conditions. Going round to people's houses, repeatedly pressing for small pieces of information in a (to the person involved) disjointed and incoherent way, is difficult to square with the development of a deeper, more mutual knowledge, required for a more sustained learning. Thus the very methodology of the study – the mixture of qualitative and quantitative data collection – was not without its problems. The way I got on with people affected the qualitative information collection, but the use of survey questionnaires itself influenced, even came to define, my relationships with a large number of people. Those relationships were also obviously constrained by my identity. Age was a factor, as was gender. But they were not, in the case of Rufiji, determinant. Among the closest relationships I developed were those with some female respondents, while those with others remained the most distant. In this case, as perhaps with others, personality was equally if not more important.

Given that fieldworkers are usually trying to find out a range of kinds of information, from a range of people, one question which immediately arises is whether it can be said that certain answers are more reliable than others. Is it possible to construct an 'index of reliability' for one's data which will guide the analysis of it afterwards? Clearly, it is impossible to do this by individuals, since it is not possible to know, say, 100 people well enough to tell what influences their replies to questions. A more promising approach would appear to be to look at *kinds* of data. This is what is attempted in 'rapid rural appraisal' methodologies, with distinctions being drawn between 'registered' or 'core' data and 'non-registered' data.[10] There is a problem, however, because core data can themselves be highly contested. Information often seen as core quantitative data, such as yields, asset holdings including cattle, and family composition, are in fact highly 'qualitative' in nature. To illustrate this point, I will take an example from my own fieldwork. It concerns a piece of numerical information – age – normally thought of as part of the core of 'hard' quantitative data.

Since my study was partly concerned with demography, recording ages was a basic step, as it is with almost any social or economic survey. I tried to take some care with measuring age, being aware of some pitfalls: the mis-statement of age for certain groups, digit preference and simple recall error. I developed a local calendar, and probed extensively to establish a reasonably accurate range for each person. Information on the ages of adult women was recorded on two occasions. There was an initial statement in the household questionnaire at the start of the study. The respondent was usually the oldest man in the house, who gave everyone else's ages. A second report was given by the women themselves in the birth and marriage history schedules, some 3–4 months later. There the interviewer was a young local woman. Table 11.1 gives the average self-reported age (age_1), the average age as reported by the house head (age_2), and the coefficient of variation of the difference between them, for different age_1-groups.

There are a number of different ways of reading this table. First, one could use various measures, such as the Whipple Index for digit preference, or a model age distribution, to assess which set of reported ages is more plausible.[11] Certainly, despite attempts to avoid it, there was definite clustering around ages ending in 0 and 5. However, since this kind of digit preference is almost universal where people do not know their ages, let alone those of other people, it is unlikely that this kind of adjudication would work.

A second interpretation involves recognising the social relationships implicit in the data. Most of the age_2s were reported by the women's husbands, a few by fathers. The male respondents consistently underestimated the ages of the women living in the same houses. Perhaps, then, we should read Table 11.1 as

Table 11.1 Differences in reported ages of adult women (Mng'aru 1985–6)

Age_1 group	Age_1 (mean)	Age_2 (mean)	Coefficient of variation ($Age_1 - Age_2$)
15–19	17.48	16.90	179.93
20–24	23.00	21.83	388.72
25–29	26.46	24.54	152.29
30–34	31.88	26.25	69.79
35–39	37.22	33.94	171.57
40–44	42.09	34.82	55.37
45–49	46.83	37.25	74.51
50–54	51.00	41.67	116.14
55–59	56.83	47.00	49.79
60–64	61.59	54.18	99.38
65+	66.50	55.00	89.95

a demographic projection of gender and kinship relations in eastern Tanzania. Surely, it might be argued, women know their own ages better than their husbands and fathers do. Their own estimates must therefore be nearer the truth, while those of their male relatives are compounded by perceptions of femininity and of their own seniority. One could go further, and try to explain the initially puzzling fact that the greatest relative mis-statement is for younger women, not older ones. This may, for example, reflect the difference between husbands reporting their wives' ages, and fathers reporting their daughters' ages.

There is a third possible reading. Since a woman's age in these circumstances is not verifiable by records of any kind, it becomes a 'cultural truth'. Its measurement is therefore not a question of getting a version closer to the truth than another, but rather an issue of how the question was asked, by who and of whom. The age_2 column represents the outcome of dialogue between myself and various older men, while the age_1 column is the product of my younger local female assistant's decisions while in discussion with the women in question. One is not more truthful than the other: they are both sets of 'fictions', made up under different circumstances. At a practical level, this brings out the effects on the collection of 'data' of employing unsupervised assistants or enumerators. Enumerators can be trained and monitored, and it is certainly important to do so. But none of this can control for the fact that they have a different identity from the researcher – often they are local, and sometimes, as here, of a different gender. Whatever the pros and cons of employing an assistant in this way (and it is sometimes almost unavoidable), the simple fact that he or she is a different person from the researcher will always have significance.

The differences between these three readings can be brought out more clearly by considering five questions that can be asked about what economists would call potential 'bias' in any set of data. These are as follows:

1. Does it exist?
2. In which direction is it?
3. How large is it?
4. What are the reasons for it?
5. Does it matter and what should be done about it?

The first reading (that of economists or demographers) lays great emphasis on the importance of questions 1, 2, 3 and 5. Since an objective truth is assumed, all the issues are about how far the data stray from that truth, and how this will affect statements about the truth. The second reading (that of realist anthropologists) concentrates on questions 1 and 4. Understanding why people give the answers they do is seen as a better way of getting at the truth than attempting to 'correct' data afterwards. The third reading (that of reflexive anthropologists) simply asserts that the questions are meaningless. There is no fixed truth that we can know of, so the concept of 'bias' is inappropriate. Rather, we have a set of representations, none of which can be afforded prior status.

What do these different views imply for the use of these data and in future studies? In economics and demography there is a tendency towards the development of techniques to correct and clean data.[12] In realist anthropology the response is to do better data collection: probe further, get more complete local calendars, take longer to search for corroborative material (Hull *et al.* 1988). A different kind of response is to make the fieldwork situation itself part of the research object – to make it less transparent. Then the relationships of the respondents to one another become important, and also eventually that of fieldworker to respondent. The problem of bias does not arise, since the concept of bias is not accepted.

11.4 Conclusions and implications

I have argued that information arising from fieldwork is important for economists and demographers. There is no absolute distinction between theory and observation, nor between quantitative and qualitative information. These issues suggest certain principles for the conduct of research. They fall into the following areas: using fieldwork to generate questions; what to do about data; writing. At each stage questions of the politics of fieldwork arise. These are explored more fully elsewhere in this volume, but should be briefly mentioned here.[13] Much fieldwork is conducted in poor communities in poor countries, while many researchers come from rich countries. There are personal and cultural consequences for both sides in the meeting. A common example is the problems raised by requests or demands for money or medicines. However, this context also raises the questions of the purpose and potential benefits of the research. The answers to these are intimately linked to the issues of who controls the research agenda, the relative values placed on the inputs of fieldworker, assistants and respondents, and who controls the product of the research and the form in which it is presented. Clearly, these are complex and important issues, and fieldworkers would be unusual if they avoided them. But they are seldom raised in the course of non-field research. And this is really the point here. Again, fieldwork relationships play a role of bringing out elements of research which can remain hidden when data arrive on tape ready to be cleaned and arranged into results.

11.4.1 *Using fieldwork to generate questions*

One of the main intellectual benefits of fieldwork for me was that it helped to crystallise a solution to the problem of how to understand fertility behaviour in

Tanzania, one which ended up being quite different from the original model. This is in itself a justification for doing fieldwork. But if all questions to be asked are predetermined by theory, this process is robbed of its potential benefit. If material gathered in fieldwork is to inform the economist's choice of questions, then it will not be of the form of direct tests of behavioural postulates (although that kind of observation may be part of the material). Rather, it is likely to arise from discussions about what those postulates imply (such as numerical preferences for children). An interesting but novel idea for economists is to present the model they are working with (in non-technical terms) to the respondents themselves and ask them what they think. Sometimes, fieldworkers find themselves being told, 'No, no, you haven't understood, you are asking the wrong question . . .'.

11.4.2 *What to do about data*

The main conclusion reached about data was that all data obtained by asking questions are 'qualitative', in the sense that they cannot be treated simply as objectively true. For the fieldworker, the immediate problem is what to do about this. The first point to note is that fieldworkers from different disciplines have different concerns, as emerged in the discussion of 'bias' above. Some anthropologists, for instance, would deny the possibility of what economists think they are doing (that is, measuring behaviour). However, the types of information obtainable through fieldwork which anthropologists focus on can be useful to the economist even on her or his own grounds.

There are at least three levels at which the fieldworker can tackle the problem. As noted above, these arise out of the different epistemologies of the economist, realist anthropologist and reflexive anthropologist. However, while these epistemologies may be logically incompatible at a theoretical level, carrying out all three kinds of practical solution at once may be possible.

For the economist and demographer, the first set of checks, such as corrective techniques and tests for bias, are perhaps the most familiar. Notably, they can usually be applied only to data in the aggregate. The use of consistency checks at the time of data collection thus becomes crucial.

The second kind of action is to learn as much as possible about the perceptions of respondents and their social relationships, as a guide to what might influence their answers to questions. In the example above, gender ideologies were argued to be relevant to the statement of women's ages by men. Another obvious instance would be the understating of the ages of young people where they become liable for tax at a certain age. Understanding the response and its direction is conditional on knowing that a tax is levied. Divining statements about cattle ownership where such ownership is not individual, or where it is bound up with contentious or costly social roles, is a more complicated business. But knowing about such things will help enormously in knowing where and how data might be 'biased', and ultimately, what the limits of truth might be.

This leads us to the last response, which is simply to recognise those limits. Data can be presented without any claims about the truth, as in the example above. What can be noted is differences in accounts, and the way in which those accounts were generated. This last point has important implications for the way in which research is presented.

11.4.3 *Writing*

In the writing of research reports based on quantitative fieldwork, a central place is usually given to data obtained from questionnaires. Whether fieldwork does have influence will depend on how much information outside of the questionnaire framework is recognised as 'data'. This can include larger questions of theory, but also information about units and categories constructed for measurement, such as 'household'. Often, this kind of information ends up outside of the questionnaire data.

More generally, I would suggest that fieldworkers may experience either poor survey design due to theoretical and categorical difficulties, or disputations over 'facts', as a problem of what, in the end, to put down in the little box in the questionnaire. One characteristic of surveys is that disagreements, uncertainties and confusions must always be resolved into a measured fact. The dispute or confusion itself may remain only as a note in the margin of the questionnaire, or as a passage in a notebook. The problem, then, is how, if at all, it can be used. An aspect of this is that disputes and confusions involve the person of the fieldworker. However, as discussed in Section 11.2 above, economists and demographers often purge literary and personal elements from their descriptions of data collection. Perhaps controversially, I suggest that the limits to the fieldworker's knowledge be shown by their presence in the written product of the research. In my example of adult women's ages, it would not be enough to apply corrective techniques and knowledge of respondents' perceptions and social relations. It is necessary to admit that the true ages could not be known, and to describe the questioners as well as the respondents.

These issues may seem extremely basic from a methodological viewpoint, since they precede the details of data identification and collection. Nevertheless, the degree to which the social and political nature of fieldwork is recognised *within the research itself* will determine its entire conduct.

Notes

1. The debate was grounded in the work of Polanyi and Sahlins. The classic works are Cancian (1966), Firth (1967), Godelier (1972), Asad (1974), and Hahn and Hollis (1979). Donham (1981) has a more recent discussion.

2. *Pace*, Leach (1967). This convergence is evident on the one hand in the appearance of village-level studies by economists in developing countries, and in the application of economic theories to subjects such as kinship and marriage; and on the other hand in the growth of anthropological studies of commodities, markets and Western economic institutions.
3. See Yanagisako (1979), Guyer (1981), Whitehead (1984) and Evans (1989).
4. For example, in Bliss and Stern's (1982) innovative and thorough work, their new approach to economic research was not matched by a change in writing style. The presence and persons of the authors were made explicitly part of the report only in the introductory remarks.
5. The insert is my addition.
6. See Lockwood (1989a) for a discussion.
7. Leridon and Menken (1979). Other researchers have noted that it is sometimes possible to probe beyond the 'Up to God' response to obtain numerical fertility preferences. As one young man said to me: 'It is a matter for God, but if it were between me and God, then I would have three [children].' But to argue that this means that decision-making models will, after all, generate interesting questions is mistaken. In such a society, people will know some individuals who have fewer children than the population average because of late marriage, primary and secondary sterility, long birth intervals or conjugal separation. They may also observe that these people have an easier, or more difficult, time than others in certain phases of rearing the children. However, this does not mean that they believe that they have control over reproduction to the degree and of the type indicated by numerical specification.
8. As Caldwell (1982, p. 21) remarks: 'This is neither an evasive nor a superstitious reply and such respondents are perfectly happy to discuss what they mean, which is really that these are matters over which they have little control and that to attempt more control would probably achieve little while bordering on the impious.'
9. Lockwood (1989b), Chapter 2.
10. See Longhurst (1981) and Hoddinott (Chapter 5 in this volume).
11. The Whipple Index gives the relative frequency of recorded ages ending in 5, 0, etc. in a population. For its calculation see United Nations (1955, pp. 40–1). For the use of model age distributions see Newell (1988), Chapter 11.
12. In demography there is a large sub-literature on how to correct biases in data. See Newell (1988) and Brass (1971, 1985).
13. See Wilson (Chapter 12 in this volume) and also Richards (1985).

12

Thinking about the ethics of fieldwork

Ken Wilson

Introduction[1]

Undertaking fieldwork inevitably becomes much more than just data collection, because the researcher enters the world of the subjects of the research. This can make fieldwork an exhilarating experience in comparison to research with secondary, archival or statistical materials. Yet it can also be distinctly unsettling, because the researcher is obliged to come to terms with the realities of the relationship between scholarship and human experience. This can be particularly difficult for Western or local elite researchers working in the so-called 'Third World', and it is to such scholars that this chapter is addressed. I aim to stimulate thinking about 'ethics' in a manner which can enable researchers to handle the personal experience of fieldwork better, and use it more effectively to generate writings that can lead to an improved existence for those studied.

While there are ethical considerations in every type of research, this chapter concentrates on those that arise because of the fieldworker's close engagement in the life of the locality studied. Researchers have to make decisions about the form and content of their involvement in 'other people's societies', and the responsibilities that this entails. Tensions are further increased by the fact that the fieldworker has to deal with the problems of getting as much information as possible out of people. This dual engagement (personal and professional) raises questions about the management of ego and ambition; about friendships; about what it is legitimate to collect data on, and how; about obligations to truth, openness and confidentiality; and about commitment to expose and transform power relations. Adams' (1979) appeal in her powerful 'open letter to a young researcher' – that research can only be legitimate if it accepts the significance of the people studied as central actors – is relevant here. Otherwise it reduces to outsiders gaining status through examining and pontificating about others within a framework in which they privilege their own role.[2]

A number of 'guidelines for ethical research' have appeared recently, and are well worth consulting (or a review of them, such as Burgess 1984). A feature of these is the notion that researchers must respect the rights of the people they study, and that the essential 'reputation' of scholarship depends upon the degree to which researchers respect those rights. They dwell less on the importance of researchers discovering and presenting the 'truth', or, more realistically, admitting to the nature of their actual evidence and its deficiencies. But I would argue that as much damage has been done by poor academic quality as by poor ethics in relation to informants. Many researchers have contributed to negative stereotypes, incorrect but fashionable ideas, exciting but unfounded theories and over-simplified notions that have supported (directly or indirectly) ideologies, policies or programmes with negative results. I am not saying that ethics demand brilliant scholarship, but surely they require a rigorous search for truth. To achieve this goal, researchers can provide local people with opportunities to comment on their interpretations, and also present readers with honest descriptions of their methods and data, and the ways in which local actors view the phenomena discussed. (See, for example, Wilson 1990.)

This chapter is divided into four sections. The first concerns general issues of research design and objectives. Section 12.2 explores the ethical issues of actually collecting data in the field, and Section 12.3 examines relationships with local people. Finally I examine ethics involved in writing up and disengaging from the community studied.

12.1 Value-free research and researchers as humans beings with values

12.1.1 *Value-free research*

An important intellectual tradition in the social sciences is the ethical necessity of engaging in 'value-free' research. Researchers have sought to achieve this through attempting to control their opinions and biases (and especially through not seeming to express them), and by 'writing themselves out of the account'.[3] This tradition encourages the presentation of empirical data and interpretations, rather than prescriptive, judgemental or polemical contributions. The 'facts' are allowed to 'speak for themselves', and the researcher explores the process and patterns of conflict in social and economic life, rather than simply trying to identify and exalt 'who is right'.

In recent years the limitations on researchers' capacities to be 'value-free' have become more generally recognised. As research on developing countries has come of age, many workers have been horrified to discover how enormously their underlying ideologies and assumptions have coloured the scope and nature of inquiry. These realisations have led to important work that challenges the racist, sexist, elitist and cultural attitudes of Western-trained intellectuals, especially those who had thought they had escaped the colonial mentality of their forebears. Even accounts that at the time were aimed at championing the values and rights of oppressed people are now seen as fundamentally racist in their assumptions. While an awareness of these problems can enable us to reduce our biases, it must be recognised that what we choose to observe, what we consider to be data, what we write about and how will always be affected by our personal and institutional values, and the underlying assumptions absorbed through our training.

In response to the realisation that values have affected the whole approach to research, some researchers have argued that if more objective values could be developed, research that is more 'value-free' could be done. Others have elaborated counter-cultural values, believing either that these are 'right', or that they might at least help to balance scholarship. But there has recently been more thinking in this area. One important advance has been through realising that the researcher is a social actor in the situation studied, with an identity and a personality, who affects what people do and say. This insight has proved relevant to a wide range of research problematics, and has been applied to such issues as agricultural development in Drinkwater and Wilson (forthcoming). Focusing on the day-to-day processes by which the understanding of situations is carved out, this reflexivity links ethical concerns about presenting 'truth' with concerns for the nature of relationships between the fieldworker and the people studied.

12.1.2 *Advocacy and truth*

The growing severity of economic and social crises for many populations in developing countries has stimulated debates about the need for 'advocacy' on their behalf. For some, research is one of the few ways to enable the voices of certain oppressed groups to be heard, and hence can provide 'weapons for the kind of non-armed struggle in which indigenous and support organisations are engaged' (Wright 1988). When I started field research I subscribed to this view, since I had already lived in rural Africa and had observed the negative effects of extraordinarily ignorant perceptions held by powerful outsiders. However, the experience of fieldwork has made me believe that there is no single, authentic, indigenous voice or reality that the researcher can discover and present to the world. Such things can often be the stuff of romantic myths, at best useless, at worst dangerous. Researching in an 'ethical manner' seems not about proclaiming good and evil, but about enabling the reader to hear the voices and appreciate the actions of as many of the different people involved as possible. Furthermore, the researcher should 'seek to comprehend the context of local interests'; that is, why people conflict over certain things in certain ways, and why and how people with different access to power interact in the way they do: indeed, this 'context' should also be presented explicitly to the reader in the analysis (Hastrup and Elass 1990).

The more 'ethical' researcher is not necessarily the most vocal and eloquent advocate for a particular cause – however noble this might initially seem – but rather is the one who makes the most rigorous application of methods enabling objective understanding (cf. Aberle 1989). This is not because we live in an amoral, relativistic world (Grillo 1990), or because everyone is approximately equally right and wrong and the 'truth' lies between them. It is because such research ultimately has the greatest potential to identify actual processes and relationships: it provides the most powerful critique of the use of power and ideology, and the greatest potential for progressive social actors to take a situation forward on the basis of real understanding. The presentation of reality is the professional role of researchers, but they also have obligations to engage themselves in political debates and social movements. It is in this wider arena, as citizens rather than directly in their texts, that researchers can best offer their understandings as a source for advocacy and action.

While arguing that 'ethical' research demands that researchers aim at 'getting to the bottom of things', so as to present an accurate and complete picture of the chosen topic, I do not wish to pass over the fact that this creates tensions with the people studied. Nobody likes to be investigated, to have somebody try to reveal ultimate truths about their conceptions of themselves, their relationships and their activities. And how can we ignore the powerful and amusing insights of Douglas (1976) into the way people have good reasons for wanting to reveal least about the things that are most important to them? (These are 'money, power and sex' according to Douglas, an American sociologist who therefore considers these to be the main focus for research.) Since people typically spin webs of misinformation and obfuscation, both intentionally and unintentionally, that are extremely hard to penetrate in fieldwork, the researcher has to delve behind what people actually admit. To help fieldworkers do this, Douglas presents a suite of 'investigative' methods for penetrating fronts and lies.

The researcher equipped with an 'investigative' methodology has both a wonderful time, and an uneasy conscience. The belief that everyone has something to hide (and that the researcher has the capacity to find this out) usually turns up excellent and often amusing material. But driven to ever greater suspicion – and discovery – the researcher can quickly become cynical. Research too easily becomes the desire to expose the smallness of people, the meanness of power, and the inability of societies to create systems sustaining their values (especially their better ones) and binding their members. While this must be recognised and dealt with, it is not the whole story of the human condition. Helpful here is work like O'Neill (1975), which is a marvellous plea for research to cease merely dissecting and judging people. In the words of one of O'Neill's reviewers (Dawe 1975):

> Modern sociology suffers nothing and celebrates nothing. It suppresses the great commonplaces of love and hate, joy and grief, time and place, care and concern. It suppresses the social world. And it is to the suffering and the celebration that [O'Neill] asks sociology to address its care; not to dominate, to legislate for or to disembowel the lives which constitute its world, but to pay its due to those lives, to converse with them, to commune with them, to respect them, to show proper humility before them.

Professor O'Neill is probably right to describe what he does as 'wild sociology'. Yet asking us to consider those we study as whole people, dwelling in a real world and seeking and deserving meaning seems to me to be both sensible and ethical. But would a study of Nazis require such a treatment, a treatment in which they are allowed to present themselves as people carving out a purpose for themselves in life? Recently anthropologists have debated work on New Zealand settlers that appeared to reviewers as 'celebratory', because it presented the people as members of a creative and environmentally sensitive society, and ignored the fact that the population and their ideology are fundamentally 'illegitimate' since they are based on the ousting of 'indigenous' people (*Anthropology Today* 1990). To me the lesson is that both the authors and the reviewers were at fault: the reviewers because we must study people as human beings and not as (judged) economic and political processes, and the authors because ethical research must critique as well as acknowledge the foundations of the society studied.

12.1.3 *Brokerage*

Researchers need to be sensitive about the role of information broker, which they are often offered during fieldwork. (By 'broker' I mean a non-controversial or non-partisan advocate.) This role can seem very attractive. Your counsel is sought by powerful outside actors, saying that they would like to do good, but simply need information. Researchers in this situation should remind themselves of the limitations of their knowledge and judgement. Besides, despite the best intentions of many representatives of governments and agencies, major decisions are rarely shaped by the actual needs or situation of powerless recipients. Even worse, information is often misinterpreted or misused. Most important of all, however, is that the real problem in the flow of information is not lack of expertise but the absence of democracy. The use of brokers, the deployment of consultants and the seeking of advice by 'area specialists' are often presented as ways of ensuring the airing of people's wishes or of 'objectively' determining their needs. Yet if policies are really to be of benefit, those people – who are the real experts – need to have a voice themselves, rather than being represented by a broker chosen and perhaps paid by outsiders. Researchers working for outside bodies play a genuine role only if they work to reorientate attitudes and structures towards allowing local people to take more power. However, as Emmanuel Marx (1987) has eloquently illustrated from his own experience, acting as a broker can, on the contrary, all too easily result both in the researcher gaining authority and initiative at the expense of local people, and in a bureaucratic incorporation of the people which brings progress to a halt.

12.1.4 *Contract research*

This brings us to a discussion of 'contract research', in which the funders or facilitators of research have specific financial or political interests in its outcome. Undertaking research on contract raises serious ethical questions about the use of scholarship, as well as occasionally providing significant opportunities to improve situations. As the 'development business' continues to expand financially and politically, and becomes increasingly institutionalised, its information needs grow. Since this information must be tailored to particular (and changing) development fashions and institutional needs, there is strong pressure to hire researchers on direct contracts with narrow terms of reference. Most 'research' of this kind is intended to justify and validate the approach of the agency involved, or to enhance its claim to the control of a particular programme. Sponsors may not accept certain research methods (such as talking to 'beneficiaries'), rule out certain kinds of evidence, quibble about emphasis and tone, and demand that the report be confidential. If a report does not support their particular line, the agency can bury it, rewrite it or bring in a new researcher to do it over again. Some consultants talk openly of having changed key conclusions to appease funders. Survival for such researchers is dependent upon future contracts, and this limits their freedom to negotiate or 'hold out' on principle. These considerable constraints notwithstanding, some researchers have found ways to conduct contract research professionally and to make valuable contributions, and some sponsors do provide independence. Clearly, however, and even more than other kinds of research, contract research requires an ethically diligent and thoughtful approach.

12.2 Being ethical while collecting data

Ethical problems always arise within the process of 'collecting data', however noble the purpose of the exercise. These involve such things as 'consent' (how and what the people studied really allow you to observe and convert into data), what actual research methods are acceptable, how to handle anonymity and confidentiality, and how people are generally involved in the research enterprise. Also important is the responsibility of fieldworkers to their research assistants.

12.2.1 *Obtaining consent*

The codes of ethics of the major professional societies are clear about the requirement for 'consent' to be obtained that is genuinely 'informed'. Fieldworkers must explain to the people being researched the purpose of their study, who has funded and supported it, how the data will be collected and how the results may be used. They should explain how they will maintain anonymity and/or confidentiality, and they should find out from the population in general, and from individuals, which matters should be kept confidential. Fieldworkers should also ensure that consent derives from the actual people involved, not just officials or leaders. Needless to say, achieving all of these is difficult. The understanding of both the researcher and the subjects about what the research is really about are likely to undergo considerable changes during a period of fieldwork, so that consent has to be continually renegotiated. As the study progresses, it also becomes harder for both researcher and subjects to make any issue 'out of bounds' for study.

To ensure that consent is really 'informed', regular meetings should be held with all concerned. It seems best to be open and detailed, but not agonising. With the help of key informants, local leaders and research assistants, fieldworkers must struggle to understand how people perceive them and the research issues so that communication on these occasions can be effective. Furthermore, to maintain 'informed consent', researchers must be prepared to spend time continually explaining to people individually and collectively why they need certain kinds of data. Finally, researchers should realise that what is said about them by local officials and the people they are personally closest to will be critical, so that such people should be especially well briefed.

To understand the research process, local people need to know more than the hypothesis or issue in question. They want to understand why people wander around the world studying it, and particularly why they want to live in their village to do so. Something I often do to provide a justification for wanting to live with people and share their world is to emphasise that most 'researchers' and policy makers do not. I can then tell people what these outsiders and policy makers are saying, and show other people's reports to those literate in English. The superficiality of these reports, their lack of consideration of the significance of local dynamics, and the absurdity of many statements made on local practices usually provide more than sufficient explanation for seeking the truth through fieldwork. Examining such studies also provides a foundation on which to discuss with people the actual current relationships between the generation of data and the design and implementation of policies. This can help to explain both the researcher's purpose and his or her method.

12.2.2 *Covert methods*

I have emphasised above that 'investigative' methods are necessary for discovering truth and hence achieving balanced, ethical research. How does this square with 'informed consent'? At an elementary level, people can be told that in order to get an accurate picture you need to see things for yourself and talk to everyone involved. This can take you far, so long as it is accompanied with humour, and is in the style neither of a policeman/court (to catch and punish) nor of a journalist or gossip (to publicise). Nevertheless, covert research is sometimes needed, because people who are aware of being observed tend to report or behave in a biased fashion, either wilfully or subconsciously. (If a researcher attempts to observe a work routine, for example, people will almost certainly alter it.) In other situations, the researcher requires information about something that those doing it would prefer to keep secret. These two contrasting needs for covert investigation require separate discussion, though many things fall somewhere in between.

Covert research techniques are not necessarily ethically illegitimate, provided that they are not too personally intrusive, that the people studied have agreed to the topic concerned being investigated, and that there is no other way of getting the data. In one study of refugees, for example, people interviewed persistently complained that they had inadequate domestic utensils for preparing and cooking food. They wanted our study to demonstrate this, because their claims were denied by the agencies assisting them. Given the nature of the dispute, refugees would not give us satisfactory answers when asked directly about domestic utensil ownership, often denying they had anything at all even if some items were visible. Our solution, given that we had no opportunity in this case to establish relations of trust, was to inform them that we wished to measure the internal area of their huts. Having gained access to their homes, we could then covertly note all their utensils. The study showed that there were inadequate numbers of domestic utensils, though there were more than people had admitted when asked directly. Given its method, the study convinced the appropriate authorities that people lacked the equipment to process the kind of food aid being provided to them. Although I have been criticised for doing the study in this way, I regard it as a difficult but ultimately legitimate way of proving something people wanted established.

Secretly researching things that people want to keep private is more difficult to justify. Undertaking fieldwork means you are always 'seeing things' and being 'told things'. I would not pretend to shut my eyes or ears whenever something seems fishy. The question that really arises is whether to investigate something further, and whether (and how) to write about it. Some of the criteria I would use are the relationship of the phenomenon to my research questions, the likely effects of revealing what is happening, and the degree to which different people want to keep it a secret. I am not sure whether it is possible to be entirely rigorous about such decisions. I seem to end up investigating and revealing abuses of power by the powerful, and neat little illegal strategies by the weak. It is very useful to be sufficiently close to people to be able to get guidance from them whether to reveal, for example, that people are only pretending to follow the livestock grazing regime stipulated by the government. It is worth noting that different individuals and interest groups will have very different opinions on the matter.

12.2.3 *Confidentiality and anonymity*

Researchers need to think hard about when and how to maintain confidentiality and anonymity. Confidentiality – not revealing facts elicited through field research – seems necessary only in particular situations. In my research, I make no general promises of confidentiality to my informants – on the contrary, I emphasise that I want people to tell me things precisely so that they can be made known. However, I generally avoid providing unnecessary details if there is any reason to suppose this could be used against the informant or population.

Anonymity – not revealing the identities of informants – is another matter. I see no virtue in revealing people's names, or even initials. Only in the case of very prominent people is it difficult to give a few cleverly chosen details that provide readers with the context for a person's activities or statements without compromising his or her actual identity. The names of people are only ever useful to other researchers in follow-up studies; otherwise printing them is simply an invitation for gossip, comment or litigation, without any academic benefits. I do not even write the names of informants in notebooks when I have no reason to do so, especially in my research on refugees. I always emphasise this to informants (and it is generally welcomed), and during research I also take care not to reveal verbally who exactly is providing me with 'good' information. (I do credit people by name when referring to their theoretical insights and explanations of phenomena, since in this case one is dealing with personal communications from fellow intellectuals. But even in this case, I maintain the anonymity of people where the remarks could be politically compromising. One of my papers (Wilson 1988) is constructed entirely from quotations of the scientific theories of named local people.)

Maintaining anonymity also includes dealing with the fact that research assistants have access to data, and are usually permanent members of the community. It is easy to tell them not to reveal anything they are discovering to others, but it is difficult for them not to learn about the people they live with, and not to use this knowledge in their relationships with the community. For example, when I started research in Zimbabwe I did not know that women's names are a secret. Several research assistants learnt their mother's names for the first time during my first-round census, but I can hardly now resolve this by telling them that they should forget or ignore anything they learnt through the study! Sometimes researchers should avoid asking certain kinds of question with certain assistants and in some cases, it they have the language skills, researchers should ask those questions without an assistant present. Fieldworkers should try to ensure that notebooks containing sensitive information are not open-access, while avoiding being rude or embarrassing close associates.

12.2.4 *Sharing experience*

Achieving consent for the research is a long way from having local people interested and committed to what is being done. While fieldworkers must accept that locals have the right to consider both them and the research topic boring, and the methods tedious, they should nevertheless make a serious attempt to generate local interest, or adapt their research accordingly. Making the research process interesting for those studied is extremely helpful to the researcher. However, it should also be done because most of the 'benefits' that will arise from the study for local people, limited as they probably will be, will come from the human contact and intellectual stimulation in the actual fieldwork process. Researchers must share of themselves and their world, and be as prepared to entertain and be studied as they hope local people will be.

But relating to people is not only about feeling free to 'share the cup of human happiness'. Researchers also need to think about how they will relate to people regarding forces threatening their lives, such as drought, economic collapse, political oppression and persecution, or forced relocation. Sanadjian (1990), for example, explores the 'gap' created by the fact that it was highly dangerous for both himself and his informants to discuss national politics in post-revolution Iran, while it was meaningless to live with people through those years pretending to have no personal or intellectual concern with the changes happening in their daily lives.[4]

12.2.5 *Some ways of being useful*

During fieldwork researchers have to make decisions about the extent to which their research can usefully address different people's needs. In terms of benefits to local people, too much stress is generally put on the value of the 'products' of research, rather than its 'process'. Engaging creatively in community life is often the most effective way of having a positive impact on an area through fieldwork.

A first priority must be to make the daily experience of the research as enjoyable as possible for all concerned. Be interested in 'them' as people as well as data, share genuinely of yourself, be prepared to grow together with people, and develop your sense of humour. Locals remember researchers and 'learn' from them through their personal relationships – not their monographs. Fieldwork as a cross-cultural endeavour is an opportunity for those studied as well as for the researcher.

Secondly, throughout your work be open in informing people about your growing understanding of the situation, and tell them what you will be writing about. In my experience, people are fascinated and engage intellectually in a highly stimulating manner. Before leaving, organise meetings with members of the community and officials (both as groups and individually) to share your main findings and elicit their reactions. In addition to enabling you to convey your thanks and learn more from them as partners in the research process, such presentations can act as catalysts to local debate. Even if your presentation is limited it can enable, for example, the views of powerless groups in the population to be articulated alongside those of the dominant, and thus contribute to the initiation of developments in the future. If possible, leave (or promptly send) a short, simple summary of your main work and preliminary findings. Try to translate this where necessary.

Thirdly, if there are community projects that you wish to support, I recommend looking into this during the latter part of the fieldwork. I would not advise moving too quickly into supporting projects – both because you may not understand some of the implications early on (for example, the project may be controlled by one faction in the village) and also because, if your aim is research, you must first establish your identity as a researcher. The argument for starting things some time before you go is that this leaves enough time for your contribution to overcome administrative hurdles. Doing something practical is really worthwhile, especially when it is simple and fits in to local institutional frameworks.

A popular way of thanking a community for their support and tolerance is through the organisation of a 'feast', in which great care is taken to ensure everyone comes and the distributors of food are carefully selected. While recommending this as an option, there is the cautionary tale of one anthropologist who reported a dismal failure due to the fact that he had not realised that in his study area people only attended the feasts of people considered superior to them!

Sometimes the ethically concerned fieldworker will be under pressure to engage directly in a situation. On one occasion, my research assistants went to rough up a man who had abandoned his semi-blind wife and her baby to slow starvation. (I was personally opposed to the use of violence, and encouraged them to concentrate on shaming him, but I never determined what exactly happened.) In another case I made the decision to visit a home at night – highly unusual in this part of Africa – in order to demonstrate to a woman that I knew she was forcing her aging father to sleep outside, as part of a range of deprivations. Being a member of another society, albeit temporarily, does not mean the suspension of a personal moral code.

Researchers should always be ready to do for the community things for which they have a particular capacity because of skills or contacts. For example, on one occasion I was able to discover a trickster who had established himself at a nearby school, pretending to be an MA student from Cambridge doing his teaching practice. I foiled him just as he was collecting what he said were the examination fees for the A-level stream he had established there!

12.2.6 *Research assistants*

Most researchers would agree that their field assistants have been absolutely key to the direction and success of their research. Quite apart from wanting to be ethical, it therefore pays to make sure they believe in the work, and feel that they are being treated fairly by you. (Note that I say 'fairly', not 'nicely', and I will point out below that the relationship can easily be compromised if, for example, the field assistant is showered with gifts that cannot be reciprocated.) A sound professional relationship is the best foundation for a good personal one, and this means demanding of them what they can do, and making the working environment pleasant and the job rewarding. It also means protecting them. Few researchers are sufficiently aware of the risks their assistants sometimes face. Field assistants are often blamed for the real and imagined crimes of researchers, and for the fact that researchers found things out that are not compatible with official views. On one salutary occasion, my field assistant was arrested after my departure from an area, because I had not adequately cleared my activities with certain local authorities. I discovered too late that he had been detained for some time and ended up losing his other job. This was an example where sloppy planning by a researcher was responsible for the suffering of an assistant. At other times the situation is almost unavoidable. One researcher working in a rural area of Zambia was unlucky enough to have the military of a white minority regime raid a thousand miles into the area to kill some refugees. This meant he was arrested on suspicion, but though he was quickly released his assistant was very badly tortured, despite his remonstrations with the authorities, and has never fully recovered.

Between the two extremes of the 'unavoidable' and the effects of 'inadequate forethought', there is much that a researcher can do to protect assistants. Strategies depend on context. In one situation, in a country with a highly developed sense of secrecy, I decided to keep the host country national (who worked with us as an equal) as an apparently insignificant subordinate, in case we inadvertently offended the government and he was blamed. In situations where research is likely to be highly critical I try to work with a large number of assistants at different times, with a variety of local statuses, so as to avoid victimisation. I once used this in a situation where a Western non-governmental agency had accrued considerable authority, and had demonstrated the inclination to engineer the dismissal or harassment of any local person they suspected of 'spilling the beans' on their many shortcomings. Finally, researchers should not put pressure on assistants to interpret events and to spell out the implications. Assistants should be allowed to feel secure that all they did was to interpret word by word, and transmit the facts according to their contracts, and did not operate as 'informers'.

12.3 Personal relationships with local people: making them work and making them ethical

One of the great strengths of fieldwork is the entry it provides into the social world of the people studied, through direct human relationships. Indeed, for long-term fieldwork such an engagement is vital if the population is to tolerate 'being studied'. The creation of relationships that are based on mutual respect and openness is essential for ethical fieldwork, because otherwise the researcher cannot hope to find out about local people's concerns, nor get advice about how to address them. It is also the most powerful way in which researchers can really learn that the people they study are human beings, not things that are 'poor', 'investing', 'oppressed', 'adapting' or anything else.

Personal relationships with the family in which one lives, with research assistants and with other close associates are a major influence on a researcher's understanding. But it is important to be aware from the outset that there will be tensions between these relationships as sources of human companionship, and as sources of data and access to the society. One researcher told me that her relationships were poisoned by her over-riding sense that she ought to be nice to everybody all the time, something she did not realise she was doing until she came back home and felt the relief of being able to be natural. Local people, too, may have prejudices that are difficult for the researcher to overcome, leading to frustration on both sides. There can also be an awkward sense of 'being studied' that makes it problematic for local people to express their true feelings. Finally, asymmetries in the power and expectations of the two parties can put relationships on an uneasy foundation. The reason why this is the case is now examined.

12.3.1 *Asymmetric friendships*

Many fieldworkers report having experienced a companionship with people that seemed greatly more authentic than that 'at home'. This may in part reflect how levels of personal intimacy are dependent upon social context, and Western elite society is notoriously individualistic, so that relationships tend towards the casual and expedient (Cohen 1961). However, further factors reflecting subtle aspects of power relations are likely to be important in making fieldwork relationships apparently attractive and meaningful for researchers.

First, relations between researchers and local people are non-competitive, because both parties retain a sense that they operate and achieve in different worlds. Secondly, researchers usually feel able to relate in a less guarded fashion during fieldwork. They often do not feel a need to act so as to impress; and they express themselves with less fear of judgement. This happens for several reasons. One is that researchers are too often engaged only at a symbolic level with the researched population: they may not even consider that the researched are actually people who are assessing and judging them. Related to this is the skilful way in which powerless people manipulate the powerful and make them feel secure, a skill developed for dealing with local leaders, officials and the police (Last 1990). I have experienced the way this increases both the enjoyment of the locals and the openness (and hence manageability) of the researcher.

Finally, in many cases the researcher cares little whether local assessments of the research are positive or not. In part this is because the people or institutions that have power and matter to the researcher will not hear or heed local views. But there is another component. The self-esteem of the researcher is derived elsewhere, rather than from what local people think of her or him. Even researchers who are perennial 'doubters' tend to take solace in the notion that at least they are 'genuine' for doubting! Yet it is still their reasoning, rather than the views of local people, that makes them decide whether they are right to be engaging in fieldwork. Working ethically with people requires the researcher to overcome this gap, generated by the fact that they do not consider themselves to belong to the same moral and social field as those studied.

Overcoming the distance between researchers and their close local associates is facilitated by moments of genuine human encounter. These might be associated with dramatic life events or even falling in love, through which symbolic barriers and structural distance are breached. Alternatively, the transformatory experience of setting and struggling to meet joint objectives can have enormous personal impact (see 'Pepetela' 1983). At any rate, people in all sorts of problematic and asymmetric situations clearly do strike up genuine friendships of enormous richness. But such relationships can still remain pregnant with tensions, to which I now turn.

Eisenstadt and Roniger (1984) explore the tension between the trust, empathy and intimacy that are sought in friendship, and the institutional order of economic and political power relations that inevitably influence it. Both researcher and local person (such as a research assistant) are under pressure to get certain things out of the relationship, both for themselves and for their own network of friends and institutions. The research assistant may be obliged to seek jobs for his or her relatives or help for his or her sick mother, and to provide a view of local history that reflects well on his or her particular social group. The researcher may be obliged to request the research assistant to work extra hard to make up for funding shortfalls and the deadlines of sponsoring institutions, and to gain access to reticent informants. This need puts pressure on a fieldworker to adopt an attitude of mind in which special help is 'traded' with assistants at the expense of themselves and the wider society. For researchers who consider themselves social radicals, individual friendships and relationships with research assistants become symbolic of their non-exploitative and non-material involvement with members of the local society. The manner in which they become 'institutionalised within the explicit political-economic order' of control and exploitation, as Eisenstadt and Roniger (1984, pp. 15–16) put it, is both disappointing and threatening. If it leads to denial or self-delusion, the relationship can become even more problematic.

The third element of tension identified by Eisenstadt and Roniger is that relationships that develop as an authentic expression of human values (in the cultural context of the society studied) become a challenge to the gulf between the powerful and the powerless, and are thus subversive to the wider social order. Exactly how each party considers the relationship as 'subversive' can add further tensions. The local person may be seeking legitimacy and the right to social elevation into equality on a higher plane. The researcher, on the other hand, may be seeking a rejection of 'status', or acceptance into the social milieu on the 'indigenous' plane. Where social movements exist that provide a distinct critique of relationships between people of different status, race or suchlike, much sharper conceptualisation by fieldworkers is necessary to construct relationships if they are to avoid stereotyping.

12.3.2 *The economics of relationships*

Fieldworkers soon realise that they cannot be social members of the community without an economic engagement. A researcher who decides to share nothing, give nothing, help nobody and demand nothing will not be considered as a member of that society. The question for most researchers is how to affirm their social membership of a community without distorting it by their peculiar access to wealth and power. Giving things in most societies establishes relations of status, and generates patronage. If it is intended to maintain a relationship as egalitarian, then only gifts that can be reciprocated should be given. For example, at one time I used to supply a fisherman with net-weaving twine following my occasional visits to the capital; for his part he would send me prize fish. In this case, we could both give, and gave only at times of special opportunity. If he had provided me with ordinary fish it would have appeared that he was under my patronage, or that he wanted me to do something for him. If I had been travelling regularly and given him a large amount of twine, he would have been unable to reciprocate, and so would have become my client.

Westerners often have difficulty in understanding local principles of gift exchange, confusing them with Western concepts of generosity, which are based on the ability of the giver and the need of the recipient. Rural societies in the 'Third World', by contrast, tend to have greater concern for the structural relationship between giver and receiver, including genealogical relations. The socialisation of a fieldworker into the community generally requires that she or he be allocated fictive genealogical relationships with people, which are hard for the researcher to comprehend fully. This adds to the difficulty of knowing what to give to whom, and when. To make matters worse, what is given (and how much) is of great importance in such societies, and a sense of insult, competition and jealousy may erupt if giving is not done appropriately. The strategy of some researchers – to give everyone the same gift in the hope that this will satisfy everyone – is therefore also doomed to failure.

I have argued that gift giving – where not reciprocated – tends to take a relationship out of a situation of equality into one of patronage. As if this is not distressing enough for the fieldworker, she or he is soon made aware that another gift is required to prevent the new relationship from deteriorating. Rather than going back to one of egalitarian friendship, a patronage relationship that falls into disrepair leaves the client frustrated: 'Does he really think I am so small and so cheap that one dress is enough for a whole year!'. To maintain the new relationship often requires ever greater gifts at ever increasing frequency. The researcher may find that the recipients of gifts seek to marginalise others – to monopolise the researcher-patron – so that resentment and bitterness can emerge in former friends who were not given gifts. It can become a most depressing scenario for the researcher, who, unlike members of the local population, usually has little experience in making something positive out of a patron–client relationship, and clings to an ideological commitment to equality.

The lesson here is for researchers to think very carefully about how and why they engage in gift giving. Practical solutions must be derived from thoughtful application of local knowledge and advice. Gifts to individuals are not a good way of saying 'thank you' to the community as a whole. I have described (in Section 12.2.5) some better ways of meeting your obligations to the wider community.

12.3.3 *Relations with local destitutes*

Fieldworkers should know the destitutes in the community studied as part of understanding the economy and society of the area. On the basis of such knowledge, fieldworkers can then make appropriate contributions to their welfare, in the same manner as other members of the society do, including, for example, giving transport to a clinic, a listening ear and an occasional gift of food or clothing. Such aid should be given quietly, but not necessarily secretly, and in the manner deemed appropriate in that society. This should be done not only for humanitarian reasons, but because if you do not it is a demonstration to local people that you are selfish and not desirous of becoming a part of the community. As in other aspects of this discussion of gift giving, being 'ethical' is advised for practical as well as moral reasons.

12.3.4 *Relations with security forces*

A final group of social relationships in the field is that of those with the local police, army, party officials and government informers. It is a mistake to assume that such people should be avoided at all costs. Assuming that you are not doing research specifically to undermine the government politically, it is wise to give such people a full account of your activities. (If you are trying to undermine the state, and still call what you are doing 'research', then you need a rather different 'thinking about ethics' paper to this one!) Locals will also want to know that the research is understood by – and receives the blessing of – the security services, so that they will not be blamed for collaboration. I have even used security officials as field assistants on occasion, and when approached in the right way, the experience has always been positive. Never forget that such people often sympathise with local concerns, are knowledgeable, and can be genuinely interested and helpful. But also do not be naive. Even if you never 'discover' anything, being open about something that is happening in an area (such as smuggling) might force the authorities into taking action when it had previously been tolerated.

12.4 Ethics in writing up and disengaging

Most fieldworkers find the shift from fieldwork to writing up difficult. One reason for this concerns the complex ethical dilemmas at this stage. There are pressures from academia requiring of the researcher 'ideas' – indeed, 'ideas' embedded in 'established theory'. Meanwhile the researcher has had a rich and confused experience, and is consumed by an enormous sense of the immediate details of real life – hardly acceptable material for academic texts. The researcher generally finds difficulties with converting real people and real events into data points, which all too often have to be uni-dimensional. These difficulties derive partly from the fact that the researcher does not yet have a 'critical distance' on events, but mainly from the fact that she or he actually remembers 'real life' rather too well. She or he still doubts the legitimacy of 'pronouncing' on what she or he knows was a profoundly messy reality. The researcher usually has to go through a process of resocialisation into the values of his or her particular academic sub-discipline. This can accentuate other ethical dilemmas faced in the process of disengagement.

While transposing the real-life experience of fieldwork into data and theories, many researchers think critically about what benefits have accrued to the people who were the focus of the study. Sometimes these questions reflect researchers taking themselves rather too seriously; wallowing in the struggle to write up. But this kind of thinking is essential if researchers wish to maintain an engagement with the world of the people they studied, which I do think is positive. If it does not start happening at this stage, then the human element of the fieldwork experience will quickly be submerged, and if any ethical considerations remain they will be dealt with on the basis of a 'sense of contract', rather than a personal commitment. Therefore, it is important to identify early on realistic ways of 'giving something back', in addition to those already discussed.

12.4.1 *Getting information out quickly*

One possible activity on departure is to seek immediate outlets for information, where this is necessary or desirable. Local or international press, radio, international human rights organisations, governments, relief agencies and concerned groups of various kinds may all be able to use your information towards clarifying and resolving problems in the area concerned. Direct field data on current events can be of tremendous value and should not be filed away without further thought. However, it is wise to be aware that 'outside' institutions are often the causes of the problems in the first place, and that any information given can be distorted and used in all manner of ways. This can happen even if they seem 'very nice' people. Also remember that little given in confidence remains private and unattributed; always be ready for it to be revealed that you were responsible for releasing it.

In presenting information, researchers need to think carefully about what is the best way to get things done. I learnt a lesson when on one occasion I thought that the international agency charged with responsibility would be more likely to see that abuses were dealt with than would the government if it was informed directly. In fact, the agency officially denied the existence of the abuses, even though some came from the files of its own officers, and the one that I had taken to local government was investigated and dealt with on the spot.

Before disseminating information through non-academic channels, carefully consider the risks and benefits for the area studied (especially to the people who assisted you). The more uncertain you are about the risks of negative repercussions, the greater have to be the anticipated benefits, and the more certain you should be about your facts. Also beware for your own 'reputation' as a scholar, and consider the reputation of 'scholarship'. Two examples illustrate this point. A researcher found that an international agency was delivering assistance to a population in a highly ineffective way, and that a large amount of the aid was going to the military. Not only did the agency deny the charges, they employed other researchers (as consultants) with fewer scruples to try to discredit her. It was only through prolonged and bitter struggle that she maintained her reputation and published. (Having support from two institutions was key, otherwise she might well have failed.) A second researcher made statements about a country that upset the administration not only because he revealed unpalatable facts, but also because he had sought permission to enter a sensitive area on entirely unrelated grounds. This led to government reluctance to permit other *bona fide* researchers into the area. Researchers should not think that their research clearance to work on millet farming necessarily extends to their having the right to investigate and protest about the arrest of prominent political activists.

12.4.2 *Depositing copies of fieldnotes locally*

Far too few researchers deposit copies of their fieldnotes in a library or archive in the host country. Yet these may be extremely useful for historical studies, or to enable future critical scholars to examine your own work. This requires consideration, from an early stage of fieldwork, of how the notes could ultimately be used. Personal information, especially that of a sensitive nature, should be recorded in such a manner as to make it as difficult as possible to trace to individuals. Where it is essential to know exactly whom you are referring to, nicknames or codes will often suffice. Protection is especially necessary for prominent people such as chiefs, expatriates, local business-people and councillors, because they are easier to trace. While many field-workers might feel little compunction about revealing the embarrassing or criminal acts of wealthy or important people, everyone deserves equal protection. It is also necessary to take into account possible changes of political regime. It is said that one west African anthropologist's fieldnotes were used to identify the main local supporters of a now deposed government. By leaving behind copies of fieldnotes and papers they write, foreign researchers can work against the stereotype (so often true) of being people who draw from a country materials and the ideas of local intellectuals, providing nothing in return.

12.4.3 *Deciding with people what to write about*

Finally, it is worth finding out what local people would like to see written about while you are still in the field. The questions locals consider important may reveal key features of their society. Responding to the challenge of 'writing for the people studied', before you are obliged to write anything, can give foundation to ethical concerns of how to represent others accurately, yet sympathetically. Most countries, however authoritarian, do have some relatively open newspapers or news magazines that can publish material of local interest.

12.4.4 *Completing the work: completing the relationship?*

The completion of writing up usually brings a great sense of relief. In addition to the academic pressures, researchers often feel that writing up data so arduously collected is something owed to the people studied. The next stage is how to get what has been written back to them. In practice, very few people have systematically sent things back or discussed their analyses with the people they lived with. But those who have, myself included, can confirm that it is a greatly enriching process for all concerned. Do not assume that local people will only be interested in the empirical and the political. One anthropologist reported that what people liked most was what he considered an obscure structuralist symbolic analysis of an aspect of their belief system. Return visits can also be occasions to review the whole research experience, bringing a new level of understanding between researchers and subjects.

Fieldwork is for life. Friendships and responsibilities are created that will stay with you forever. Many researchers still correspond with people from the area they worked in decades later. Several have made follow-up studies, a re-engagement that catapulted them back into the personal relationships of previous years. A few researchers have never made the break and ended up abandoning academia altogether and going back to live with the people they studied.

It is increasingly possible for research assistants or members of the local community to come to visit the home countries of researchers. The visits of my former assistants to the United Kingdom have been tremendous occasions, and I will continue to hope for and organise these in future. It certainly helps to complete the circle, and takes the personal relationship forward significantly. You never dispense with the responsibilities of having done fieldwork, or the opportunities for learning and social experience that it generates.

12.5 Conclusion

I entitled this chapter 'thinking about the ethics of fieldwork' because doing ethical fieldwork – and indeed living ethically in general – is not about following prescribed formulae, but precisely about *thinking* over the processes and situations that you are involved in. Although we engage in thinking to seek answers, and without answers we are more likely to behave in a perplexed than an ethical manner, learning can only occur if we start from admitting that we do not know. Therefore this chapter has aimed to encourage thought on ethical issues in fieldwork; the concrete suggestions that I make about how to resolve the dilemmas are perhaps of secondary importance, although I hope they are useful.

Notes

1. The thinking of this paper has been influenced over several years, particularly through discussions with B.E. Harrell-Bond and Florence Shumba. Readings provided by Jayantha Perera for the recent *Social Research Methods* course at the Refugee Studies Programme were also extremely useful, as were his comments on the manuscript.
2. Florence Shumba, who has been a member of a much-researched community, and who has done fieldwork in her own right, commented on this paper by observing:

   > The kind of behaviour researchers have towards locals tells us that really they just want to exploit them and take from them their ideas and information. It also tells us that they don't really care at all. They want the information to use in front of a group of people at home, so that they can be seen as clever academics. Then in the end they publish books, reviews, articles etc., in order to spread their popularities. So what is this, and what is research really about? Not all researchers are exploiters, but most are, and I think it is time up now for this, and that these researchers should also be exploited by local people.

   This is the challenge that we must face up to.
3. Lockwood (Chapter 11 in this volume) discusses this in detail.
4. See also Razavi (Chapter 10 in this volume).

13

Contrasts in village-level fieldwork: Kenya and India

Judith Heyer

Introduction[1]

This chapter contrasts village-level fieldwork in 1961–2 in two very different parts of Kenya, and in 1980 and 1981–2 in Tamil Nadu, south India. It draws on these experiences to argue that no single method is applicable to every fieldwork setting. Every fieldwork situation is different, as are every fieldworker's personality, personal circumstances and research objectives. It follows that much of the advice that is given to fieldworkers beforehand may turn out to be irrelevant or even positively unhelpful. Knowing this, however, and knowing how different people have solved different problems, can prepare fieldworkers for solving their own problems when the time comes. This argument is illustrated in this chapter by focusing on relatively straightforward examples – relationships with government officials; choice and management of research assistants; relations with respondents; and interviewing techniques. The penultimate section comments on similarities and differences between fieldwork in east Africa and south Asia, and briefly considers how one fieldwork experience better prepares one for the next. The chapter concludes with a discussion and restatement of the rationale for fieldwork, arguing that, while fieldwork raises important ethical and political problems, it is also a rich, valuable source of data that usually cannot be obtained in any other way.

The contrasts in this chapter are not only between Africa and India, but also between two very different fieldwork experiences in Africa. In 1961–2 I was doing fieldwork for my Ph.D., I was young and single, and I was full of the confidence that comes from lack of experience as much as anything else. Kenya was on the verge of independence, which made the environment in which I was working exciting. The terms under which the research was financed (by the Colonial Social Science Research Council) were a help at a period during which colonial rule was drawing to a close. Had the fieldwork not been financed by an official body, it is unlikely that I would have received permission to undertake it. The fieldwork was part of an economic study of constraints on African agricultural production. What was novel at the time was my decision to obtain the relevant material using methods influenced by anthropology. I worked in two contrasting locations – one Kamba and one Kipsigis – spending a total of 4–5 months in each. Crucial to the success of my fieldwork was the fact that I lived in each area continuously for 2–3 months at the start.

When I set out to do village-level fieldwork in western Tamil Nadu, India, I was an older, more established academic, with three young children who accompanied me. I began with a short period of fieldwork over the summer vacation in 1980, and followed this up with a more substantial period during 1981–2 while on sabbatical leave. I conducted an exploratory study, on the borders of several disciplines, examining the dynamics of the accumulation and distribution of wealth. I was working in an easier political environment with village people who were familiar with the concept of research. My personal circumstances made it necessary to commute daily (by car), rather than living in the fieldwork villages.

13.1 Relationships with government officials

The expatriate fieldworker's first encounter with officials is usually in the course of attempts to obtain visas and research clearance. Once in the country, relationships with national, regional and district level officials can be crucial. They can give useful and sometimes indispensable support, advice and access to information, but they often need to be treated with care. Relationships with the police, internal security and immigration officials may be more difficult than those with technical departments. Interactions with officials living in or frequently visiting the research site can be equally delicate. In some situations it is important not to be seen to be closely associated with officials at the village level, but in others a close relationship can be beneficial.

There is a temptation for village-level fieldworkers not to spend enough time on relationships with officials or on obtaining the secondary information that they can provide. Fieldwork can be very compulsive – it is easy to get into a frame of mind in which it seems to have the only valid claim on one's time. But officials can provide an entrée into many valuable sources of information, as well as being important in all sorts of practical and sometimes unforeseeable ways. Fieldworkers always find themselves having to spend more time than they would like visiting and revisiting offices, sitting around, waiting to complete essential business with officials. Time spent on relationships with bureaucrats over and above this can seem tedious or unnecessary, but can also be unexpectedly productive.

It is increasingly the case that a condition for research clearance is affiliation with a local university. Even where this is not insisted upon, it can be very sensible to obtain an association with a local academic institution. Relationships with people in local universities provide useful inputs into one's research and a link to the local research community. Some of the above points are illustrated below.

In Kenya, in 1961, I had great difficulty obtaining clearance from those involved at the district level with internal security. Local government officials were reluctant to let a solitary white woman move around in the African rural areas, let alone live there. After a point-blank refusal by the District Commissioner in the Kamba case, I had to go to the Deputy Governor in Nairobi to get the District Commissioner to negotiate a compromise that would enable me to go ahead. We eventually agreed that I could work away from the District Headquarters if I took a bodyguard. The bodyguard could be chosen by me but had to be approved by the District Commissioner.

I found a very satisfactory answer to this. A local Indian businessman with whom I had made friends offered me a driver, whom he thought (correctly) would be both suitable and acceptable to the District Commissioner. I went off with the driver, who drove my car, taught me Swahili and kept me company. After 2–3 weeks, I quietly sent him back. I never heard any more from the District Commissioner or anyone else in his office. I suspect that once I was out of the way, they were glad not to have any further dealings with me. By contrast, I never had any difficulties with the technical people, such as the staff at the Department of Agriculture, who were all extremely helpful and cooperative. They took me on some of their field trips and gave me a great deal of their time and access to a substantial amount of material. They understood and supported my project wholeheartedly. At the very local level in Kenya, I had little contact with officials (such as agricultural extension workers or community development assistants). I kept a deliberate distance from them because it was so important at that time not to be seen to be associated with the government in any way.

In Tamil Nadu, I had no problem obtaining permission to work in the areas concerned, despite the fact that my official research clearance never came through. The local university with which I was associated was satisfied by the fact that I had *applied* for clearance. The same was true of the District Collector. It was fortunate that my source of funds had not insisted on clearance before releasing money. (Some do.) However, I had some problems getting information from government offices. Obtaining access to official records involved endless visits to senior officers, towards whom I had to be extremely deferential. Once access was granted, it was usually in the form of information copied by clerks according to my instructions, rather than direct access to the information itself. When I did, occasionally, see original records, this proved immensely valuable.

The local officials who were most important for my research in Tamil Nadu were the village headmen and the village accountants. The village headmen were responsible for tax collection, but the tax records proved not to be especially useful for my purposes. The village accountants maintained records of land ownership and land transfer and were also responsible for estimating acreages under different crops from season to season. This information would have been very valuable for my study. Despite endless attempts, all I ever managed to get from one village accountant was a series of village maps and map references of titles to land without any ownership information, and one year's cropping estimates. Superficially, we were always on good terms, but he had his own reasons for not allowing me to see the records most useful to me. He used a strategy of endless procrastination until the end of my stay, at which point he gave me what turned out to be only a small fraction of what I had hoped to obtain.

13.2 Choosing and working with research assistants

The role research assistants play in fieldwork will differ from study to study. In both my studies (Kenya and Tamil Nadu) I wanted, above all, someone who would work with me as an interpreter – someone through whom I could speak and through whom others could communicate with me. In all my fieldwork sites, I decided against learning the local languages well enough to be able to work in them. One certainly misses a lot not knowing the language – all the subtleties in respondents' answers, and the additional information that is picked up by understanding conversations that are going on around one in the field. But the costs associated with achieving fluency may be sufficiently high to justify a decision not to give priority to this.

Though interpreting was their principal task, my research assistants performed a number of additional functions. They introduced me to rural people, familiarised me with local customs and sensitivities, did a great deal of vital public relations work, provided me with explanations that went far beyond interpreting, gathered information independently, and passed on a wealth of information to which they already had access. They also gave useful advice, and criticism, on many occasions. Because of the importance of these tasks, I have found it useful for my assistants to have a good understanding of the goals of my fieldwork.

Given their role, I have always tried to get my assistants to interpret literally during interviews and conversations with respondents, and then to add insights and additional information afterwards when we are alone. I find it very unsatisfactory if interpreters elaborate on responses during the course of the interviews and interject views of their own. As there is a great temptation for interpreters to do this, I have been very strict in stopping them when there appeared to be any danger of slippage in this respect.

It can be difficult to know how literally research assistants are interpreting, and general tendencies will be easier to spot than particular inaccuracies. (I was especially uneasy about this before I started work in the Indian villages, because I felt that I knew so little about the culture and the setting. I had started with as little, even less, information about the Kenyan rural areas, but I do not remember being as worried.) One soon begins to spot some of the misinterpretation as one picks up key phrases and sentences in the local language. Further, one quickly builds up a sense of consistency, and this makes it easier to pick up quickly things that do not make sense. Although this does not guarantee that there are no problems in this regard, it certainly reduces them.[2] Working with interpreters has the important practical advantage of enabling the researcher to write things down in full, while the interview is going on. In terms of their other responsibilities, the main difficulty I have found is getting my assistants to communicate *all* the most relevant information. It required continual prompting to be sure I obtained as much as I could. It also requires a great deal of understanding and commitment on the part of assistants before they can pick out the particular aspects that are really valuable for the researcher to know.

Given the importance of the research assistant, it is worth spending time choosing one carefully. It is vital to choose someone with whom one can get on. It may be necessary to try out and reject several candidates before finding a suitable person for the job, and to allow for the possibility of letting the individual go if she or he does not work out. But it is not always possible to find an ideal assistant. There can be instances when there is hardly a choice! Sometimes it is necessary to make the best of a bad choice, but this is not always a disaster. There are senses in which this was the case in one of my Kenya areas, as will become clear shortly.

The contrast between the pool of possible research assistants available in Kenya in 1961–2 and those available for fieldwork in India in 1980 and 1981–2 could hardly have been greater. In Kenya, the choice was extremely limited. It was difficult to find people with enough basic education and sufficient command of English who were willing to live and work in the rural areas in which I was interested. In the Kamba area, I ended up with a Nairobi primary schoolteacher who had retired to live in the community in which I worked. In the Kipsigis area, I employed a young community development assistant who was between jobs.

The ex-primary schoolteacher worked well despite the fact that he turned out to be very unpopular locally. This only emerged rather late in the fieldwork. People began telling me that they would not normally speak to him or welcome him into their homes. They were only talking to him when he was with me because he was my mouthpiece. Eventually, I was told (through him!) that they were willing to discuss more sensitive issues with me but only through a young and well-liked primary schoolteacher with whom I had become friends. I continued with the unpopular old man for everyday purposes, and used the young man in his free time for the more sensitive discussions. It was amazing in retrospect how little the old man's unpopularity appeared to affect the bulk of the fieldwork. This was so particularly at the beginning when I was being introduced into a suspicious community.

The first assistant I tried in the Kipsigis area would not interpret literally, and I had to let him go. I then employed the community development assistant. He was not from the locality and resided in a neighbouring market centre for the duration of the fieldwork. He acted as a straightforward interpreter, without intruding his own personality too strongly. He established good relationships in the community, though none of them independently of me. With hindsight, it may have been an advantage that he lived outside the immediate area in which we were working. Although I did not get the benefits of having him living in the community and getting to know some of what went on outside working hours, people did not react adversely to him in his own right. It certainly avoided the problem of being associated with someone who was distinctly unpopular. This could have been more disastrous in the Kipsigis area than in the Kamba area, as my relationships with the Kipsigis were always more problematic. It would have been good, on the other hand, to have had someone whose popularity was a positive advantage.

The other interesting group of 'research assistants' I employed in Kenya were Kamba schoolchildren. I asked them to keep time budget diaries in great detail while I was away working with the Kipsigis. They did this for their own households or their neighbours (only a minority of households in my study had literate schoolchildren at that time). The schoolchildren wrote down everything everyone in the household did each day, in the vernacular. This provided a rich source of information on labour inputs, and on all sorts of other things. Having the diaries in the vernacular opened up a wealth of unexpectedly useful information about crops and agricultural practices that I would not otherwise have encountered.

In Tamil Nadu, the range of possible research assistants was much greater. There were many university graduates, often with masters' degrees, willing and able to work as research assistants at the village level. Some had experience of village-level fieldwork already, if only for their masters' theses. I selected from among people suggested by professors at local universities, but I could also have advertised.

A major problem with the Indian research assistants was that they were also applying for places on further degree courses or for permanent jobs. Consequently, there was no guarantee that they would stay with my project. In the event, I employed three different assistants. I thought it would be devastating to change, but in practice I found it relatively unproblematic. I worked with an agricultural economics student who knew a lot about technical aspects of agriculture, and with two sociologists who provided background information on cultural aspects. Each contributed in a different way to my knowledge and understanding of the area. All were good at performing the role of interpreter. The fact that I was the person who was there all through, while my research assistants were the ones who were changing, reinforced my feeling of direct relationship to the people among whom I was working and gave me added confidence in the lack of interpreter bias.

A second problem concerned caste. The research assistant with whom I did most work with untouchables was someone who, though a member of one of the higher castes himself, had done a master's thesis on untouchables in neighbouring villages. I assumed that he would be able to straddle the communities without any problem. However, when I did get to interviewing untouchables, the most he would do was stand about 10 feet away from the house concerned while I sat on the doorstep or inside. When it came to food, the taboos were especially strong. There was absolutely no question of my assistant eating with untouchables. When I did this, very much against his advice, and at some risk to my relationship with others in the village, he stood outside, waiting patiently, until I had finished eating and 'we could go on with our work'.

Finally, it is worth noting that I have always worked with research assistants who are men. I have appreciated the protection they gave if circumstances were awkward, and the counterweight to the fact that I am a woman. In my fieldwork, the gender of my research assistants has not been of critical importance. In other contexts, of course, gender can be crucial.[3]

It is obviously important to take time over the recruitment and (to a lesser extent with interpreters) training of research assistants. But it is not always clear in advance which particular attributes are important, and other factors, such as their personal standing in the community, will not become apparent until interviewing is well under way. On reflection, it is surprising how little, as well as how much in unexpected ways, the characteristics of my assistants have affected my fieldwork.

13.3 Relationships with rural people

Other contributors to this volume have discussed aspects of the fieldworker–respondent relationship, and it is apparent that these will differ in various locations – and not only because of the unique personality of the fieldworker in each case. Below, I illustrate this point by comparing my relationships with rural people in the two Kenyan locations and in the Indian villages in which I worked. There were many positive aspects to each set of relationships, but for purposes of comparison I will focus here on some of the problems I encountered.

My relationships in the two Kenyan locations were very different. In the Kamba area, one of the main difficulties was being white in a place that was on the verge of independence. This meant that I was an object of great suspicion, variously portrayed as a colonial representative or a spy. The only parallel case of white people living and working in rural areas with which the Kamba were familiar was missionaries, and at my particular fieldwork site they were rather remote. Being a white woman living with a local family was quite outside anyone's experience. But this may have been an advantage. As a woman, I was taken less seriously and hence was not seen as a threat. (It also meant that I had access to both men and women.) It was a great help, too, that I was introduced by the main nationalist political figure in the area at political rallies. I did all I could to dissociate myself from the colonial government. This involved, among other things, asking government officials not to come anywhere near me in my fieldwork area.

It also became clear that any trips I made outside the area were regarded with suspicion. The best I could do, to get myself accepted, was not to go away at all. I stayed in the village without travelling anywhere for several months. However, I quickly learnt that I had friends as well as enemies. Many local people were interested in having me do my study in the area, and from an early stage people anxious to help came to tell me if there were problems, and where. I made it a priority to drop everything to deal with rumours and hostility, by tackling them head on the moment I heard about them. That was what kept the project going.

The Kipsigis among whom I worked were more familiar with the idea of someone doing research. They knew of anthropologists who had lived with and studied other Kipsigis communities. They were not as overtly hostile to the idea that I might be a representative of the colonialists, either. But they were implicitly hostile to the idea that I might represent change, to which they were strongly opposed. Resistance was passive rather than active – the level of cooperation was not as high as among the Kamba. Being more traditional, the Kipsigis also found it difficult to place me in the community. Unlike the Kamba, they seemed unable to treat me as an outsider. I had to have a role that was identifiable in their terms. They ascribed to me the role of an unmarried daughter in the household in which I was living. It was not always easy to live up to this, but by and large it worked.

In Tamil Nadu, people accepted my intentions but were interested in who was behind my research. I had long and interesting discussions in response to questioning about who would pay such obviously large sums to enable me to conduct such work. I also had challenging and rewarding discussions about what research involved, why I was doing it the way I was, and in particular why bi was asking the same questions over and over again. I presented the research as enabling me and others to teach students. This was very different from the way I described my work in Kenya in 1961–2, when I really thought my research might be of some use to the people I was interviewing. I used this argument successfully then, at least in the Kamba area.

A major issue in the Indian villages was caste. I started out thinking it would be a good idea to act as if caste did not exist, and then see how strongly it emerged. This was a mistake. It turned out to be extremely important to be sensitive to caste, right from the beginning. On my first visit to the villages, my research assistant simply refused to let me walk more than a certain distance down one of the village streets, without explaining why. He later told me it was because the upper-caste people in the village would be hostile if they thought I had been to the wrong end of the village before I had established a relationship with them. It took time before he considered that I was well enough established to be able to *walk* to the far end of the village without completely ruining my relationships with the upper-caste group. As for *visiting* the lower-caste groups and untouchables at the far end of the village, that was out of the question for much longer. When the time came, we decided to discuss the problem with some of the more sympathetic upper-caste people. After several rounds of discussion and consultation with others in the village, they recommended that I visit lower-caste households, particularly untouchables, only at the end of the day, and that I then leave the village by the back route and return after at least a night away (to ensure that I had the chance to rid myself of the 'pollution' before setting foot in the upper-caste area again). We did not keep to this very strictly as time went on, but it was a salutary beginning, bringing home to me how careful I had to be where caste sensitivities were concerned. In some parts of India it is impossible to do research that involves visiting households in all caste groups in the same villages.

Problems also arose in the Indian villages from the fact that I was a widow. My research assistants tried to persuade me (unsuccessfully) not to admit to this. Another early problem was a rumour that I was a child-stealer. This was quickly squashed by a couple of visits with my children to the village. Indeed, having my children with me, and taking them to the village from time to time, was extremely helpful in building up village relationships.

It is possible to find ways around many of the problems that arise if one takes the time to do so. Sometimes this is not possible and one has to learn to accept that fact also. In general, I have had overwhelmingly positive experiences of relationships with respondents in the communities I studied.

13.4 Interviewing

13.4.1 *Respondent cooperation*

I obtained nearly all my information in the field through interviewing, supplemented on a few occasions by participant observation. In common with others, I found that rural people like being interviewed far more than might be thought, and that people frequently asked to be interviewed if they were not on the list. My interviews were often not unlike extended conversations, particularly in India. I did not find it a major problem to keep respondents interested, even though, in Kenya at least, I was doing a lot of quite tedious and repetitive work. It is obviously vital to keep interviewees interested and concentrating on the subject matter. This is more difficult if repeated rounds of interviewing are involved, or if the interviews are long and tedious. Solutions to this must be found.[4]

I found it well worth going out of my way to be polite and considerate; to interview people at their convenience; to be prepared to go away and come back again if need be, even if the interview was prearranged; and not to rush people. Much interviewing does not take these things sufficiently into account, partly because research is done on too tight a time schedule, or on too tight a budget. Some interviewers can be domineering, insistent or even bullying. The quality of the material collected is obviously influenced by the interviewer's attitude.

Many fieldworkers have found a willingness to accept food from people in the field a valuable first step in establishing relationships of empathy and trust. Among the things I tried in cases where cooperation was a problem were: staying overnight in one Kamba household that was particularly suspicious; joining a party of old Kipsigis men sitting round a pot of local beer and drinking from a straw that was passed round the circle so that everyone had a turn to drink; letting a group of Tamil women teach me to wear a sari. Seemingly trivial acts like these can make an enormous difference where one needs to break down barriers or establish relationships of trust.

There were many gaps in my data because I did not always retain the interest, cooperation or patience of the people concerned. Such gaps are inevitable, but they can be considerably reduced by doing everything possible to maximise the quality of the interview time.

13.4.2 *Social time during interviews*

In my Indian research sites the concept of work was very much to the fore, and this was most helpful. We would arrive at a house, greet people, sit down and be encouraged to proceed with 'our work'. Only if we wanted to, if we had time, and if we were invited, would we stay on for a social visit. We did so frequently, and learnt a great deal from doing so, but 'work' always had priority in our respondents' minds.

By contrast, in the Kenyan fieldwork (particularly among the Kamba), it was extremely difficult to get people to curtail the social aspects of our visits. Socialising always preceded any possibility of an interview, and it could be rather unproductive and drawn out. We would arrive at a compound, be greeted and seated, whereupon everyone would disappear, leaving us on our own for quite a long time. At the very least our arrival would be the occasion for fetching water and firewood to make tea. Often it would also be the occasion for finding a chicken to kill, prepare and serve, however hard we tried to prevent this. There were times when the interviews seemed endless. It was a continual struggle to try to get people to make compromises, as far as their normal social activities were concerned.

In India, the number of interviews we did in a day, and the amount of ground we covered, never ceased to amaze me after my experiences in Africa. The difference in attitudes towards 'our work' was undoubtedly a major factor.

13.4.3 *'Public' v. 'private' interviews*

It is generally assumed that interviews are best conducted in private. There are in fact advantages as well as disadvantages in having an audience. In practice, there may be little choice either way. In my Kenyan fieldwork, I seldom had anyone other than members of the household present. Compounds were fairly far apart in both Kamba and Kipsigis communities, and passers-by did not come into compounds uninvited. The problem in Kenya was one of getting a public discussion.

In the Indian villages, this situation was reversed, although it varied for different caste and class groups. Because most people lived at close quarters in the villages, many interviews could only be conducted in the presence of onlookers. There was a particular problem with interviews in the centre of the village when school was not in session. The audience would then be augmented by large numbers of schoolchildren, crowding round to listen in. Onlookers would often add to the information provided by the interviewee. They would also correct it. Moreover, surprisingly little of the information I was collecting proved not to be publicly known. Even topics that I expected would be private – credit, dowry gold, etc. – were quite readily discussed in the presence of others. It is important to discover what is and is not in the public domain. This itself is very culturally specific.

It was also the case that the few really powerful, potentially secretive people always ensured that they were interviewed in private, and it was relatively easy for them to do so. Privacy, or lack of privacy, in Indian villages, is very much a matter of location and class. Among the elite, onlookers would be close kin, or neighbours who were also members of the elite. Among the poor, onlookers were rarely a difficulty: most people were simply too busy to listen in. It was the large group in the middle for whom onlookers could be a problem. To get over this, we used to stop people on the road, in their fields, or anywhere where we came upon them on their own, if only for a few minutes before a crowd congregated. This required us to be alert for such opportunities at all times, but we were able to pick up a lot of the 'private' information we needed this way.

13.4.4 *Difficulties with concepts*

A striking contrast between my Kenyan and Indian fieldwork was the difference it made if respondents were used to thinking in similar terms to myself about the subject of the interview. In Kenya, I found that endless questioning was necessary to obtain any of the individual aggregates in which I was interested. I could never get over how much easier it was interviewing people in Indian villages about their economic activities. They used similar concepts and categories to the ones with which I was working, and discussed things among themselves in similar terms. This was undoubtedly related to the greater degree of monetisation of their economy.

An example of this can be taken from questions on purchased agricultural inputs. It took ages in the Kenya locations in 1961–2 to establish whether these were used, in what amounts, how much was spent on them and how much labour would have been involved in applying them. In India, people would respond immediately to similar questions by giving a figure for the total spent on inputs, usually by crop, adding on the cost of the labour associated with their application, if asked. They were continually adding these figures up in their heads for their own purposes, and often also discussed them with friends and neighbours, so they could reproduce them for us quite easily. Another example is the cost of building a house. In the Kenyan locations, we had to go laboriously through every possible item of expenditure to arrive at a rough estimate of the total cost. In the Indian case, the cost would usually have been calculated already, discussed on many occasions and remembered, often for decades after the event.

In neither of these Indian examples was there any reason to think that the aggregated information was any less accurate. But I had to be careful to understand exactly what was or was not included in the calculations. It is obviously important not to accept aggregates unquestioningly, but to follow up with further discussion and questions to be sure that both oneself and one's respondent know precisely what is being talked about.

13.4.5 *Structured v. unstructured interviews*

I have used unstructured interviews much more than structured, but I have always used a combination of both. Some data need to be collected on a systematic basis, and a questionnaire can be crucial to ensuring that they are. It is also a great deal more efficient than having notes in fieldbooks that must be transcribed later. I usually work with a list of questions in my mind, and often also an order in which to ask the questions, building up from easier to more sensitive and difficult information. I have always found it extremely fruitful to keep open the possibility of 'asides', often even inviting them. What appears to be a digression is always worth listening to. Digressions frequently reveal that the assumptions on which the question is based are wrong. They can suggest connections and additional aspects that one had not thought of. Listening to and recording 'asides' has given me many of the surprises that have been most illuminating and crucial. The significance of some of these has only become apparent much later, when doing the analysis. Such material also comes through 'off-the-record' or 'social' conversations. This is the value of really *living* in the community, as opposed to simply working there.

I have also undertaken a limited amount of participant observation. This was an extremely rich source of additional information on the occasions when I chose to engage in it. For example, I learned a great deal from weeding finger millet with a group of Kipsigis women and from picking cotton with groups of Kamba men and women. These experiences gave me a completely new attitude to recorded 'hours of work'.

In summary, it is worth taking time and trouble to get the most out of interviewing. There is a lot one can do to improve its quality, and there are enormous gains from doing so.

13.5 Contrasting fieldwork experiences

13.5.1 *Similarities and differences between Kenyan and Indian fieldwork*

In both my periods of fieldwork I worked in areas in which transport and communications were mostly on foot and by word of mouth, and among people who lived at a very basic level where material goods were concerned. These were people who lived in close proximity to each other and to their work, and who knew a great deal about each other; who were, on the whole, and once they had got over their initial suspicions, open, friendly and hospitable to strangers like myself; who were generous with their time; and who were as curious about me and my world as I was about them and theirs. The interviews were often as interesting to respondents as they were to me; and most people were pleased to be interviewed rather than the reverse. I was working in situations in which a great deal was visible, and in which most people seemed to have no guile, no desire to hide what I really wanted to know. Pockets of hostility were relatively easily dissembled. Openness on my part was nearly always accepted at face value. Few people had any difficulties in accepting my project. Everyday relationships with research assistants were easy as well. My assistants were generous and supportive in their commitment to my work.

Many of the differences between my experiences in India and in Kenya have already been mentioned. The more general points are as follows:

1. The Indian villages in which I worked were less isolated than the Kenyan, despite the extent of migrant labour in Kenya (the migrants were never there, and members of their families rarely left to visit them).
2. The Indian villages were much more differentiated, and self-consciously so. Differentiation had many aspects: caste, economic status, history and experience all played a part. There were a few relatively rich and sophisticated individuals in the Indian villages, and many at the other extreme who were both poor and completely subordinated. The differentiation that existed in the Kenyan environments in which I worked was much less extreme, and much less self-conscious.
3. There was an assumption in Kenya that things I did differently were superior. In India it was the reverse, and cultural differences were more

formalised and difficult to manage. Not knowing how to behave with respect to eating, dress, sitting or moving around was a matter of some importance in India. In Kenya it could not have mattered less.
4. Fieldwork was much quicker and easier in Indian villages.
5. Indian village society was generally more opaque; there were more nuances that were not apparent on the surface.

Overall, the similarities were as striking as the contrasts. There was as much that was common to all three experiences as was different.

13.5.2 *Later v. earlier fieldwork: learning from experience*

My own experiences of fieldwork suggest that there is less direct learning from past experience than might be thought. Many aspects are specific to particular situations for which previous fieldwork provides little or no preparation, especially if one thinks all will be easy the second time round. What succeeds in one place often fails in another. What is a problem in one locality is not in the other – new, quite unexpected problems emerge instead. But in a general and indirect sense, one certainly does learn from prior experience of doing fieldwork. One learns confidence, and an assurance of the value of fieldwork. There are also a number of somewhat more specific lessons.

One learns to take seriously maintaining good relations with the community, even if this takes up a good deal of time. One learns not to be over-ambitious, not to expect too much (or too little). One finds that patience is often called upon, and nearly always rewarded, and that persistence pays off. One learns to welcome being surprised, and being proved wrong. One gains the confidence and the knowledge that there are usually ways around what at first seem insuperable problems – and that there will always be aspects that will go better than planned, as well as those that might go unexpectedly wrong. One also acquires practical fieldwork skills such as interviewing techniques and how to get the best from research assistants. Most important of all, one learns the value of being flexible and ready to learn, and to improvise.

13.6 Conclusion: the case for fieldwork

This chapter refers to non-action, non-participant research, and to research done in an academic context. It is normally justified as advancing understanding of rural communities, and informing policy relating to them. The fieldworker never quite knows what influence the research will have, or even whether it will have any influence at all. The hope is usually that it will have some influence and that this will be benign.

The important moral and political questions concerning the ethical responsibilities of researchers doing fieldwork are addressed by Wilson in Chapter 12. Here I consider the academic case for, and the policy implications of, fieldwork, again by reference to my own experience. Before doing that, however, I make a very brief comment on the effect of fieldwork on respondents, researchers and research assistants.

For respondents, fieldwork may be valuable in getting their predicament more widely publicised and understood – but not everyone will benefit from this. Respondents also often derive entertainment and broad educational value from having fieldworkers in their communities. For researchers, in addition to being of direct value for doctorates and other forms of recognition, fieldwork is a unique personal experience. It provides the basis for additional appreciation and insight that they are able to bring to work on broader problems thereafter. For research assistants, there may be similar benefits, including help in their careers too (and researchers often have an important influence on the extent to which this is so).

The case for fieldwork, if one is satisfied that it is legitimate in moral and political terms, is that it enables valuable information to be obtained that cannot (or cannot easily) be obtained by other means. Where academic research is concerned, this could include data that suggest new ways of thinking about existing problems; information helping to explain, or question explanations of, data that have been obtained in other ways; information about processes, or the mechanics of relationships that can otherwise only be guessed at. The fact that fieldwork does not allow one to generalise (a recurring criticism) is not a major objection. Case studies and small surveys are valuable in their own right. Besides, if one does want to be able to generalise, village-level fieldwork can be combined with information from other sources, such as large-scale surveys. Examples illustrating some of these points are now taken from the fieldwork to which the rest of this chapter refers.

In the Kenya study, I analysed constraints on 'peasant' farm production at the individual farm level. At that time, it was believed that farmers were capital and credit constrained, but peasant producers were not responding to injections of capital. Previous attempts to address this issue had used experimental farm data, without much success. The key data that could only be obtained through fieldwork were detailed measurements of critical inputs and outputs on farms that were operating under normal, not experimental, conditions. I used case studies to obtain the required information. I preceded these with extensive discussions with people in the rural community to try to identify the critical inputs and outputs on which data needed to be collected. The fieldwork resulted in the development of alternative hypotheses, the most important of general application being that labour was a more significant constraint than capital.

Hypotheses more specific to the Kamba area included: (1) that cotton cultivation did not provide an adequate return to labour; and (2) that the maize pricing system distorted resource allocation between regions, and contributed to famine. In fact, these were more than hypotheses – they were preliminary findings that could be tested in later work. The village-level case studies were followed by more extensive work confirming many of the preliminary findings in a wider context.

In the Indian study, fieldwork was used to explore unfamiliar territory of a different kind. I started by looking at a programme aimed at getting assets to poorer households in the study villages, but I soon became interested in the processes of asset distribution over time. I pursued this by conducting a village-level study of the mechanisms by which wealth was transferred between households, particularly through inheritance and marriage, as well as the processes through which wealth was generated and dissipated. The research brought out the central role of marriage and kin-based relations in the rural economy, and the role these played in determining the accumulation and distribution of wealth. It also revealed how kin networks were used to provide insurance, and for the circulation of credit and finance. It would not have been possible to discover how these networks operated in this highly commercialised agricultural economy without doing fieldwork at the village level.

In these examples, fieldwork produced results that had important implications for the understanding of how agrarian economies work. The results were strengthened by the larger body of research work to which these studies could be related. Fieldwork should not be seen on its own, but as contributing to a continually expanding body of research that produces a better understanding of rural (and urban) life in general, as well as in particular countries like Kenya and India.

Ultimately, the case for fieldwork can be made most strongly through its results. It is one thing to discuss fieldwork as a research method – equally important is the way in which data are analysed and used. The onus is on those of us who have done fieldwork to demonstrate, not only that good data can be collected, but also that important results can come out of this research if the data are skilfully exploited at the processing and analytical stages.

The last word must be that fieldwork can be an extremely rewarding and rich experience, as well as a most valuable source of information that cannot be obtained in any other way. There is an element of luck in how it turns out. Those of us who have had good experiences are aware of all the things that could have gone wrong. But when it goes well, as it usually does, fieldwork is immensely worthwhile and immensely enjoyable.

Notes

1. The British Government Colonial Social Science Research Council, the Leverhulme Trust and the George Webb-Medley Fund all contributed financially to my different periods of fieldwork.

Tamil Nadu Agricultural University and the Madras Institute of Development Studies gave me generous support when I was doing fieldwork in India, as did Barbara and John Harriss, who were working in Coimbatore when I first went there in 1980. Queen Elizabeth House, Oxford, provided me with the time I needed away from teaching and administrative responsibilities in Oxford to get that fieldwork underway.

Government officials in both Kenya and India gave me help without which I could not have done the fieldwork at all. My three research assistants, I. Ganesan, E. Shanmugasundaram and V.S. Mohanasundaram played a vital role, as will be clear from much of this chapter. The rural people among whom I worked must always be those to whom I am most indebted.

Finally, I owe a particular debt to Stephen Devereux and John Hoddinott for organising this volume and persuading me to write on this subject in this way, as well as for their exceptional skill as editors.

2. I once had the salutary experience of having a Tamil-speaking friend accompanying me on some interviews late in my fieldwork and commenting on all the mistranslations that were going on. This did not completely shake my faith in the undertaking, but it did remind me to continue to treat the interpretation with caution.
3. Lockwood (Chapter 11 in this volume) has an example of this, while Razavi (Chapter 10 in this volume) discusses the implications of the interviewer's gender in Islamic societies.
4. See Olsen (Chapter 4 in this volume) for some suggestions.

References

Aberle, D. (1989), 'Can anthropologists be neutral in land disputes? Reply to P. Whiteley', *Man* (n.s.), **24**, pp. 340–1.

Abu-Lughod, L. (1988), 'Fieldwork of a dutiful daughter', in S. Altorki and C. F. El-Solh (eds.), *Arab Women in the Field: Studying your own society*, Syracuse, NY: Syracuse University Press.

Adams, A. (1979), 'An open letter to a young researcher', *African Affairs*, **78,** pp. 451–79.

Alexander, J. (1987), *Trade, Traders and Trading in Rural Java*, Singapore: Oxford University Press.

Altorki, S. (1988), 'At home in the field', in S. Altorki and C. F. El-Solh (eds.), *Arab Women in the Field: Studying your own society*, Syracuse, NY: Syracuse University Press.

Altorki, S. and El-Solh, C. F. (eds.). (1988) *Arab Women in the Field: Studying your own society*, Syracuse, NY: Syracuse University Press.

Anthropology Today (1990), articles on 'Cultural politics in New Zealand', **6**, no. 3.

Asad, T. (1974), 'The concept of rationality in economic anthropology', *Economy and Society*, **3**, pp. 211–18.

Athreya, V. B., Gustav, B., Goran, D. and Lindberg, S. (1987), 'Identification of agrarian classes: a methodological essay with empirical material from south India', *Journal of Peasant Sudies*, **14**, pp. 147–90.

Attwood, D. W. (1979), 'Why some of the poor get richer: economic change and mobility in rural western India', *Current Anthropology*, **20** (3), pp. 495–516.

Barker, P. (1986), *Peoples, Languages, and Religion in Northern Ghana*, Accra: Ghana Evangelism Committee.

Barley, N. (1983), *The Innocent Anthropologist: Notes from a mud hut*, Harmondsworth: Penguin.

Barnes, J. (1977), *The Ethics of Inquiry in the Social Sciences*, Delhi: Oxford University Press.

Bernard, H. R. (1988), *Research Methods in Cultural Anthropology*, Newbury Park: Sage.

Bleek, W. (1978), 'Envy and inequality in fieldwork: an example from Ghana', *Mimeo*, Accra: Institute of African Studies, University of Ghana.

Bliss, C. and Stern, N. (1982), *Palanpur: The economy of an Indian village*, Oxford: Clarendon Press.

Bowen, E. (1964), *Return to Laughter*, Garden City, NY: Doubleday.

Bozzoli, B. (1985), 'Migrant women and South African social change: biographical approaches to social analysis', *African Studies*, **44**, pp. 87–96.

Brass, W. (1981), 'Methods for estimating fertility and mortality from limited and defective data', Occasional Publication, Laboratories for Population Statistics, University of North Carolina, Chapel Hill.

Brass, W. (1985), 'Advances in methods for estimating fertility and mortality from limited and defective data', Occasional Publication, Centre for Population Studies, London School of Hygiene and Tropical Medicine.

Breman, J. (1985), 'Between accumulation and immiseration: the partiality of fieldwork in rural India', *Journal of Peasant Studies*, **13**, pp. 5–36.

Burgess, R. (ed.) (1982), *Field Research: A sourcebook and field manual*, London: Unwin Hyman.

Burgess, R. (1984), *In the Field: An introduction to field research*, London: Allen and Unwin.

Caldwell, J. C. (1982), *Theory of Fertility Decline*, London: Academic Press.

Cancian, F. (1966), 'Maximisation as norm, strategy and theory: a comment on programmatic statements in economic anthropology', *American Anthropologist*, **68**, pp. 465–70.

Carruthers, I. and Chambers, R. (1981), 'Rapid appraisal for rural development', *Agricultural Administration*, **10**, pp. 407–22.

Casley, D. and Lury, D. (1987), *Data Collection in Developing Countries*, 2nd edn, Oxford: Clarendon Press.

Chayanov, A. V. (1966), *The Theory of Peasant Economy*, eds. D. Thorner, B. Kerblay and R. Smith, Homewood, IL: Richard D. Irwin.

Clifford, J. (1986), 'Introduction: partial truths', in J. Clifford and G. Marcus (eds.), *Writing Culture: The poetics and politics of ethnography*, London: University of California Press.

Clifford, J. (1986), 'Contemporary problems of ethnography in the modern world system', in J. Clifford and G. Marcus (eds.), *Writing Culture: The poetics and politics of ethnography*, London: University of California Press.

Coale, A. (1973), 'The demographic transition', in *Proceedings of the International Population Conference 1973*, **1**, pp. 53–71, Liege: IUSSP.

Cohen, Y. (1961), 'Patterns of friendship', in Y. Cohen (ed.), *Social Structure and Personality*, New York: Holt Rinehart and Winston.

Cohen, D. W. and Odhiambo, E. S. Atieno (1989), *Siaya: the historical anthropology of an African landscape*, London: James Currey.

Crow, B. (1989), 'Plain tales from the rice trade: indications of vertical integration in rice markets in Bangladesh', *Journal of Peasant Studies*, **16**, pp. 198–229.

Crow, B. and Murshid, K. A. S. (1989), 'The finance of forced and free markets: merchants' capital in the Bangladesh grain trade', Open University, Development Policy and Practice Working Paper No. 18.

da Corta, L. and Olsen, W. (1990), 'On the road to Nimmanapalle: an empirical analysis of labour relations in drought-prone villages in south India', Discussion Paper 66, Department of Economics, University of Manchester.

Dawe, A. (1975), Review and comments on J. O'Neill, *Making Sense Together: An introduction to wild sociology*, London: Heinemann.

Deane, P. (1949), 'Problems of surveying village economies', *Rhodes-Livingstone Journal*, **8**, pp. 42–9.

Devereux, S. (1989), *Food Security, Seasonality and Resource Allocation in Northeastern Ghana*, ESCOR Report R4481, Overseas Development Administration, London.

de Waal, A. (1988), 'The sanity factor: expatriate behaviour in relief operations', *Refugee Participation Network*, No. 2b, Refugee Studies Programme, Oxford.

de Waal, A. (1989), *Famine that Kills: Darfur, Sudan, 1984–85*, Oxford: Clarendon Press.

Dewey, A. (1962), *Peasant Marketing in Java*, Chicago, IL: Free Press of Glencoe.

Donham, D. (1981), 'Beyond the domestic mode of production', *Man*, **16**, pp. 515–41.

Douglas, J. D. (1976), *Investigative Social Research: Individual and team methods*, Beverly Hills, CA: Sage.

Drinkwater, M. J. and Wilson, K. B. (forthcoming), *A Question of Perspective: Re-interpreting environmental and social relations in Zimbabwe*, London: James Currey.

Eisenstadt, S. N. and Roniger, L. (1984), *Patrons, Clients and Friends: Interpersonal relations and the structure of trust in society*, Cambridge: Cambridge University Press.

Eldridge, J. E. T. (1970), *Max Weber: The interpretation of social reality*, London: Michael Joseph.

Ellen, R. (1984), *Ethnographic Research: A guide to general conduct*, London: Academic Press.

El-Solh, C. F. (1988), 'Aspects of role during fieldwork in Arab society', in S. Altorki and C. F. El-Solh (eds.), *Arab Women in the Field: Studying your own society*, Syracuse, NY: Syracuse University Press.

Epstein, T. S. (1967), 'The data of economics in anthropological analysis', in A. L. Epstein (ed.), *The Craft of Social Anthropology*, London: Tavistock Press.

Evans, A. (1989), 'Gender issues in rural household economics', Discussion Paper 254, Institute of Development Studies, University of Sussex.

Firth, R. (ed.) (1967), *Themes in Economic Anthropology*, London: Tavistock Press.

Fox, R. G. (1969), *From Zamindar to Ballot Box: Community change in a north India market town*, Ithaca, NY: Cornell University Press.

Freilich, R. (1977), *Marginal Natives: Anthropologists at work*, New York: Harper and Row.

Friedman, M. (1979), 'The methodology of positive economics', in F. Hahn and M. Hollis (eds.), *Philosophy and Economic Theory*, Oxford: Oxford University Press.

Giddens, A. (1974), 'Introduction', in A. Giddens (ed.), *Positivism and Sociology*, London: Academic Press.

Giddens, A. (1976), *New Rules of Sociological Method*, London: Hutchinson.

Godelier, M. (1972), *Rationality and Irrationality in Economics*, London: NLB.

Graham, D., Aguilera, N., Keita, M. and Negash, K. (1988), 'Informal finance in rural Niger: scope, magnitudes and organisation', *Economics and Sociology Paper No. 1472*, Department of Agricultural Economics and Rural Sociology, Columbus, OH: Ohio State University.

Gregory, C. and Altman, J. (1989), *Observing the Economy*, London: Routledge.

Grillo, R. (1990), 'Comments on Hastrup and Elass', *Current Anthropology*, **13**, p. 311.

Guyer, J. (1981), 'Household and community in African studies', *African Studies Review*, **24**, pp. 87–137.

Hahn, F. and Hollis, M. (eds.) (1979), *Philosophy and Economic Theory*, Oxford: Oxford University Press.

Harriss, B. (1981), *Transitional Trade and Rural Development*, New Delhi: Vikas.

Harriss, B. (1984a), 'Analysing the rural economy – a practical guide', Discussion Paper No. 164, School of Development Studies, University of East Anglia.

Harriss, B. (1984b), *State and Market*, New Delhi: Concept.

Harriss, B. (1990), 'The Arni studies: changes in the private sector of a market town, 1973–83', in P. Hazell and C. S. Ramasamy (eds.), *Green Revolution Revisited*, Baltimore, MD: Johns Hopkins.

Harriss, J. (1983), 'Making out on limited resources: or, what happened to semi-feudalism in a Bengal district', in B. Harriss and J. Harriss (eds.), *Papers on the*

Political Economy of Agriculture in West Bengal, Reprint No. 170, School of Development Studies, University of East Anglia.
Hastrup, K. and Elass, P. (1990), 'Anthropological advocacy: a contradiction in terms?', *Current Anthropology*, **13**, pp. 301–10.
Hill, P. (1982), *Dry Grain Farming Families: Karnataka and Hausaland compared*, Cambridge: Cambridge University Press.
Hill, P. (1986), *Development Economics on Trial*, Cambridge: Cambridge University Press.
Hoddinott, J. (1989), 'Migration, accumulation and old age security in western Kenya', unpublished D.Phil. thesis, Oxford University.
Hull, T., Hull, V. and Singarimbun, M. (1988), 'Combining research techniques in the study of fertility and family planning in Java: theory and practice', in J. Caldwell, A. Hill and V. Hull (eds.), *Micro-Approaches to Demographic Research*, London: KPI.
IDS Bulletin (1981), articles on 'Rapid Rural Appraisal', **12**, no. 4.
India, Government of (1917), *Re-Survey and Re-Settlement Register of the Village of Nimmanapalli*, No. 102, Madanapalle Taluk, Revenue Settlement Office, Chittoor.
Jackson, M. (1989), *Paths Towards a Clearing: Radical empiricism and ethnographic inquiry*, Bloomington, IN: Indiana University Press.
Last, M. (1990), 'The deep rural economy: a Hausaland village over twenty years', seminar, Queen Elizabeth House, Oxford.
Leach, E. (1967), 'An anthropologist's reflection on a social survey', in D. Jorgmans and P. Gutkind (eds.), *Anthropologists in the Field*, Assen: Van Gorcum.
Lele, U. (1971), *Foodgrains Marketing in India: Public policy and private performance*, Ithaca, NY: Cornell University Press.
Lenin, V. I. (1899/1977), *The Development of Capitalism in Russia*, Moscow: Progress Publishers.
Leridon, H. and Menken, J. (1979), *Natural Fertility*, Liege: IUSSP.
Levi-Strauss, C. (1973), *Tristes Tropiques*, London: Cape.
Lockwood, M. (1989a), 'The economics of fertility and the infertility of economics: theory and demographic reality in Africa', Working Paper No. 12, Centro Studi Luca D'Agliano/Queen Elizabeth House, Oxford.
Lockwood, M. (1989b), 'Fertility and labour in Rufiji District, Tanzania', unpublished D.Phil. thesis, Oxford University.
Longhurst, R. (1981), 'Research methodology and rural economy in northern Nigeria', *IDS Bulletin*, **12**, pp. 23–31.
Marx, E. (1987), 'Advocacy in a Bedouin resettlement project', in M. Salem-Murdock and M. M. Horowitz (eds.), *Anthropology and Rural Development in North Africa and the Middle East*, Boulder, CO: Westview Press.
McCall, G. and Simmons, J. (1969), *Issues in Participant-Observation: A text and a reader*, Reading, MA: Addison-Wesley.
Mines, M. (1972), *Muslim Merchants: The economic behaviour of an Indian Muslim community*, Delhi: Shri Ram Centre.
Morris, M. L. and Newman, M. D. (1989), 'Official and parallel cereals markets in Senegal: empirical evidence', *World Development*, **17**, pp. 1895–1906.
Morsy, S. (1988), 'Towards the demise of anthropology's distinctive-other tradition', in S. Altorki and C. F. El-Solh (eds.), *Arab Women in the Field: Studying your Own Society*, Syracuse, NY: Syracuse University Press.
Nagar, A. L., and Das, R. K. (1983), *Basic Statistics*, 2nd edn, Delhi: Oxford University Press.
Neale, W., Singh, H. and Singh, J. P. (1965), 'Kurali market – a report on the economic geography of marketing in north India', *Economic Development and Cultural Change*, **13**, pp. 129–68.
Newell, C. (1988), *Methods and Models in Demography*, London: Belhaven Press.

Olsen, W. (1988). 'Overview of extended census results', *Mimeo*, Oxford.
Olsen, W. (1991), '"Distress sales" and exchange relations in a rural area of Rayalaseema, Andhra Pradesh', unpublished D.Phil. thesis, Oxford University.
O'Neill, J. (1975), *Making Sense Together: An introduction to wild sociology*, London: Heinemann.
Patnaik, U. (1976), 'Class differentiation within the peasantry', *Economic and Political Weekly*, **11**, pp. A82–A101.
Patnaik, U. (1987), *Peasant Class Differentiation: A study in method with reference to Haryana*, Delhi: Oxford University Press.
Patnaik, U. (1988), 'Ascertaining the economic characteristics of peasant classes-in-themselves in rural India: a methodological and empirical exercise', *Journal of Peasant Studies*, **15**, pp. 301–33.
Pelto, P. and Pelto, G. (1978), *Anthropological Research: The structure of inquiry*, 2nd edn, Cambridge: Cambridge University Press.
'Pepetela' (Artur Carlos Mauricio Pestana dos Santos) (1983), *Mayombe*, trans. by Michael Wolfers, Harare: Zimbabwe Publishing House.
Rabinow, P. (1977), *Reflections on Fieldwork in Morocco*, Berkeley, CA: University of California Press.
Rahman, A. (1986), *Peasants and Classes: A study of differentiation in Bangladesh*, London: Zed Books.
Richards, P. (1985), *Indigenous Agricultural Revolution*, London: Hutchinson.
Rudra, A. (1989), 'Field survey methods', in P. Bardhan (ed.), *Conversations Between Economists and Anthropologists*, New Delhi: Oxford University Press.
Sanadjian, M. (1990), 'From participant to partisan: an open end', *Critique of Anthropology*, **10**, pp. 113–35.
Schendel, W. van (1981), *Peasant Mobility: the odds of life in rural Bangladesh*, New Delhi: Manohar.
Sen, A. (1979), 'Rational fools', in F. Hahn and M. Hollis (eds.), *Philosophy and Economic Theory*, Oxford: Oxford University Press.
Sen, A. (1981), *Poverty and Famines: An essay on entitlement and deprivation*, Oxford: Clarendon Press.
Shanin, T. (1972), *The Awkward Class: Political sociology of a peasantry in a developing society*, Oxford: Clarendon Press.
Shanin, T. (1980), 'Measuring peasant capitalism: the operationalization of concepts of political economy: Russia's 1920s–India's 1970s', in E. J. Hobsbawm, W. Kula, A. Mitra, K. N. Raj and J. Sachs (eds.), *Peasants in History: Essays in honour of Daniel Thorner*, Calcutta: Oxford University Press.
Smith, M. J. (1975), *When I Say No, I Feel Guilty*, New York: Bantam Books.
Spiegel, M. R. (1972), *Schaum's Outline of Theory and Problems of Statistics*, Schaum's Outline Series, London: McGraw-Hill.
Spradley, J. (1980), *Participant-Observation*, New York: Holt Rinehart and Winston.
Srinivas, M. N. (1976), *A Remembered Village*, Delhi: Oxford University Press.
Swaminathan, M. (1988), 'Growth and polarisation: changes in wealth inequality in a Tamil Nadu village', *Economic and Political Weekly*, **22**, pp. 2229–34.
Tapsoba, E. (1981), 'An economic and institutional analysis of formal and informal credit in eastern Upper Volta: empirical evidence and policy', unpublished Ph.D. dissertation, Michigan State University.
Taussig, M. (1987), *Shamanism, Colonialism and the Wild Man: A study in terror and healing*, Chicago, IL: University of Chicago Press.
Thompson, P. (1978), *The Voice of the Past: Oral history*, Oxford: Oxford University Press.
Twumasi, P. (1986), *Social Research in Rural Communities: The problems of fieldwork in Ghana*, Accra: Ghana Universities Press.

United Nations (1955), *Manual II: Methods of appraisal of quality of basic data for population estimates*, New York: United Nations.

Vaughan, M. (1987), *The Story of an African Famine*, Cambridge: Cambridge University Press.

Vierich, H. (1984), 'Accommodation or participation? communication problems', in P. Matlon, R. Cantrell, D. King and M. Benoit-Cattin (eds.), *Coming Full Circle: Farmers' participation in the development of technology*, Ottawa: IDRC.

Von Pischke, J., Adams, D. and Donald, G. (eds.) (1983), *Rural Financial Markets in Developing Countries: Their use and abuse*, Baltimore, MD: Johns Hopkins.

Werner, D. (1980), *Where There Is No Doctor*, London: Macmillan.

Whitehead, A. (1984), 'Beyond the household: gender and kinship based resource allocation in a Ghanaian domestic economy', paper presented at the workshop on 'Conceptualising the Household', Harvard University.

Wilson, K. B. (1988), 'Indigenous conservation in Zimbabwe: soil erosion, land-use planning and rural life', in R. H. Grove (ed.), *Conservation and Rural People in Zimbabwe*, Cambridge: Cambridge African Monographs.

Wilson, K. B. (1990), 'Ecological dynamics and human welfare: a case study of population, health and nutrition in southern Zimbabwe', unpublished Ph.D. thesis, University of London.

Wright, R. M. (1988), 'Anthropological presuppositions of indigenous advocacy', *Annual Review of Anthropology*, **118**, pp. 365–90.

Yanagisako, S. (1979), 'Family and household: the analysis of domestic groups', *Annual Review of Anthropology*, **8**, pp. 161–205.

Yeomans, K. A. (1982, original 1968), *Statistics for the Social Scientist. Volume 2: Applied Statistics*, Penguin Education Studies in Applied Statistics, London: Penguin.

Index